Key Account Management
Second edition

. . . .

To Dorothy and her friends

Key Account Management

Second edition

John Rock

Business & Professional Publishing

Business & Professional Publishing Pty Limited

Unit 7/5 Vuko Place
Warriewood NSW 2102
Australia

Email: info@woodslane.com.au

First edition first published 1994
Reprinted 1995
This edition first published 1998
Reprinted 1999

National Library of Australia
Cataloguing-in-Publication entry

Rock, John.
   Key account management.

   2nd ed.
   Includes index.
   ISBN 1 875680 59 4.

   1. Selling - Key accounts. 2. Marketing - Key accounts. 3. Sales management.
   4. Marketing - Management. I. Title.

658.8

Publisher: Robert Coco
Text design: Judith Summerfeldt-Grace
Cover design: Miller Hare
Set in 10/12.5 pt Palatino
Printed in Australia by Australian Print Group

Distributed in Australia and New Zealand by Woodslane Pty Limited. Business & Professional Publishing publications are available through booksellers and other resellers. For further information contact Woodslane Australia on +61 2 9970 5111 or Woodslane Ltd, New Zealand on +64 6 347 6543, or email info@woodslane.com.au.

Contents

Part 4: Selling to End Users

Part 5: Making Key Account Management Work

Tables

Figures

Introduction

Sales force productivity and effectiveness

For most companies, the sales force is a large cost centre. Looking at it in another way, it is one of the most valuable investments a company makes. If the sales force is considered as a cost, its management evokes words like 'cost containment' or 'cost control' leading to 'limited head count'. It tends to focus on only one side of the equation. On the other hand if we talk about investment, the immediate response would be 'return on investment'. Now we are focusing on both sides of the equation. What is the return in terms of sales performance for the investment made in the sales force?

A very significant part of that return is the activities of the sales force. What does each sales person do with the time available? How well do they use it? Are they spending it with the right customers? Are they seeing the right people within an organisation? And are they talking about the things that are really going to make a difference to sales, while they are there? This question has been of interest to me for some time.

As a consultant designing and running training courses for sales and marketing people, I have over the years had the opportunity to know and work with very many sales forces in all sorts of different industries. I have found that there are very few lazy sales people. Most are very hard working, and they put in far more hours than most people in the company, but they tend not to be as productive as they could be. A large part of the investment the companies have made in their sales force is not providing the return it should. This is because not enough thought has gone into their business dealings with each individual customer. There is no structure to the way they do business with each particular account. There is not sufficient attempt to see the mutual business through the eyes of the customer. There is no dedication to helping the customer meet his or her particular objectives. Instead, there is a series of ad hoc activities, many of which are responses to situations which arise. It leads to a barren unimaginative relationship.

Above all, there is poor focus on the right markets and products, and the priority customers. Even when such focus does exist, there is no mechanism which ensures that these priorities are reflected in how and where the sales force spends its time.

Key account management is the answer

There is, however, an alternative. It requires insight, dedication and a lot of hard work. It produces cooperative relationships, creativity and more profitable business for both of the trading partners. It builds stability and reduces vulnerability. It makes it easier to keep the business you already have, and allows you to target business you aspire to. That alternative is called account management.

The process of account management is a total approach to business with an account. It is specific to an individual account. It has a preparation phase, a planning phase, an implementation phase and a review phase.

The concept is valid for any selling situation, but because it requires involvement by the supplier in contributing to the profitability of the customer or account, it operates differently, depending on the type of business. For example, selling through a distribution network of distributors, agents, outlets, dealers, resellers, retailers etc. requires a response from the supplier which understands their relationship to the product. They buy it, sell it and hope to make money out of the process.

On the other hand, products might be sold to a customer who uses the product directly or as part of a further manufacturing process. Such products could be technical products or services, either consumables or capital items. Here, the customer cares specifically how the product or service performs for them in its operation or usage.

Not only does account management differ between these two types of business (distribution and direct), it varies within each type. The detail of information you need on the customer, and the ways you add value to your package, will depend on the type of products and how they are used.

How this book is organised

This book has been divided into five parts. The first and the last parts are common to every situation and should be read by all those interested in account management. Parts 2, 3 and 4 refer to the business segments described above, and the reader should at least concentrate on that part which covers the type of business their company operates in. However, often what is happening in one area of business eventually influences others, and ideas can be taken from one area to another. Furthermore, implementation is not as easy as one might think. I would strongly recommend to all readers that to get the best from the book, they should read all the chapters—even those about businesses which seem quite different from their own—and study Part 5 in particular to learn about successful implementation.

So far in this introduction I have talked about 'Account Management', yet the book is entitled 'Key Account Management'. In nearly every business there is some kind of Pareto principle operating. In some businesses 80 per cent of the business comes from 20 per cent of the accounts, or 70 per cent from 30 per cent, or 90 per cent from 10 per cent. The point is that there are some accounts which are fundamental to the ability of the company to meet its sales objectives. These are the accounts where priority must be placed in investing the sales effort to get the best return. Too many sales forces spend too much time with the wrong customers. 'Key' suggests that in the process of account management we should be focusing resources on those customers who really are going to produce the sales results.

There are some businesses where this principle does not apply. Examples might be the selling of residential real estate, life insurance or for fleet motor vehicle sales. However, there are very few businesses which fall into this category. Account management principles can be applied even to the medical detailing of pharmaceuticals, either to large medical practices and groups, or to pharmacies and especially hospitals.

This book is therefore applicable to anyone who has an interest in selling and sales effectiveness and productivity. This includes those at the front line, such as account managers, account executives, sales representatives, and sales managers. It is also recommended as important reading for marketing people, market managers and product managers.

I know from my experience over the past fifteen years that key account management *works*. It is itself an investment and it requires time and effort. The return on that investment is better quality of business through a mix of higher prices, higher volumes and longer-term, more stable relationships. Your personal time investment in reading this book will pay off too, as long as you do something about it when you have finished. Selling is, after all, about action. I have also learned that implementation is not as easy as one might think. Part 5 on implementation is possibly the most important section.

PART 1

All About Key Account Management

1

Philosophy, discipline and commitment

. . . .

The philosophy of account management

The introduction talked about the need to get the best return on the investment made in the sales force. This means the best sales results. More enlightened companies measure this in terms of contribution to profit rather than in volume sales or dollar revenue. In other words, they take into account the value of a sale and the amount of money the company makes from it—including the gross margin net of all discounts and allowances, if possible, adjusted for packaging, transport and even the cost of inventory and credit.

These results depend on the effectiveness and the productivity of the sales force. The effectiveness of the sales force is largely a function of their skill level, how well they handle themselves each time they are in front of a customer. The skills involved are selling skills, presentation skills, negotiation, analytical, communication skills, interpersonal skills and problem solving. Increasingly important is the ability to argue the case on the basis of financial benefit to the customer.

It also depends on the knowledge the sales people have, involving product and product application, the marketplace and the competition. It also includes knowledge of the customer base.

Part of the sales manager's job is to ensure that these skills and knowledge are developed in his/her sales people. This is a significant part of the subject matter of my book *The Effective Sales Manager*. Account management assumes that these elements of sales effectiveness will be developed in the sales people.

The issue of sales productivity says that even given satisfactory sales effectiveness, there will be a wide variation in sales results depending on the activities of the sales force. Account management is a mechanism that ensures sales people spend their time on those activities which are going to give us the best chance of maximising sales results.

The problem of price

There are very few businesses which do not claim to be in a very competitive marketplace, with constant downward pressure on prices. At the same time, manufacturers in particular have high fixed costs and usually high working capital requirements through inventory and provision of credit. You can try as much as you like to control these elements, and there have been cycles of campaigns to reduce inventory, or get receivables down and then cut back on costs, but they never have as much effect as getting the price up.

The left-hand column of Table 1 shows the overall figures making up the net profit before tax (NPBT) for a company. In the columns on the right the effect on profit of a 5 per cent change in the main items is calculated. It shows what happens to profit if the price is raised 5 per cent, or the volume 5 per cent, or the variable costs reduced 5 per cent or the fixed costs reduced by 5 per cent. In the last column the effect of doing all those things at the same time is demonstrated. It shows that the single best way to boost profit is to raise the price. This suggests that selling on price creates a real

Table 1: The effect of price

	Now	Price	Volume	Variable cost	Fixed cost	The lot
Sales revenue	1250	1312.5	1312.5	1250	1250	1378.12
Variable cost	800	800	840	760	800	798
Gross profit	450	512.5	472.5	490	450	580.12
Fixed costs	200	200	200	200	190	190
Depreciation	100	100	100	100	100	100
NPBT	150	212.5	172.5	190	160	290.12
% Increase in NPBT	N/A	42%	15%	27%	7%	93%

$000s changes of 5 per cent
If you manage a 1 per cent change in each of these items the increase in profit will be 18 per cent.

problem for most of us. (That is not quite the same as saying that price itself is a problem, as we will see.)

The problem is that many businesses are very volume-sensitive, especially those with a high breakeven point because of the high fixed costs. Such companies are always trying to get the balance right between the highest price they can manage, and the need to secure the volumes to keep the plant going. It ought to be possible to lower the price, and as a result increase the volume. This does not work very often, and certainly not for long. This is because most customers do not buy primarily on price, although they may tell you they do. Furthermore, the competitors are not going to stand by without reacting.

For every company which is not the lowest cost producer, the downward price spiral is a disaster. If you are the lowest cost producer, is selling on price, to lead the prices down, a viable strategy? If there are considerable barriers to entry and you can push competitors out of business, the answer is probably 'yes'. But otherwise, you will find that the extra business you pick up has cost you so much in profitability on the rest of your business that the whole exercise is not viable. Another strategy would be more profitable.

The conclusion is that we must try and keep prices up.

The effect of dropping the price

If you are making 30 per cent gross profit, and you drop your price 5 per cent, you will have to sell 20 per cent more to retain the same gross profit.

This is the equation to use if working with percentages:

GP = gross profit as a per cent
  x = percentage by which you drop the price
  y = the percentage amount more you have to sell to make the same gross profit as the original case

$$y = \frac{GP}{GP - x}$$

Working with actual numbers:

gp = gross profit per unit in dollars
  x = the amount you drop your price in dollars
  z = the number of units of the original sale
  y = the number of units you would need to sell to make the same gross profit

$$y = \frac{gp \times z}{gp - x}$$

This calculation has a depressing effect on most sales managers, financial controllers and far-sighted sales people. In the case of a 30 per cent gross margin, you would be better off if you put your price up by 5 per cent but lost 14 per cent of the volume. The breakeven is where:

$$y' = \frac{GP}{GP + x}$$

where x is the percentage by which you increase the price, and y' represents the maximum percentage drop in volume you can withstand without losing profit at the higher price.

For actual figures, rather than percentages, the equation is:

$$y' = \frac{gp \times z}{gp + x}$$

This does not mean that you should never defend business on price; neither does it mean that you are always better off to lift prices even if you lose volume. There may be strategic market share implications which must be considered. However, the calculation shows very quickly the effect of dropping price.

Is price the main purchase criterion?

6 Customers are bound to say price is the main criterion: they have nothing to lose by saying so, but much to gain especially if you believe them. But the facts are that by far the largest majority of purchases are not made on price; they are made on the basis of value for money.

This we know from our own experience to be true. In certain cases a lower price may even be a barrier to a sale. It can create a lack of trust, the customer thinking 'There has to be something wrong with it at that low price.' Most of us will realise that we make most purchases on the basis of value for money. Only when there is no discernible difference between the offers, including the product and service, will we opt for the lower price.

There are many studies in different industries which show that only a very small number of customers buy with price as the main criterion.

Many readers will be thinking that their industry is different—that I should go and visit their customers, and I would quickly change my mind. I have two comments.

The first is that the customers may tell you that they buy on price, but in fact do not. Let us assume that you provide good quality products, maybe better than the competitors. Your delivery service is at least as good as the competition. The same for your administration. If the customers have a better price from a competitor who performs less well than you, are they going to tell you that you perform better? Or are they more likely to ignore the areas where you are performing well, and attack you on the weaker area of price? What they really want is your product and service, but at some one else's low price. If they can get it, they have really won. And you have just given away all the cards you had in your hand. If they do not have a better price from the competition, it is still in their interests to tell you that your price is too high. You might be frightened into giving them a lower price.

In a distributive business, your product may sell better and there may be fewer customer complaints but there is more margin out of the competitor's product. The customer is going to concentrate on getting a better margin on your product by beating you down on price. That way they win twice. They will be stressing to your competitor that your product assures more volume, and to justify using the competitor's product the customers would need a lower price still. Then they can use that lower price against you again!

The second possibility is that the customers believe that there is no discernible difference between what you are offering and what your competitor is offering. In that case they will concentrate on price. If there is a difference between what the products can do for the customers, or what you can make the product do, and the service you provide, you will have to identify that difference and sell it. You are taking the focus away from price, and demonstrating different value for money to the customer.

7

The me-too world of the 90s

Years ago life was much easier. Most companies had at least some products which were clearly better than the competition, or they had technology which gave them an edge in product application. Many had virtual monopolies in parts of their range. Imports were not a significant threat.

In the 1990s the situation is quite different. There is a trend towards less and less product differentiation. Customers know more about the world market. There is easier access to application technology, and to products from a wide variety of countries. All this leads to suppliers offering increasingly similar packages. The only way the decision-making process can go is towards price, especially when the competition is from a country with lower labour costs and fewer operating requirements, particularly on environmental issues. Local manufacturers cannot always lower their prices to match.

As the product and technical content of selling becomes more similar, the emphasis must change to the non-product, non-technical areas, which for the moment we will call 'service'.

That is not to say that we should accept that there is going to be less technical or product differentiation. The most powerful way of showing the customer an advantage is having a better product. This must be the major goal where possible. But even where this is achieved, the sales people have to learn how to sell a complete package of goods and services.

The changes to selling

The need to sell more of the package than the product requires an enormous change in emphasis in most companies, at all levels. The directors need to recognise it, marketing must make it a cornerstone of their planning, and the sales force must learn how to sell the package. The traditional sales force that sold just the product is going to be at a distinct disadvantage. They tend to lack creativity and be inflexible in their approach. The same can be said about the whole organisation in some cases. This is one of the most important issues in the whole implementation of an account management program, and we will return to it in more detail later.

What if you simply cannot find or create any positive difference?

Very often sales people tell me at the start of a training session that there is just no scope to provide customers with anything—product, advice or service—which is better than their competitor's. In most cases, a little creativity and opening of minds, and a lot more knowledge of the customer and how they operate, can find ways where differences do exist or where they can be created. Or we can find stronger parts of the range which are able to pull through the weaker ones. Generally, a company in an overall sense can provide customers something which is more valuable to them than what other suppliers are offering. The degree to which this can be capitalised upon depends largely on the ability of the sales force to sell the value of the package to the customer, and in their negotiation skills.

But there are some cases where it simply cannot be done; the competitors do it better across the board. In such cases, unless you are the lowest cost producer, there is a clear message. Get out of the business quick, before it goes broke! If you are a sales-person from such a company, my strongest advice is to look for another job while you have time on your side.

The sad thing is that much of overseas investment in Australian manufacturing, and quite a bit that is locally owned, decided to do this without fully investigating the options of providing a differentiated package. People may make the wrong decision if they get out too soon. The businesses where people really should get out because they are without hope are relatively few.

Differentiation

The word 'differentiation' has cropped up on a number of occasions in the last section. This is not surprising, since it is the basis of account management.

Differentiation is the provision of goods and/or services such that there is a positive, desirable and discernible difference in the customer's eyes relative to the customer's other purchasing options. This is the process of adding value to the total package from the customer's point of view, so that the customers are prepared to reflect the added value in the quality of the orders placed (higher price, more volume or longer-term commitments).

There are a few key words in this definition which should be remembered.

- **goods and/or services.** This suggests that as products move more to a me-too status we may have to look beyond the product to the service aspects of supply in order to differentiate.
- **a positive, desirable and discernible difference.** The difference created must be sufficient for it to weigh in the decision making process. We should be able to convince customers of the extra value of our package so that it more than bridges our price premium.
- **in the customer's eyes.** It is critical not to get carried away with an idea for creating differentiation only to find that although we believe that it is of value to the customers, they do not. Differentiation is only useful if it is perceived by the customers.
- **relative to the other options.** Differentiation is a difference; it is relative to something else. That something else is the offerings made by the competition. We may not know what those are in detail, although we should do our best to find out. The key issue is to convince customers that they should be comparing value for money rather than price. This may require some education of buyers, although it has been the trend in purchasing organisations over the last few years. As offerings keep changing and as customers' needs change, the existing differentiation is constantly changing. As we will discuss in the implementation of account management, we should stop from time to time and assess the current differentiation at each account.

If we are going to avoid having to sell on price, differentiation is the mechanism whereby we add value to our offer. If this cannot be done directly through better product or product application, it has to be done in other areas. These might include delivery systems, packaging, technical or non-technical advice, some sort of special assistance, or anywhere where we have some expertise which can contribute to the profitability of the customer. It might be the ability of a supplier in selling product for a distributor or dealer. It could be market knowledge that shows a supermarket how to create more sales.

9

In a general sense, it is matching our corporate abilities to customer needs or capitalising on customer opportunities.

Account management is the structure and the process, for managing individual accounts to create this differentiation and capitalising upon it.

Business needs and personal needs

This section has primarily been about business needs, and the relative value in dollar terms of the offers of various suppliers. But there is another dimension to account management. Customers are composed of people with emotions and personal needs, likes and dislikes. The decisions they make will tend to include a component of whether their personal needs are being satisfied. In some cases such considerations override the logic of the dollar. A supplier who has the best package may lose the business if the customer feels uncomfortable with them for whatever reason. There are internal politics, power plays, the desire to punish a supplier who has let them down or not done the right thing. Sometimes decisions are logical and rational, but they can also be emotional reactions not based on logic. Account management has to recognise the importance of the role played by relationships between the two companies, not just at the sales person–purchasing officer level, but at all levels within both companies. The supplier must ensure that the individual personal needs of the customer are being met.

An individual process

We have been talking about the customer's options and the relative value to them of those options. The issues will be different for each customer because each will have different business needs. Furthermore, these needs will vary depending on the priorities of the company at any given time. Account management is a process, but it needs to be applied on an individual customer basis. It requires thought and planning for an individual account.

It is astonishing to find that in many cases the only planning that ever happens on an individual customer basis is call planning, and even that is sparse in some organisations!

There are market plans and there are product plans, there are state plans and territory plans, yet less time and effort is expended on Account Plans. When we consider that it is customers (accounts) which place orders, not markets or products, this is extraordinary. We are not talking simply of setting a budget for annual sales by customer, but about a plan for how to create differentiation at this account, how to establish and maintain the right relationships. The document must be capable of serving as the guide for how we run our business at a particular account.

The key to focus

It is clear that the sales force cannot be all things to all customers. There is a tendency for the smaller customers to use proportionately more of our time than they should. There are several reasons for this. They are usually less well organised, and errors occur which have to be sorted out. In technical-based industries they have less technical expertise, and rely on the supplier to help them or even to solve their problems. One customer of mine, ran a very lean operation and used to place a claim on our company every time there was a problem with their operation. They always said that it was the material we sold them. There was usually a dollar figure on the claim high enough to get the most recalcitrant technical manager rushing out there to make sure that we could prove that we were not at fault. In doing so, of course, the technical manager always solved the problem for them and told them how to overcome it.

If we look at a matrix such as the one in Table 2, with urgent tasks along one axis and important tasks on the other, and divide the matrix into four boxes as shown, clearly the box which shows urgent and important is the one which is attended to first. The box with unimportant and non-urgent tasks probably never gets attended to. The interesting question is, which

Table 2: Urgent–important priority matrix

1 What tends to happen

	Urgent	Not urgent
Important	Priority 1	Priority 3
Not important	Priority 2	Never gets done

2 What should happen

	Urgent	Not urgent
Important	Priority 1	Priority 2
Not important	Priority 3	Never gets done

of the two remaining boxes is attended to before the other, and is that the way it should be?

The chances are that the urgent but not important tasks are attended to before the important but not urgent ones. This is because of the squeaky wheel syndrome—there is some one out there yelling. The important non-urgent tasks include planning and thinking, the sorts of things which to many sales people are less interesting. The urgent tasks are likely to involve action, which many sales people feel more comfortable with. Sales people can be very busy doing these urgent but not important tasks, and feel that they have spent the day as productively as possible.

The fact is that we must try to put higher priority on the tasks which are important rather than urgent. Generally this means doing more planning and thinking about the larger and more critical accounts, rather than solving problems at the smaller accounts which are not going to give us such a large return.

These smaller accounts neither can nor should be ignored. Their business is valuable, and we need to back up our product and provide service. But we must try to change the emphasis from providing so much service to these smaller accounts that it prevents us from doing the job we should and must do at the larger accounts which are going to provide us the major part of our sales results.

Focus on the key accounts

This is where the concept of key account management comes in. It means that we should categorise our customers into four or five categories, and decide which of these categories are going to be account managed and which not. The work involved in account management is such that we cannot do it effectively for all the customers. Account management is a process, and when it is done correctly it involves an investment in time and effort. For smaller or less complex accounts there is an abbreviated form which can be used. You may decide to have five categories of accounts.

- **Category A**—that handful of accounts (for most companies half a dozen) whose business is fundamental to the success of the company—take priority over every other customer.
- **Category B**—those very important customers whom we need and want, and in whom we will invest the time in applying account management, as with Category A. A and B accounts generally will make up 60–85 per cent of our business.
- **Category C**—those accounts whose business we would like, and whom we will visit and service, but at a reduced level compared to A and B accounts. We may use an abridged version of account management for larger C accounts.
- **Category D**—those accounts whose business we will accept if it comes our way. We will service them on a needs basis only, but we will not

expend energy in account management and we will limit the service we supply.

- **Category E**—those problem accounts, bad payers etc., who we would prefer to purchase from our competitors.

There may also be some value in certain businesses of differentiating between an account where you have a good share and high penetration (their usage of the product is close to their maximum possible usage), and one where there is still some growth for you within that account. You could use R for retain and D for development accounts.

In some businesses there is a need to bring in new accounts, and there is therefore some 'prospecting' to be done. Such accounts where we have no business, but where we must get some business, could be designated as P accounts. Clearly you should not be spending time trying to get business at a P account unless you are sure it will be capable of growing into a B or A account eventually. Early on, the task with these prospects is to qualify them. Only when you can be sure they have the right potential should you designate them as a P account.

A key account may not just be one of the largest accounts. There are other factors to be taken into consideration, such as innovation, growth potential, technical development and whether it is part of a larger and important group.

It can be useful as a starting point to measure the existing skew, ranking customers in order of dollar revenue and contribution to profit. The curves will have a shape similar to those in Figure 1.

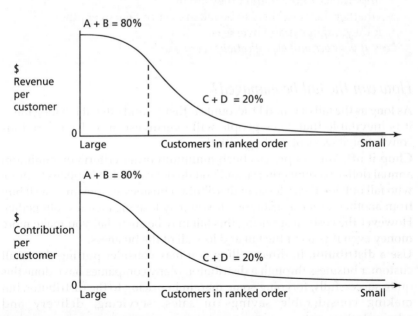

Figure 1: Customer contributions to revenue and profit

The contribution curve is a little flatter since large customers often depress prices, whereas with smaller customers the margin can be higher.

These curves do not tell you which customers should be your key accounts, but they do tell you something about the profile of the current business.

It raises the question of where the sales force spends its time. Does it spend 80 per cent of its time with the top 80 per cent of the business, or the bottom 80 per cent of the customers? The answer of course will be somewhere in the middle. But generally we will find that the sales force will be distracted in to relative trivia at the right-hand side of the curve, thus reducing the ability to invest the time required to develop the right relationships with the large A and B accounts.

The A and B accounts are more competent yet we often try to get by by doing little more than a housekeeping job on them. Yet they are the accounts which should be producing most of our revenue and profit. We need to ensure that the appropriate effort is directed to these customers.

> **Other factors to consider in deciding account classification:**
> * growth trend and potential
> * technical innovation
> * complexity of the account and business
> * strategic importance
> * part of a national account
> * association with other companies
> * importance of the market they are in
> * whether they are likely to be taken over or take over others
> * if they might expand overseas.
>
> *Look at your account classifications every year.*

How can the tail be managed?

As long as the tail of C and D accounts is there—and often it is a long tail—it is inevitable that sales people will overinvest in it. There are four conventional ways of dealing with this.

Chop it off. You simply establish minimum order criteria or minimum annual dollar account criteria, and you do not care what happens to those who fall outside the criteria. In distribution businesses they may well buy from another larger distributor. Or you may lose the business altogether. However the costs in servicing this tail may be such that you make more money even if you cut the tail and lose all of the business.

Use a distributor. In direct selling you may consider putting the small customer business through a distributor. Many companies have done this quite successfully, forgoing some margin in pricing to the distributor, but making considerable savings in sales, servicing, delivery and administrative costs.

Use teleselling. If the product does not require a large amount of technical support, it can sometimes be handled very effectively through a separate telephone selling facility. This allows you to retain contact with the customers and makes it easier to identify any D accounts which might be capable of growing into a C or even a B or an A account.

Reassess sales force organisation. You may also consider ensuring that A and B accounts are looked after by different sales people from the smaller C or even D accounts. You need to free up those looking after the A and B accounts so they are not dragged into handing less critical issues with the C and D accounts. This implies two tiers within the sales force, perhaps what we can call either Account Managers and Sales Representatives, or Key Account Managers and Account Managers. In fact several of my clients have made this distinction, creating both a career opportunity and different salary levels, as well as recognising the different requirements for the two jobs. In most sales forces not all existing people are capable of growing into the real Key Account Manager role.

15

. . . .

Sales force productivity measures

A major impediment to productivity in the sales force is the series of distractions into non-sales-productive tasks which many sales people are asked to perform. The rationale is often that if things requiring customer contact or customer focus need to be done, the sales people should do it since they are visiting customers anyway. Sales people may find themselves servicing or installing equipment, collecting money, delivering samples and so on. We might well ask if there is a better way of handling such needs. It is not easy to find good sales people and we should avoid wasting their time when other more appropriate people could do it.

There are several ways you could measure sales productivity. The basic measure should be the contribution to profit per dollar invested in sales (return on investment), but contribution per person per annum is another measure. Other measures could be the revenue per person or the revenue created for every dollar invested in sales. You could also measure sales productivity per person, per state, overall, and see how it changes with time.

A very rough calculation of cost per call can have a useful 'shock value'. Take the annual remuneration of a sales person, and multiply it by 2.5 to give you the 'salary overhead'—what it actually costs the company to employ a sales person, taking into account factors such as payroll tax, superannuation, car expenses, mobile telephone expenses, training, customer entertainment, travel, and workspace. Divide that figure by the number of calls that person makes in a year to give an approximate cost per call. Do not take the highest daily call rate as an average! Look at the number of calls actually made in a year.

Results with my clients vary from $50 a call to $550, depending on the type of selling. For Key Account Managers a common figure is $200 to $300. Do we get value for money from each call? And does the knowledge of the cost per call make us determined to get better value for money from each call?

One of the key factors in sales productivity overall is, of course, the number of calls an account manager makes—what we can define as call productivity. It is astonishing how few companies measure this. The reason might be that the quality of calls is much more important than the number of calls. But this fact does not mean that the number of calls is irrelevant. After all, the most important work an account manager does is done face to face with customers. Some companies measure face-to-face time with the customer in minutes per week or in percentage terms. The results are usually sobering in the extreme.

The account manager can set standards for the number of calls she or he plans to make. In fact for A and B accounts this will be specified as part of the individual account plan. But for rough calculation purposes, assume there will be a visit to someone within an A account once a week, to a B account once every two weeks, and to C accounts maybe once every three months. Further assume that each visit takes the same time (which given travelling time is possibly not far from the truth). You can work out based on current levels of call productivity whether you have the resources to meet planned needs of customer contact.

As an example:

	A Accounts	B Accounts	C Accounts	Total Accounts
Number of accounts	6	40	125	146
Visit frequency per annum	50	25	4	n/a
Total visits	300	1 000	500	1 800

If current call productivity per person is 500 calls per annum, you need 3.6 people to handle the sales task as you have defined it.

If in fact you only have three people, these are your options:
• put on an extra person—an option which can be very hard to justify
• increase call productivity without prejudicing call quality
• reduce planned service levels where you think it will have least impact on the business.

Not only should each account manager set standards and targets for call productivity and sales productivity, they should also measure what actually happens. Many account managers are reluctant to do this because they fear that their call productivity is indeed lower than it should be and are nervous about exposing it.

However, we need to understand the reasons behind low call productivity, and we need to analyse performance to see how we can achieve higher productivity. We could consider reducing what the administration sales people do, streamlining reporting, providing some internal support to make the external people more productive. It is hard to find good sales people, and they are expensive, so they should not spend their time chasing deliveries, writing sample request forms and so on. It is also clear that information systems play a role. The account manager needs access to the information in the most useful format he or she needs to run the business.

Senior sales and marketing people may be vaguely aware that call rates and face-to-face time with customers are not high enough. But they do not have sufficient 'hard evidence' to act. No manager is going to make changes or spend money if there is only anecdotal evidence. It is useful, therefore, every six months to keep a log for two weeks to see where in fact you spend your time. The results may shock you into doing something about minimising these non-sales-productive tasks. Combined with analysis of call productivity, this log provides the justification for looking at sales productivity overall. And being aware of it is an improvement in itself.

17

Time management is associated with examination of sales productivity: for this, see Figure 11.

Summary

The philosophy behind account management is that it is not in the interests of the supplier to sell on price. It is often not in the long-term interests of the purchaser either. To avoid this, the supplier must find ways of adding value to the package by creating a differentiated package of goods and/or services. This process is individual to an account. It must include aspects of how to meet the personal as well as the business needs of the account by ensuring the right relationships exist at all levels in both companies. Through key account management it focuses time, effort and resources onto those accounts who we anticipate are going to provide most of our sales results. It forces sales people to address sales productivity and call productivity.

. . . .

Discipline

Account management is a process; it is a systematic way of approaching business at a single individual account, based on the fundamental concept of differentiation. It should proceed step-by-step, rotating in a cycle of activities, which repeat every few months.

Many of the steps of account management are already carried out to some extent by a considerable number of sales forces. But the strength of the account management process involves making sure that it is carried out completely and correctly on all occasions. Otherwise, what happens is that a step is missed out, which might be so important that its omission means the negation of all the other work done.

A classic example might be not to have recognised that future decisions are going to be made by a different person, even a newcomer who knows nothing about the work you have done with this account. The customer may have some changed priorities, and some urgent ones. Cashflow might be an example. If you have not realised this, and your competitor walks through the door at the right time with an offer which specifically addresses the customer's cashflow needs, you may lose the business despite the good work you have done.

If you have been account managing an account for some time, and have been doing it well, before committing to an alternative supplier the customer may tell you what is happening and give you another chance.

Account management implies the discipline of getting it right on an ongoing basis. Another way of saying this is that it takes years to build up a relationship of trust with a customer, but it can be destroyed in a minute.

Account management is not a part-time activity. It is something which, if you are dedicated, you must keep doing, forging stronger and better relationships with the customer. It needs to be integrated into the job descriptions of the sales force, both at the sales person level and at the sales management level. It must be part of the appraisal system for the sales force.

There are several aspects to the discipline which should be adhered to. The strength of the approach is in getting them all right. Failure in one area will lead to failure overall.

These areas are:

- information
- planning
- analysis
- presentation
- getting agreement
- implementation
- review.

We will be dealing in detail with each of these areas under the three sections for the different business types, namely distribution network selling, supermarket chains and direct end-user selling.

. . . .
Commitment

The only way a discipline will be adhered to is if there is commitment to it. The companies which have been the most successful with account management are those which had a total commitment to it from the top down. Otherwise the sales force sees it as yet another management idea which will run its course in a few months, after which the sales force can get back to doing things the way it always has.

The first step of commitment is to have the account management process written into job descriptions and for it to be seriously assessed as an important part of the appraisal process, and hence, at least in principle, reward for performance.

You should never underestimate the power of the chief executive of a company to influence the way people think and do things, and even influence value systems. This can be directly through their excellent leadership qualities, such as when James Strong led Australian Airlines into a clear leadership position over Ansett. It can also be a passive process, where employees emulate the views of the boss as a matter of survival, even if they do not believe in them. The main point is that when the chief executive speaks, the troops listen.

If you really want to demonstrate commitment to account management, make sure that the chief executive talks about it. Get him or her to attend training meetings or work sessions on account management and to ask questions about it in the corridor.

Mention account management in the company magazine. Offer an incentive tied to account management. Integrate the plans into the appraisal system; since the account plans represent both the activities and the results wanted from the major accounts, and they are proposed by the account managers themselves, they serve as an excellent mechanism for assessing whether sales people are doing their job.

Build some of the training round account management, refer to it in sales meetings and conferences. Just keep talking about it.

Have a timetable for the plans to be written, and make sure that it is adhered to. Set standards for the gathering and keeping of information to support account management and make sure they are followed. Sales managers must manage the implementation of the account plans, by making sure that the sales people are following them. Ensure that the account plans are live documents, not a work of art which is then put away in a drawer somewhere to gather dust. Make them the subject of 'quality time' reviews. The sales manager should keep copies of the plans, and regularly review progress with the sales people.

Commitment of company resources outside sales

Finally, we must recognise that account management requires time and effort not only from the sales people, but also people resources from other departments, and financial resources.

Account management implies using the abilities of the company, whatever they are, to assist a customer to make more money. Usually such abilities are drawn from the sales and marketing departments, but they could also come from outside. For example, if your Distribution Manager has expertise in setting up a facility similar to one a customer is intending to set up, it may be valuable for your Distribution Manager to talk to the customer about his or her experience, and how to avoid some of the pitfalls.

You may have expertise in information technology which would assist a customer. You may have expertise in environmental issues which could help a customer meet requirements more cost effectively. You may have material on energy conservation which could save your customers thousands of dollars every year on an ongoing basis.

While you have to be careful not to commit resources outside your area of control without agreement of the individual concerned, the company should develop a culture which says that any part of the company might be required to participate in the account management process, as long as it allows the company to differentiate itself as a supplier.

There is a further advantage in involving parts of the company that would not normally be involved with customers. That is, that it demonstrates to them that, whether they realise it or not, every part of the organisation is involved in satisfying the needs of customers. Taking a broad definition, everyone is involved in sales.

Account management may require more cash investment than normal ad hoc selling. There may be meetings to fund, and more interstate visits to be made. There may be things which have internal costs, or which may require the expenditure of money on external services. There is no point in going into account management unless there is a preparedness to make this extra initial investment. The payback at the end of the day is handsome, as those who operate account management will testify. But you have to be prepared to commit people resources and some financial resources to get that return. Generally the amounts involved are not enormous but the value of account management is greatly reduced if in a cost-cutting exercise a decision is made to cut back on key account activities such as visits, meetings, promotional campaigns and so forth.

20

. . . .
Summary

We have described key account management as a philosophy, a discipline and a commitment. It is a philosophy which is based on the sound marketing concept of differentiation, focused on those accounts whose business is going to be responsible for most of our sales results. It is a discipline in the sense that it requires the dedication to adopt key account management completely and consistently to get the best results. Commitment is required from the whole company to make sure it happens, through integration into the company culture and the job descriptions of those directly and regularly involved, and by the provision of resources required.

2
Integrating marketing strategy

. . . .

Introduction

So far we have said very little about the role that the marketing department might be expected to play in account management. In a strict sense the answer should perhaps be 'not very much'. From a purist point of view marketing is strategic and selling is tactical. Account management is clearly a customer-related activity and as such it is the sales force which has the prime accountability, authority and responsibility for it. Account management is a process for managing the company's business with an account. This is a sales function.

However, sales should always be directed towards the marketing objectives set by the marketing department. Furthermore, much of the differentiation we create as a company should be part of the marketing strategy. The marketing department will set the strategic direction and provide or develop the corporate ability to differentiate itself, then put together marketing programs which are designed to assist the sales force to achieve the objectives. Simplistically, marketing makes the bullets for the sales people to fire.

Sales should have some say in the type of bullets which marketing are going to make, because after all they are the ones who are going to have to fire them. Equally, marketing are paying for them, so they have a right to know and comment on how and where the sales force is going to fire them.

(In some consumer products companies there are bullets fired at the consumer, media advertising for example, and some which are fired at the supermarket chains. This has given rise to two strands of marketing, trade marketing and consumer marketing. See Part 3.)

Marketing people are still a resource, and their knowledge and expertise can be useful in creating differentiation at individual accounts. Marketing people must have first-hand experience of the market, otherwise they will formulate plans on the basis of hearsay and the opinion of others. For this reason, marketing people should be visiting customers as part of the account management process. But this should be planned and controlled by the sales people, in particular the person responsible for that account, the account manager.

. . . .

Setting the strategic direction

How does the sales force decide which should be the key accounts? It is easy to say, that they should be the accounts which make up the top 60 per cent or 70 per cent or 80 per cent of turnover. But does that take into account where the company expects to be in three years? Are the accounts we have now the same ones we want for the future? Is the distribution network right? Are our major accounts viable and returning us the right profitability? If there are going to be new products, will they be sold to the same accounts? Do we expect the mix of our business to change so that the business at some accounts will decline and at other accounts will grow? Do we need to reallocate resources between market segments?

The choice of which accounts are going to be key accounts will depend on marketing's view of where the company is heading. This provides the focus of where the sales force should be developing the business and which accounts should be in which category, not just for now but for the future as well.

When account managers are planning the business for their accounts, how do they decide which products to promote, given that different products have different margins, and which products are the key ones to develop now in order to secure the company's position in the future?

For that matter, how do the marketing people know which programs to develop to support sales? How do they know in which direction they should push market development and product development? How do they know what company goals their strategies are designed to support?

Unless there exists a strategic plan for the company (or Strategic Business Unit), they can only guess. If we want to ensure that the sales force is really being productive in contributing to the corporate goals, those goals need to be defined and the intermediate planning and communication processes, to the point where a sales person is talking to a customer, need to be in place.

If the account management process, implemented through the account plans, is going to have direction, it must be backed up by some fundamental strategic thinking. That way you ensure that everyone in the company is heading towards a defined and desirable goal. The alternative is a sales force who may be doing things with customers that contradict where the company wants to go, and which could create problems in the future. Failure to have this focus means at best that much of the effort of the sales department might be wasted. It gives rise to productivity leaks.

. . . .

The marketing plans

One of the first questions I ask sales people in an account management workshop is whether they know what their marketing plans are. The responses are varied. Few of them are encouraging. They range from, 'What marketing plans?' to 'Some plans have been issued, but they do not really help me decide the direction I should be heading the business.' In the consumer products area things are somewhat better structured. The worst area is the industrial area with companies selling direct to end users.

When the marketing department is asked if they have written marketing plans which provide clear direction for the sales force, they invariably claim that they have. How do we reconcile these two pieces of information?

My experience is that too many marketing plans are long on statistical analysis of today's market, supplemented with some budget numbers, but very short on setting direction. There may be some statements of where the company wants to go, but very little guidance on how to get there. It is this 'how' which is so important for the sales force to know, and which is so often missing. To state a result without being specific on how it is going to be achieved risks failure to achieve the result.

Part of the problem in the industrial market is that nearly all marketing courses are geared to consumer marketing. Another part of the problem is that many industrial manufacturers are limited to how much they can respond to the market needs by the nature of the manufacturing process they use, and in which they have enormous amounts of money tied up. As a result they tend to abandon a market orientation and do their marketing through Product Managers, whose job it is to champion a particular product. This risks losing a focus on the total business, and presents to the sales force a fragmented and often contradictory set of instructions.

The marketing plans need to:
- be clear and concise
- set clear desirable and achievable goals
- be in enough detail for the sales people to interpret them, and know how the goals are going to be achieved
- keep supporting data in an appendix
- have quantified and timed elements
- clearly detail the major thrusts
- make a statement about the six 'Ps': place (or distribution), product, packaging, price, penetration, promotion
- be consistent with the corporate objectives
- be based on input from sales and preferably with their agreement
- clearly show the agreement of other departments whose operations may be affected
- managed by marketing to make sure the plans are implemented on time.

25

. . . .

The corporate strategic plan

In a workshop with a group of account managers from one of Australia's largest companies, the subject of marketing plans and strategic plans came up. The account managers said that it was left to them to do the marketing, and they had never heard of a strategic plan. That morning the Managing Director of the company joined the troops for morning tea. One of the account managers told the MD that we had just been discussing strategic plans, and asked him what the company's strategic plan said.

The Managing Director replied, 'It is funny that you should ask that. One of our directors has just come back from a course in the USA, and on his return he said that we should have one of these strategic plans.' That was nearly four years ago, and as far as I am aware, they still do not have one!

They have always made what they make and, because of the high-freight component, they have in effect a market protected from direct competition. They purchase technology from time to time. But there are some serious threats to their business in the future and they have not addressed them in any consistent way. What will happen is that when a problem crops up they will try and solve it on an ad hoc basis. But by then it will probably be too late for them to take any action to prevent a very large reduction in the volume of sales.

An experienced strategic planner bemoaned that since his company had been sold by its professional overseas owner to another company, the strategic planning process which had been in place as a world requirement had fallen into a void. His concern was about investment. The sort of plant that this business requires takes years to build. The failure to do any strategic planning caused them not to know whether they should be investing. If it turns out that they should be, then it will be too late to do anything about it. The competition will have stolen the lead.

Strategic planning has a rather frightening ring to it. It seems to be at the pinnacle of marketing wizardry, the sort of things they do at Harvard, MIT or Swiss business schools. It is seen as something for the top echelon companies who can afford to pay consultants exorbitant rates to tell them what they should be doing, and then get it wrong!

That is not at all what it should be. To start with, strategic planning is a company activity, not just a marketing activity. Certainly much of the input will be of a marketing nature, and the plan will have implications for how the company will interact with the marketplace. But it is an activity which should be performed by the senior executives of all of the corporate functions—manufacturing or operations, finance, human resources, marketing and sales, maybe distribution, research and development or technical departments, information technology, depending on the type of business.

The order in which a strategic plan reads is not necessarily the order in which it is generated. The box shows some of the headings of a typical five-year strategic plan in the order in which they are likely to be written.

Background: brief history of the business

Corporate mission—not the company mission statement which is for public consumption, but a statement which states what the company is all about, and what it is trying to do

Business definition—sounds easy, but broader business definitions open up considerably more horizons

Key financial figures

Major SWOTs

Key gaps

Summary strategic statement

Positioning statement

Detailed strategy

Major thrusts by functional area

In appendix as working sheets:
    Consolidated strengths
    Consolidated weaknesses
    External analysis
    Internal analysis

The steps involved in the strategic planning process are:

- assessing the current position and trends in the external environment
- auditing the company's strengths, weaknesses and resources
- identifying those activities where the emphasis must be changed by reduction, expansion or redirection
- setting corporate objectives.

The process is about assigning weights and priorities to the major elements of production, finance and systems, organisation and HRD, and marketing. The first step is one of analysis, requiring thinking about the business, the marketplace and where it is going, and about the company. This requires the input of everyone at the meeting representing all the functional areas. They must come well briefed.

The exercise is exhilarating and exhausting. There is often lively discussion. An issue like the business definition may have major impact on the way the company develops, and may provoke heated argument. Imagine the difference between seeing yourself as a TV hire company versus one in the business of processing enormous numbers of small amounts of money, or a newspaper publisher versus a disseminator of information, which opens up electronic storage and transmission. Is a blow moulder of plastic bottles primarily a plastics moulder, or a transporter of fluids? In my own training business it makes a difference whether I see the business as designing and running workshops, or business education which might include making and selling training videos, writing books and lecturing at business schools, or helping business to be more productive and effective, which might also include consultancy services.

Because all participants bring to the meeting their own views of the company and the business, one of the major benefits of the strategic planning exercise is that it creates better understanding about the total company, its operations and the market in which it operates. Everyone has the chance to speak their mind, it is an excellent communication system. The process should aim for the agreement of all the participants. This may not be possible, but at least everyone's view will have been heard, and everyone will understand why decisions have been made. As one client said after such a strategic planning exercise, the most productive part of the whole thing was that the management team is working together as one unit for the first time.

The output of the process includes strategic thrusts for each of the key functional areas, which are consistent because they have been derived from the same thought process and at the same time and are all supporting the corporate goal.

The heads of each functional area should take away their major thrusts and write plans for their own department on how they are going to be

27

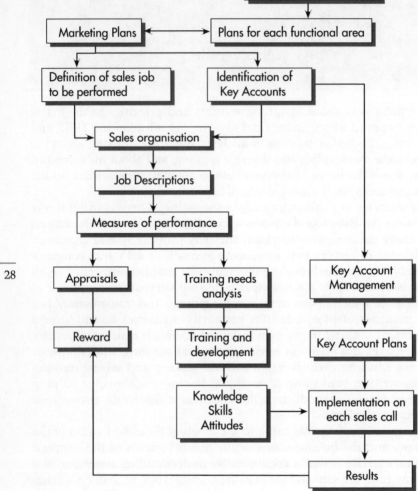

Figure 2:   The flow of business direction from corporate plan to each sales call

carried out. In the marketing department these thrusts will lead to the marketing strategies which will get passed to the sales force to give the direction they need for their selling activities in general and account management in particular.

Strategic planning does not normally come up with major surprises. If it did, that would suggest that the company knew nothing about the business it is in. But it should reaffirm the key priorities. It indicates the key few things which the company must achieve. Too many companies try to achieve too many things at the same time, and because of conflicting priorities do not do any of them completely or well. We should take the view that if a major activity or expense is not supportive of a core priority as defined by the strategic plan, we probably should not do it.

Many companies are now expressing this as the Corporate Vision supported by what are described as core values.

Figure 2 (opposite) shows the flow of plans which ensures that what a sales person is saying to a customer (the micro level), is consistent with and supportive of where the company wants to head (the macro level).

The balanced corporate scorecard

There has been considerable interest recently in a concept called the 'balanced corporate scorecard', pioneered by Robert Kaplan and Robert Norton from Harvard Business School. Some reviews were printed since 1993 and a book on the subject was published by Harvard Business Press in 1996. It is an approach to managing business by looking at a number of key elements. The elements a particular business will choose depends on its strategies, objectives and competitive demands. It allows the company to focus on those key elements which are most consistent with its overall strategy, it sets specific goals and then allows progress to be monitored.

29

They point out that most companies use countless measures to monitor progress, and that these measures tend to have been developed on an ad hoc basis. They suggest that companies tend to concentrate as a priority on financial results, and that this leads to short term focus and a failure to build a long term sustainable business. Money is invested in short term fixes rather than genuine value creation.

The balanced scorecard looks at other elements which will influence the achievement of financial results, and forces the integration of the whole company towards achieving the company vision. There are four 'perspectives' to the balanced scorecard. They are the:
- **Financial perspective**—the achievement of bottom line results
- **Customer perspective**—how the company will approach customers and the marketplace
- **Internal business perspective**—the processes to achieve the objectives
- **Learning and growth perspective**—the infrastructure the company needs to build for long term growth, and improvement of systems and organisational procedures.

This approach has a very strong customer focus. It looks not only at results but also at how a company goes about achieving those results. Whilst the balanced scorecard approach does not help decide the strategic direction, it certainly is a very useful tool in implementing it. The main issue with respect to key account management is that the two approaches dovetail. Key account management should be a key component in how the customer perspective is implemented.

Summary

For account management to be most effective, those managing the process, the sales force, need to know what the marketing plans are. The plans should be derived from a corporate strategic planning process. Account plans are sometimes written without having a clear marketing direction. In this case the sales people have to assume that nothing will change, or will make the assumptions for change themselves.

If you want to get account management operating in your company and there are no existing marketing or strategic plans, start lobbying for them. But at least get some account plans written now to gain expertise in account management ready for when you can add into the process the marketing direction your company has decided upon.

3

The key account management cycle

. . . .

Introduction

Key account management is a process; it is a series of events which leads to the goal of a better quality business with a particular account. So far we have been discussing the thinking behind the process. Now we will talk about the process itself. There are several steps which lead towards the result, and these steps are repeated in a cycle. The periodicity of this cycle will vary with how dynamic the business is at that account, and on the type of account. In selling through a distribution network, it may be convenient to look at the business on an annual basis with quarterly adjustments. In other businesses, such as the agricultural sector or the hospitality industries, it may make sense to plan around seasons. Generally, the cycle will last three months to six months, and can be varied as the business at that account becomes more or less dynamic. There do not have to be any fixed rules in this regard. In the case of a client on contract, the cycle may revolve several times during the currency of the contract. There is a danger that once a contract has been agreed, the supplier relaxes efforts at that account in order to concentrate on other business. This is a mistake. It should be easier to retain the business you have than create business or steal someone else's. It is therefore critical to account manage those clients who are on contract, as it is then likely that you will retain them when the contract comes up for renewal.

The core of the account management cycle is the account plan, which is the document which commits us to action and sets goals and activities for a defined period. However, there are several preparatory steps without which the quality of the plans will be poor, and some follow-up steps, without which you will not get the best out of the plans.

The concept of the account management cycle is that it is a series of chronologically sequenced activities. It starts with collecting the basic information necessary to do the planning, some analysis of the current situation, and an investigation of the opportunities to add value to our package and hence differentiate ourselves. Then comes writing the plan, followed by its implementation.

There is a fundamental difference between selling to accounts who then resell the product, and selling to an account who will use the product or service themselves. In the case of the direct customer who uses the product, the plan will remain an internal document of the supplier, describing a series of activities which when complete will add value to the package through a process of differentiation, and achieve the objectives set for this account. In the case of selling through distribution, the plan is a commitment to joint activities to sell the product out, as well as gain distribution by selling the product in. As such, the plan is a joint external document which should be the basis of the presentation and negotiated agreement on how the supplier and the reseller will work together.

This leads to plans which are different in their construction and format. They will be dealt with separately in the text for this reason.

The next step is the implementation and management of all the elements of the plan, which should lead to results. The last step in the process is for a review session of the progress made, and consideration of the implications for the next planning cycle, both external with the customer, and internal.

The account management cycle is shown in its variants, both external with the customer and internal for direct selling and for selling through distribution, in Figures 3 and 4.

Now let us look at what is involved in each of the steps.

. . . .
Understanding the marketing plans

We have talked about the fact that we must ensure that what the sales force is doing at the customer interface must be consistent with the direction in which the company intends to head. The first part of ensuring this is for the company management to have gone through some radical strategic planning which defined the key issues for the business. This corporate strategic plan will have implications for each of the functional areas of the

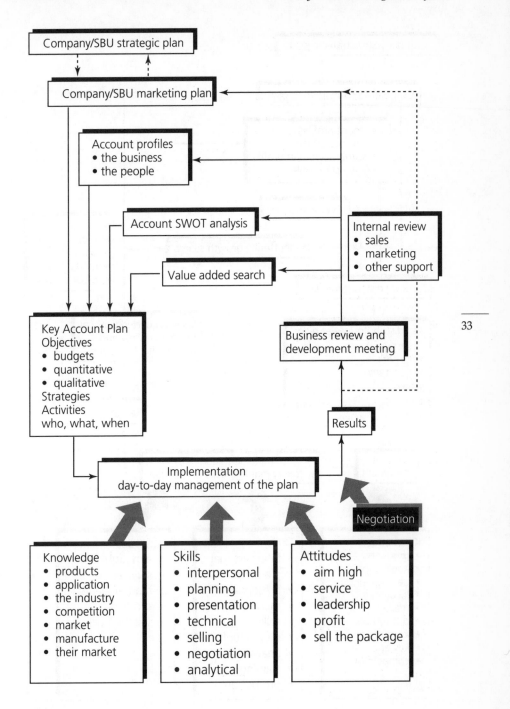

Figure 3: Direct account management

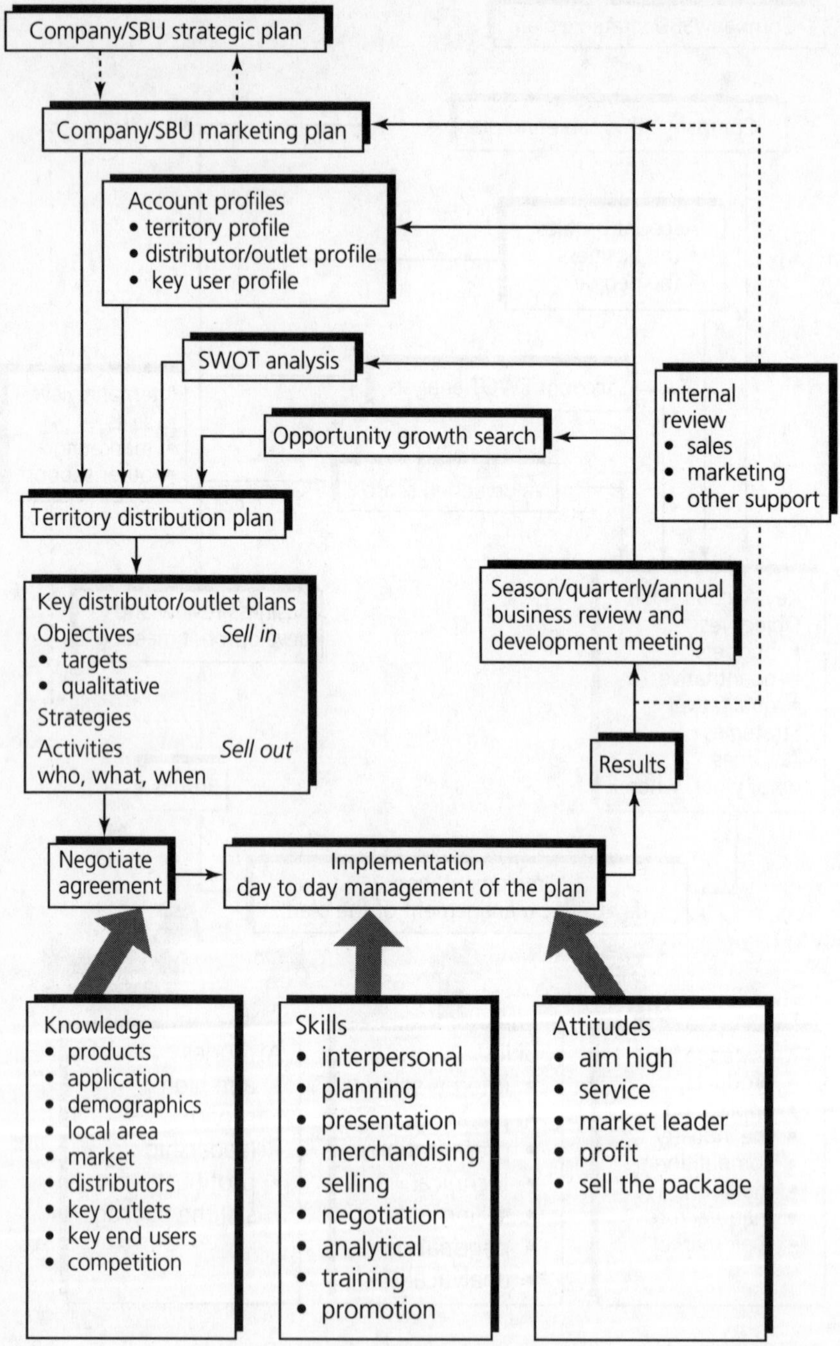

Figure 4: Distribution account management cycle

34

company. In particular, there will be implications which the marketing department must take into account when writing the marketing plans.

These marketing plans will have implications for how sales people are going to interact with the marketplace. Typically they will at least include a statement about each of the six 'Ps' or the classic four 'Ps'—product, place, price and promotion (the six Ps include packaging, penetration and sometimes people). The sales force needs to know which products the company is concentrating, and how they will be packed, despatched, transported and delivered. There will be a statement on product positioning and on pricing. (The question of who should be responsible for pricing is complex. Marketing should define the price positioning, in other words set the strategic guidelines on price. The sales department should implement the pricing policy within the agreed guidelines. A mechanism is required for agreeing price when action outside these guidelines is being considered, as there is a need for a system for managing price on a daily basis within sales authority guidelines. The national sales manager will normally be the person with the authority, some of which may be delegated to the more junior sales managers.)

'Promotion' means much more than just advertising. It should include a statement about the preferred customer base, and the thrust of how the sales force are going to sell. For example, will it be on the basis of a differentiated service, technical back-up, or the company's ability to develop new products or new business? This decision may influence the customer base where we are going to sell and influence where the sales force will spend most of its time. It will also define the sort of activities the sales people perform, and the content of sales calls.

Generally, consumer companies are far better at defining the marketing programs than are those selling technical products or those selling direct to customers. Too many marketing plans for these latter groups do not give clear enough direction to the sales force. They concentrate on market analysis and definition, and do not tell anyone what the company is going to do about it. The sales department must discipline the marketing department to ensure that the marketing plans have clear statements about these points so that the sales department can incorporate them into account management.

Sales input into marketing plans

The sales department should be involved to a certain extent in the process. There is no point in the marketing department devising plans which the sales people feel they cannot implement. There needs to be good two-way communication while the marketing people develop their plans.

Sales input should be through some formal review process, which ensures that the marketing people really know what is happening out in the marketplace. This can involve the sales department making recommendations for consideration by the marketing department. The marketing department should then devise the plans, and obtain agreement in principle from the sales department, usually the national sales manager, that they are achievable. This should happen before the detailed plans are formalised.

The marketing plans should then be formally presented to the sales department, and checked for understanding. In businesses where there are promotional programs which change regularly, consideration should be given to a quarterly meeting between sales management and marketing. This allows for review of the success of past programs and learning from them, and presentation of the next period's marketing and promotional programs. This could best be achieved with an immediate period for fine tuning, and a later period for plans to be addressed. For example, at the end of December you may review what had happened in the quarter October–December, then fine-tune plans which had been discussed three months earlier for the period January–March. Then there would be presentation of the plans for April–June. Those plans will be fine-tuned at the next meeting at the end of March. The key point is that in many businesses where there are marketing programs which change over a few months, there needs to be a formal mechanism for review and presentation, allowing an appropriate lead time, and enabling some last-minute fine-tuning. Figure 5 illustrates this process.

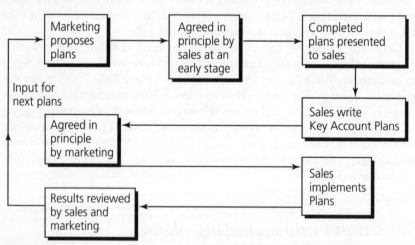

Figure 5: The process of sales and marketing agreeing on each other's plans

The message for marketing people working for companies selling industrial products is this: nearly all marketing courses, whether academic or formal training refer to consumer marketing rather than industrial marketing. There is more to industrial marketing than meets the eye. It is not just a question of analysing the market, identifying trends and market sizes and shares. Neither is it only a question of setting goals in terms of financial and commercial objectives. It is about setting priorities for the various market segments and allocating resources between them and then creating the marketing strategies to achieve these goals. Each marketing plan must have a substantial portion devoted to how objectives are going to be achieved, and it should be expressed so that the sales force can interpret and implement it, through the account management program.

. . . .
The account profile

If we are to plan our business by key account, especially if we are seeking to add value to our package or differentiate, we clearly need to know something about our accounts. If you ask account managers to compile a list of things they think should be included in the account profile, as I often do in workshops on account management, they will come up with a formidable list. Much of it falls into the 'it would be nice to know' category. The question is, whether the information is important or useful in running the key account management program. The danger is that account profiles can get out of hand, to the extent that so much energy is devoted to collecting and storing information that there is none left for the more important activity of writing and implementing a plan. Some information (see box) is critical.

37

Basic information includes:
- basic details, address etc.
- something about the corporate entity—who they are
- the people, the organisation chart, key influencers and decisiom makers, what sort of people they are
- operations: what they do, how they do it, what they use
- their marketplace, their customers, competitors and issues in their business
- how they do business, contractual agreements, systems and procedures.

What information you decide to collect on your key accounts will vary with your type of business. This will be discussed further in Parts 2, 3 and 4 of the book, with more detailed suggestions on what is appropriate.

Decide what you really need to know to manage the business.

The account profile is a reference document and should be fairly stable. The most dynamic part will be customer personnel. Issues like competitive performance are better handled in the SWOT.

Account profile formats

Have a company-wide format so that each account profile collects information under the same headings and in the same order. This makes it much easier for everyone to find their way around the profiles. An outline example is given in Figure 6.

Allow flexibility so that the appropriate quantity of information under any heading can be accommodated. Some accounts may have a short sentence under a particular section, whereas for others you may need space for two or three paragraphs. Under some headings there may be nothing at all.

It can be useful to have a menu of prompts for things which are important for your particular business. I have provided some standard formats and headings (see Figure 6), but take the 'boxes' and add the appropriate menu items for *your* business.

Many companies have considerable information on their customer base, but most of it is in the heads of the sales people. The company needs to collect this information in something more durable than a sales person's neurons. The formal collection and recording of this information can seem unnecessary. That is, until a sales person leaves and the company discovers that there are no records in existence—that all our information walked out the door with the sales person.

Establishing a database

The task of establishing a database is daunting. The worst thing you can do is focus for a prolonged period of time (a month or more) on just getting account profiles up to date. It interferes too much with the daily business, and is a demoralising chore for sales people. It is much better to take it in steps and to build up the database over time. This requires some discipline from the sales manager in chasing it up, otherwise after the first burst of enthusiasm there will be little activity.

My recommendation is to take it slowly, recording a bit at a time what you already know about your accounts. Set goals of doing that for, say, two accounts a month until you have recorded everything you already know and need to record. Then, as part of the call objectives to these key accounts, define what you do not know and still need to know, and make sure that on every call to a key account the account manager looks up the profile and finds something to add to it. It may take a year to get the account profiles in the condition you want them, but you will have created a considerable asset to the business without turning the sales department upside down in doing it.

Account Profile For The East Coast Company

Address

Phone

Fax

A.C.N.
Customer number:
Account Manager:

Date prepared:

Last date amended:

The Company

The business they are in:

Ownership:

Who owns them, who they own, affiliations and associations

Brief company history:

Company objectives:

Company dimensions:

sales turnover, profits made, how many people employed

Business with associated companies:

theirs:
ours:

Financial standing and results

39

Figure 6: An outline Account Profile Format. The first three pages would be the same for both direct and distributor accounts. The last three will differ, and two formats, one for distributor and one for direct are given.

40

Operations - manufacturer

Description of operations

Equipment and facilities

Processes and results

Relative importance to them of purchases from us

Purchase history

shares and volumes, key issues
Choose selected total figures for the last three years from the stats.

Purchase criteria

Any special issues

Organisation and people

Organisation

* influencer on our business
** decision maker

Organisation Chart

Key People Profile

1

2

3

4

5

6

Contractual arrangements

Special pricing

Period of the arrangement

Any special clauses or conditions

Payment terms

Special delivery instructions

Budget schedule

Other

41

Sales and marketing - manufacturer

Their marketplace

shares, size of business
Australia:
Export:

Their positioning

Major sales and marketing thrusts

Their key customers

Key purchase criteria of their customers

Key competitors

Potential for growth

Sales and marketing - distribution

Their marketplace

Their clientele

Products they sell

range of products sold, shares, size of business

Their positioning

Major sales and marketing thrusts

Their key customers

Key purchase criteria of their customers

Key competitors

Potential for growth

Other

Operations - Distribution

Description of operations

Number of stores and warehouses

Delivery and transport arrangements

Relative importance to them of purchases from us

Purchase history

our shares and volumes in their business, key issues
Choose selected total figures for the last three years of the stats.

Purchase criteria

Any special issues

Contractual arrangements - distribution

Special invoice pricing

_____

Promotional funds

_____

Rebate arrangements

_____

Period of the arrangement

_____

Any special clauses or conditions

_____

Payment terms

_____

Special delivery instructions

_____

Other

_____

43

You may be surprised about the gaps in your knowledge. They do not matter, as long as you fill them in. You must also guard against what you know to be the facts, and what you believe to be a fact because someone told you or the company has always believed it. The task of keeping account profiles up to date involves questioning whether there are any changes in the account which you are not aware of. Beware of accepting folklore about your accounts as facts, just because you have always believed it.

It is important to remember that account profiles are a tool, not an end in themselves. They are there to be used whenever you write account plans, before business review and development meetings (see later in this chapter), and whenever you do a SWOT analysis on an account. They are also used whenever the account manager is not there and some action needs to be taken at an account, or when a new account manager is appointed and needs to familiarise her/himself with the account.

Account profiles are also useful to marketing people, including product managers. They may also be useful to other employees who may be involved in providing a service to the customer or have some contact with the customer. Technical service, research and development and product distribution personnel could all fall into this category.

It is the responsibility of the account manager to keep the account profile up to date. However, it is also the responsibility of anyone who has contact with the account and who finds out any useful information to make sure that such information is recorded, either by doing it themselves or passing it to whoever is able to do it (account manager, secretary or sales people).

Customer personnel and the account profile

One of the common areas where companies collect information is on their customers' personnel. Since much of the success of selling and account management depends on the relationships between us and our customers, it makes sense to prepare ourselves as much as possible by knowing about the people involved. The question is what we need to know. This depends to a certain extent on cultural issues of the industry in which you operate and the culture of your own company.

Some organisations like to collect personal information on their customers, such as the name of their spouse and children, birthdays and home addresses. Some care needs to be exercised here in terms of the law and privacy, and the possibility of causing offence. You should certainly never record information which has not been volunteered by the individual. Rumour and gossip is out! If we look at it from the point of view of making it easier to establish the right relationships and being able to predict the behaviour of a customer, the sorts of things which could be useful are:

- previous jobs and career history
- interests and hobbies
- their business and management style
- how they tend to decide
- any particular 'no-no's'
- personality.

In constructing these personal profiles you must guard against subjective feeling. A person you dislike, or one who is negative about our company, products or even our own people is not necessarily a 'bad' person. This is where the question of personality characterisation can be problematical. You may find a person unresponsive and uncooperative, but another account manager may have a totally different experience.

'Empathy selling' depends on an approach described in his book of that title by Christopher C. Golis. It is the characterisation of customers according to a personality profile, and modification of the sales person's behaviour to appeal to the characteristics of the person. The theory is good, based on the reputable Humm-Wadsworth tests operated in Australia by Chandler and Macleod. What is doubtful is whether sales people, even those who have done a few short training courses on the subject, are able to correctly assess the salient elements of a customer's profile. Getting it wrong could lead to disaster.

It is useful to know what their career path has been, and what they achieved in previous positions and how they went about it. Someone heading a negotiation team is likely to take a different approach depending on whether they have had experience as an accountant, a marketing person, a sales person or a production person with experience negotiating with unions. Knowing whether a person tends to want to appear decisive or whether they seem to prefer others to make decisions, or even seem unable to make a decision, is important.

45

. . . .

Account SWOT analysis

The account profile is about the account and how they operate, but we need to know how they perceive us as a supplier, especially relative to other suppliers in the market place. A SWOT analysis (see Figure 7) looks at our strengths and weaknesses at that account at a point in time, relative to other suppliers. It also looks at any opportunities for us at that account, and any possible threats to our business. Such an analysis can change very quickly and dramatically, depending on what is happening in the marketplace. Clearly the aspect of the analysis which deals with our strengths and weaknesses is about differentiation: it is asking what differentiation exists between suppliers, in the eyes of the customer.

Key Account SWOT Analysis

Date ....

Key Account ....

Key Account Manager ....

1. Strengths

Our strengths versus the competition

              seen by us   seen by the customer

2. Weaknesses

Our weaknesses versus the competition

              seen by us   seen by the customer

3. Competitive performance at this account

Criteria	Supplier	Competitor 1	Competitor 2	Competitor 3	Weighting/10

Menu of criteria:
- technical back-up
- technical innovation
- credit
- representation
- delivery
- responsiveness
- availability
- price
- promotion
- relationships
- flexibility
- administration
- professionalism
- product quality
- materials handling

4. Relationships matrix

Customer	Purchasing	Operations	Technical	Research	Marketing	Management
Supplier						
Account Manager						
Sales Manager						
Marketing						
Technical						
Head Office						
General Management						

5. Opportunities for us at this account

6. Threats to us at this account

7. Items for action

1   4

2   5

3   6

46

Figure 7: Account SWOT analysis

It is appropriate to do a SWOT analysis on a key account whenever you are about to negotiate a supply agreement, or whenever there is a commercial situation which requires some action or at least once a year before you start writing the major account plans for the period. (In distribution businesses you might do a SWOT before writing the annual plan, but not before each quarterly action plan. In direct accounts you might do a SWOT once or twice a year before each major set of account plans is written.)

It helps to have a format to guide the questioning and analysis, but in putting together a format, remember that this is not a form filling exercise. The form exists only to guide you through the process. Figure 6 is an example of a format. It is suggested that you design your own form to meet your particular requirements. You may select the criteria which seem to be the ones which the customer takes into consideration when making a purchasing decision or evaluating suppliers. Even just asking yourself which are the main purchase criteria may force you to ask if you *really* know. It can be useful to examine whether there is a difference between our view of our performance, and their views. This implies that we should be getting feedback from them on how they see our performance. One of the best ways to do this is formally through the business review and development meetings which is the last step in the account management cycle.

Even harder is to make an objective assessment of how they see other suppliers. This is because it has traditionally been believed that it is in the interests of the customer to only tell you about the things which your competitors do better than you, and which they therefore would like you to improve on. It is not in their interests to tell you what they think you do well, as it weakens their negotiating position and allows you to better assess and build the strength of your total package. However, as you forge better relationships with customers and build up trust, you will find out more about how they really see the relative performance of suppliers. With quality programs measuring performance against criteria considered important in supply by customers, such as delivery performance, product quality etc., it is easier to be more objective. This coincides with a philosophical shift away from the mechanistic competitive paradigm towards a more cooperative approach of doing business, such as is practised particularly in Japan. As cooperation replaces competition as a management style within companies, it will also begin to extend outwards to relationships between purchaser and supplier, and will lead to more frank and open dialogue, and thus to more objective input for SWOTs.

47

Other ways of finding out how your customers regard you

Market research

Many companies commission market research from time to time to get a general feel for how they are seen by their customers, and to identify aspects of customer regard of which they may have been unaware. (Depending on the design of the project, you may or may not get information from individually identifiable customers.) Most companies who commission such research find it expensive but useful, but there are also a few companies who do not learn anything they did not already know. The pitfalls to watch for are:

- poorly designed questionnaires
- market research interviewers who have not been trained in how to conduct interviews
- inappropriate interviewees
- a tendency for respondents to generalise problems they may have had with a supplier, so that they 'mark them down' on everything
- respondent fatigue, if the exercise is repeated too often (once every six months is too frequent).

By their nature, market research questionnaires are restrictive: they focus on specific questions posed normally by the supplier commissioning the research, so that there is a bias in them. The questions look through the same eyes as the supplier and concentrate on how they see the business. Focus groups can be a useful way of generating ideas on new ways of doing things and meeting customer needs, especially under the stewardship of a skilled facilitator.

One client of mine who has been successfully operating account management for several years had a questionnaire professionally designed, but has used their own account managers to do the interviews. The immediate objection of course is that this reduces objectivity and introduces bias (since the customer is responding directly to the supplier)—and is more likely to lie in order to achieve some commercial advantage. However, my client feels that having operated in 'account management mode' for some time, the customers trust their motives in conducting the research and generally will give open and honest answers. The fact that the interviewee knows the business and the customer actually assisted in the value and the meaning of the responses. It is clearly a less expensive option, and the company was quite satisfied that, for them, this was the right way to go.

A final point. Most good market research companies will readily admit to the margin of error inherent in such projects. Since people often do not act the way they genuinely believe they would, market research is more reliable at finding out what *has* happened than in predicting what *will* happen.

Agreeing measures of performance

With total quality programs abundant in the community—and in spite of more recent criticisms of their achievements—both customers and suppliers are measuring more and more of the elements of supply. (ISO 9002 has played a role in this.) Sadly, more often than not it is the customers who have taken the lead in applying certain criteria to their suppliers. The pity is that the suppliers lose the opportunity to take initiative in this area, and end up by having to dance to the customer's tune.

When you and the customer measure things such as delivery, quality, availability of supply, administration and any other factors affecting supply in your business, objectivity enters the relationship. So if there are areas of your performance pertinent to supply which you can measure, then you should measure them. If the story such measurement tells is good, then agree standards of performance to your customer and provide feedback on how well you do. If the story shows you are not performing as well as others, or not well enough, then fix it up first!

The appropriate time to review performance is during an external review with the customer—typically, a Business Review and Development (BRAD) meeting. Don't be afraid to find out how good or bad you are, it can only lead to either capitalising on a strength or fixing a weakness. Take some initiative, blaze a trail!

49

Doing the SWOT analysis

A SWOT analysis is a desk operation. It relies on input which you will be soliciting from the customer through business review and development meetings and in the course of your normal calls. If you can identify things which are important to the customer and where you perform better than your competitors, you have identified some positive differentiation. Furthermore, if this is in an area where it is hard for competitors to meet your performance through product differentiation or geographic circumstances, the differentiation is more useful and enduring, and is thus more valuable to you. Those are items you need to build up and stress in your dealings with the customer. On the other hand, if there are strengths which you perceive that you have but which the customer does not recognise, you need to either persuade the customer that you have a strength which is of value to them, which is a selling job, or accept your belief is less important than the customer's perception.

If the customer believes that you have weaknesses relative to competitors, in other words negative differentiation, you must seek to overcome these weaknesses. If you cannot, you must look for other things which you can do, other opportunities to differentiate positively, in order to compensate for this weakness. If you do not believe there is a weakness but the customer does, you need to either persuade them that in fact you do not have the weakness, which is again a selling job, or accept the customer's view.

Items 1 and 2 in the analysis (the strengths and weaknesses) are where you can express in words your strengths and weaknesses. In item 3 you can try and quantify performance. Be careful here. If you decide to give scores out of 10 for how the customer rates the suppliers on a particular criterion (10 being a high score) and then you again assign weightings out of 10 for higher or lower importance to the customer of that item, you could multiply out the scores for each supplier and then total them to give an overall score. Do not do it! These measures are not necessarily linear scales, and such a score is not terribly meaningful. What this matrix does is force you to think through the important purchase criteria for the customer, and how well the various suppliers perform against them. Remember that the point of the exercise is to identify actions you need to take.

The relationships matrix encourages you to think through the relationships you have at several levels in both organisations. You can do it as a comparative analysis (better, same, worse) or on the basis of the quality of your actual relationships (good, poor, excellent, non-existent).

This account SWOT is not meant to be a form-filling exercise. It is designed to work as a series of prompts to ensure that you think through properly your competitive position so that you can decide what actions to take to improve it. If you never use the forms at all, but manage to systematically and critically think about the competitive situation, fine. But most people find that having the account SWOT format helps guide them through the analysis.

When SWOTs show no positive differentiation

If, at the end of the analysis, you find that you are negatively differentiated and you believe there is nothing you can do about it, you have defined a very weak position. Unless you are the lowest cost producer and can therefore establish a position by compensating for your weaknesses through a sustainable lower price, you had better consider leaving that customer, and you may even need to assess whether you should not get out of that business altogether. More common is a situation where there seems to be no significant difference between most of the suppliers. This is happening more as products move towards commodities and more me-too products. The most common differentiation, and indeed some of the best, has been product differentiation, but this is gradually disappearing.

We are left with the challenge of creating differentiation in the services we provide rather than in the product. This requires defining the services which are really of value to customers. Having identified the opportunities to create such differentiation, and then created the differentiation on a total or a customer-by-customer basis, the sales force has to learn how to sell the total package of product and service.

The challenge in a low differentiated product situation is to define the opportunities to create some kind of other differentiation. It may still be in the product area, but is more likely to be in other areas. This quest for more differentiation is the subject matter of the next step in the account management cycle, namely the 'value-added search'.

Before we consider this next step, a few words need to be said about opportunities and threats. This is a question of looking at our business at an account and identifying any opportunities to gain business where we do not currently have it. They may occur as growth takes place in the account through new products they are introducing or a planned growth in their own market share. They could occur in selling more of our own range of products to the customer. It could be an opportunity to replace the business of another supplier with our own products or services.

Equally, we must accept that every customer of ours is also a prospect for our competitors, and that they will be planning to take business away from us. We need to identify any weaknesses in our own position or any potential situations which could threaten our business. This should be considered down to the level of what might happen if there were to be a change in the management structure and the decision making process within the customer, to what would happen in the event of a takeover of the customer by another company.

The dangers are epitomised by the story of Acmil's takeover by ACI Plastics. One supplier had sworn to ACI that ACI got the lowest price on a certain product because their volume was the largest in Australia. However, Mr Alan Swain, who was the head of Acmil at the takeover, was an excellent negotiator. Acmil was several price rises behind everyone else, and was buying at a lower price than ACI. When information on prices were pooled and ACI found out that its supplier had been lying, it took the business away from that supplier altogether for a time. Several other suppliers were pleased to pick up some extra business.

The SWOT analysis is not just an analysis of the situation, but also the identification of actions which need to be taken as a result of the analysis. Item 7 in Figure 7 is therefore the most important item of the whole

51

process. Actions need to be addressed in the account plan, and the SWOT analysis is part of forcing the thought processes which should take place before the account plans are written, and which ensure that these plans are correct.

. . . .
Value-added search

For those of us who would prefer not to sell at the lowest price (and that should be most companies), the secret of success is to provide added value to our package of product and services, such that the customer is prepared to reflect this extra value in the type of commercial arrangements they make with us. It is creating positive differentiation.

There should be a marketing position on this subject which is addressed in the marketing plans. Part of the marketing program will be to provide general ways of differentiating ourselves in the marketplace. However, the exact way this position is implemented at an individual account may well be unique, and as such needs to be thought through and planned on an account-by-account basis. Equally, there may be specific things which we can do at one account which might not apply at another.

The process of 'value-added search' is one of creatively identifying what we can do to add value to our package, preferably in areas where our competition is not doing it and cannot match it.

Most opportunities to do this will directly revolve around our products and services. Apart from the product itself, there is the way it is packaged, transported, stored and delivered, and in what quantities. There may be aspects of helping the customer get the best performance out of it. There could be minimisation of risk through technical back-up and quality guarantees. There could be elements of making the buying and selling process easier through improved administration systems. An opportunity could focus on our ability to help the customer with their own quality programs. There might be financial issues of cash flow, inventory costs or contribution to profit. It might involve our experience in marketing to help customers achieve their marketing and sales objectives. In distributive businesses, opportunities could be our ability to help customers define market opportunities and then to provide assistance through training, promotion or even physical help in selling the product out to their own customers. There is an enormous list of things suppliers can do. These will be dealt with in more detail in Parts 2, 3 and 4.

Differentiation beyond product and service

There are also opportunities to do things outside the normal avenues of activity and discussion. Here are examples of some areas where suppliers have creatively added value to their package in areas totally divorced from the normal operations. ICI Group had its own plant engineers carry out an energy audit of a customer's plant. Several recommendations were made and implemented. These actions saved the customer tens of thousands of dollars a year in energy bills. In another case Union Carbide Australia, which had had its share of industrial trouble through some tough and not very successful negotiations, was able to give some good advice to a customer facing similar challenges. From Union Carbide's experience, it was able to recommend some things to do and some things not to do. In another case one ICI Group was able to help a customer draft a commercial presentation to secure a large contract. Issues of safety, ecology and the environment, communications, marketing, management systems, quality programs, legal interpretations and computers are all areas where suppliers can contribute to a customer's business by sharing experience.

To be able to identify where the opportunities exist to add value, we must have a very thorough knowledge of the customer, how they operate and what their objectives are. If a supplier can demonstrate that they can make a contribution to a customer's business, the customer is more likely to identify more opportunities. The more times the account management cycle has successfully rotated, the more the customer is going to respond, and the better the whole process operates.

Conducting the value-added search

A value-added search is basically a desk job where one or more people generate ideas about what we could do to add value to our package to differentiate ourselves, or contribute to the customer's bottom line in some way. It may be useful to have a list of possible areas where we could help. This should be geared to the customer. It might be designed as a checklist of items which affect the customer's profitability in a number of areas, including operations or manufacturing, sales and marketing, physical product distribution and inventory, financial effects, or management issues. (In a distribution business the value-added search focuses more on how the customer can improve their ROI through identification of missed opportunities. This will be dealt with in more detail in later sections. The principles are the same, but in the case of distributive businesses market analysis can lead relatively easily to identifying the opportunities.)

For the type of business you are involved in you could make a checklist. Under the general headings, place the items which could affect the profitability of the customer or where we can help them save or make money. An example of such a checklist for a company selling packaging material is given in Figure 8.

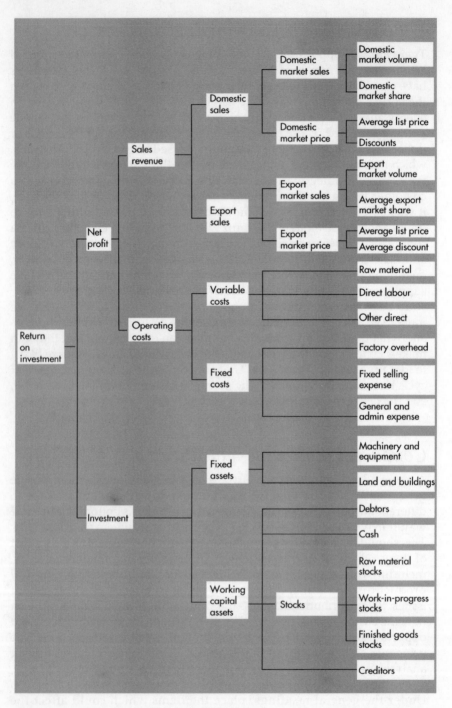

54

Figure 8: Value-added search
Source: John Fenton, *How to double your profits within the year*, William Heinemann, London.

Sales and marketing

Improve their market share

Grow the market share

Higher quality end product

Extra volume sales

Higher prices for their products

Added value services

Differentiate from their competitors

New products

More environmentally friendly

Safer products

New markets

New applications

Higher performance end product

1

2

3

4

5

6

7

8

9

10

Operations

Lower material costs

Cheaper alternatives

More effective end product

Faster throughput

Better yield

Less downtime

Less wastage

Longer plant life

Less labour

Safer work practices

Less damage

Lower energy costs

Less wear and tear

Cheaper formulation

1

2

3

4

5

6

7

8

9

10

Financial/inventory/materials management

Range rationalisation

Lower stock holding

Lower transport costs

Better forecasting

Less storage space

Lower interest charges

Cheaper handling costs

Product flexibility

Delivery flexibility

Less labour in materials movement

Easier administration

Less damage to stock

Lower insurance costs

Cash flow conservation

1

2

3

4

5

6

7

8

9

10

Management and administration

Systems

Communications

Training

Financial understanding

Legal

Industrial relations

Marketing

Promotion

Exporting

1

2

3

4

5

6

7

8

9

10

Special issues

- new projects?

- takeovers?

- relationships?

- others?

Information deficit

1

2

3

4

5

Priority value-added opportunities

1

2

3

4

The checklist is purely a prompt and a guide to help generate ideas. It should not be seen as a form-filling exercise. This is fundamentally a brainstorming activity, and the more ideas you can generate the better, because each idea might lead to a new and better one. You should write down every idea without qualifying it in any way. It does not matter if an idea is against company policy, too costly or impractical to be considered, or if it contradicts the previous idea. Just keep generating ideas. Use the checklists particularly if you are getting stuck.

The process is better when there are a few people. It helps to have someone, usually the account manager, who really knows the customer well. It can also be useful to have someone who does not know the account and therefore comes with a more open mind, and might ask that dumb question which leads to a brilliant idea.

During such a process, ICI Explosives Group had a couple of frankly awful ideas which prompted us to identify that a mining customer had a capacity problem. The customer was using the same shaft to take explosives down the mine and to bring product up, and was on the limit of the shaft's ability to cope. It is very expensive to sink new shafts, but a much smaller shaft existed for utilities. If a way could be found to get the raw materials down this smaller shaft, and then mix down the mine, they may have been able to continue operating for the life of the mine without any new shafts. This would be an enormous saving for the mine.

The customer should not be directly involved in the process. The reason for this is that if you have a meeting which aims to generate ideas of how you could help the customer, they will probably come up with all the items in their too hard basket. They may list items which for a variety of reasons you will need to reject. All this is likely to lead to raised expectations which can never be fulfilled. It is better to attempt two good ideas and be successful, rather than have four ideas and only be able to address three of them. Perceptions are created by your achievements measured against expectations, not so much what you achieve in factual terms. In the case of distributive businesses, where the opportunities are going to exist in a common external market, there is less danger in searching for opportunities with the customer. But in direct accounts, it is not recommended. (I counselled against doing this value-added search with the customer for one of my clients. The client chose to ignore my recommendation, created a lot of customer interest, generated large lists of items they could not easily do, and eventually lost all credibility by not meeting the expectations they had created.)

If, in going through the process you identify some areas where you believe there might be some opportunities but you are not sure, it is appropriate to follow up with the customer by asking some questions, but not promising or raising expectations in the process.

If it seems hard to come up with ideas

The first time people do this exercise for a key account, they discover that it is impeded by the fact that there are many things they do not know about the way the customer operates. In other words, the account profile is incomplete. The more we know about the customer, the easier it will be to do a value-added search.

Another possible avenue for identifying opportunities once the account management cycle is up and running, is through the review process, the last step in the cycle. This is also true of distributive businesses where an analysis of the sales made by the dealer/reseller/retailer will lead to identifying opportunities, and this will be part of the regular review process.

You will find that there will be some areas of your customer's operations where you appear unable to generate any ideas. This may be a function of the business or it may be because you do not know much about that side of the customer's business. This does not matter. It is the quality of the ideas which matters, not the number. For most businesses it will only be possible to work on two or three ideas at a time. If you generate quite a few ideas, you have to decide which you are going to work with.

Selecting the few items you will work with

Selecting ideas should be done on the basis of consistency with the marketing plans, and the ROI of the idea, that is, the extent of the added value you create (as seen from the customer's point of view) relative to the cost to you in creating the differentiation. You will find, when you do a value-added search, that many of the items which you identify as being able to contribute to the customer's bottom line imply a transfer from our own. This is obviously true with pricing and terms, so they are not good items to select when you choose the ideas you will work with. Even though there are many elements of the relationship which are by nature competitive (any item which suggests a transfer of funds from us to them), there are many more elements where supplier and purchaser have joint goals. This is particularly true of distributive businesses, where increased sales is in the interests of both parties, and therefore is an ideal area to look for opportunities.

61

It is poor business to invest more in creating differentiation than will be reflected through the customer's perception of added value. However, once again it is probably in the customer's interests to minimise the value to them of what you are doing. They may therefore understate it in their dealings with you. Fairly often, however, sales forces say that they know they are positively differentiated from their competitors, but that their customer does not value this differentiation. This suggests that the sales force is either not able to sell a package or that they are weak on negotiating skills. If a company really is investing money, time or other resources into creating a differentiation to which the customer ascribes no value at all, the supplier should stop doing it.

Negotiating skills are needed to get the best out of account management.

There is no point in adding value to your package unless you can get something back in return, and that should be higher prices, more volume or longer-term commitments, and preferably a combination of all three. Account managers must understand the importance of this and have negotiating skills and the ability to sell a total package rather than just the product.

. . . .

The account plans

All the steps so far have really been preparation, forcing the thinking through of business and issues so that the plan we write is the right one.

The account plan is the responsibility of the account manager, that is, the person who is directly responsible for that account. Certainly he or she may ask for the input of other people and involve them in the process, but the accountability for getting the plan written and approved is that of the account manager.

The account plan is an accountable document in the sense that it expresses a commitment to the investment of resources and often money. The plan needs therefore to be signed off by someone in a supervisory position in the organisation, usually the sales manager. The sales manager needs to get the agreement of the marketing department to these plans, in the same way that the marketing people need to get the agreement of the sales department, in principle, to their marketing plans.

The account plan will contain objectives or goals which may be quantitative and qualitative. It defines some overall strategies, and then a series of sequenced and timed activities covering the period, which together will lead to the objectives, or at least are most likely to do so.

Accountability and appraisals

Since the plans are accountable, that is signed off by the manager, they become an excellent basis on which to appraise people. If an account manager writes plans covering 80 per cent or 70 per cent (or some Pareto principle figure) of the business for which she or he is responsible, and the plans define both the activities to be conducted and the results expected, then writing and implementing these plans expresses a very large part of the job's function. A further advantage is that the plans are written by the account manager and then implemented or managed by her or him. The account manager is nominating the actions and results, gaining agreement from the sales manager, then controlling progress of the plan with some guidance from the manager and with periodical reviews with the manager to ensure that the plans are on track. This meets the key elements of what is considered to be a good basis for an appraisal system. It also takes much of the subjectivity out of an appraisal system, because it deals with a tangible item—a plan—rather than a manager's opinion.

What the plan should look like

The largest single difference between account management for selling direct to those who use the product or service and those who resell it is in the account plan. In the case of direct selling the account plan remains an internal document which is prepared by the company and implemented by the company. The customer may be aware that you are operating to a plan, and may even have had input to it. They will see things happening as a result of it, but they will not actually be involved in writing it and neither should they read it!

63

In a distributive business the plan is about the basis on which we do business, that is the terms and conditions, but it is just as much about the activities which are important to sell the products out.

In the consumer business selling to supermarkets, it will include the deal and the cooperative advertising, positioning, facings and so on. In selling through distributors, resellers or dealers it will include items like training, identification of target markets, agreeing a sales campaign, local promotions, customer evenings and meetings, and so on. The exact nature of the different types of plans will be discussed under each chapter.

In each case, however, you should ensure that the front page includes the name of the customer and the period covered by the plan. For direct selling the front page will include the name of the account manager and signatures as part of accountability. For distributive businesses the front page should, if possible, include a desirable end result which you will attempt to sell first. It might state 'A $30 000 Profit Improvement Plan for 1998', and have the name of both companies, and even the logos. Remember that this plan is to be used as the basis for agreeing actions for both the supplier and the dealer/reseller/retailer through negotiation. It is your Aim High document, the presentation which forms the first part of a negotiation.

There should be the facility to collect all the items to be addressed, which derive from the previous processes already described. This makes sure that any actions which need to be reflected in the plan are not forgotten. This will form the second page of the direct account plan, and may be on a separate sheet of paper for the distributive plan, in the sense that it will not appear in the plan which is to be the presentation step of your negotiated agreement with your trading partner.

On the next pages will appear the objectives then the strategies, and these will be followed (often on the last page) by a sequenced series of activities. See the individual chapters for details on how this might look for various types of businesses.

The most important page of all is the one which defines the actions to be taken. These might be actions for either or both supplier and dealer/reseller/distributor, in the case of distributive businesses. In the case of direct selling accounts, the activities will usually mainly involve the supplier.

The activities must all be consistent with the plan and the objectives and strategies, as well as the marketing direction. They should be chronologically sequenced, and they should be timed and expressed in a way that the action can be determined to have been completed. They should also state who is accountable for the action—usually the account manager, but not necessarily.

The activities should be spread over the period if possible, so that the account manager's workload is evenly spaced. Any deadlines in meeting advertising programs or other project requirements must be adhered to.

It is also worthwhile including somewhere in the plan a target for the frequency or number of visits. This might include visits by the account manager and other key people within your organisation, and might also define the people to be visited in the customer's organisation.

What the account plan for direct accounts should look like

The format you use should be whatever best meets your needs. It can be useful to have the plan on database, especially if the account manager has a laptop or computer at home which can be networked with the company system.

Consider having two different formats. The one for the major customers would be a complete and fairly substantial document consistent with the importance to the overall business of that account. The other format would be an abridged version of one sheet which would be used for those accounts which are not quite as important, or ones where the business is not very dynamic or where the plans are very simple. Layouts for these two types are given in Figures 9 and 10.

Let us consider the more complete format first. The front page should include the name of the account and information such as address, telephone numbers and fax numbers. It should state the period the plan is

SUMMARY OF PREPARATION

PRIORITIES FROM VALUE ADDED SEARCH

1
2
3

INFORMATION DEFICIT

1
2
3

ACTIONS FROM ACCOUNT SWOT ANALYSIS

1
2
3

RELATIONSHIP BUILDING OPPORTUNITIES

1
2
3

PRIORITY OPPORTUNITIES FROM BRAD

1
2

SPECIAL ISSUES

1
2
3

DIRECT ACCOUNT PLAN

FOR

EAST COAST COMPANY

ADDRESS:

TEL:
FAX:

ACCOUNT MANAGER............

PERIOD FROM .... **TO** ....

ACCOUNTABILITY:

PREPARED:

ACCOUNT MANAGER.........SALES MANAGER....... DATE ....

COMPLETED:

ACCOUNT MANAGER....... SALES MANAGER....... DATE ....

Figure 9: Direct account plan

ACTIVITY SCHEDULE

WHO	ACTION TO BE COMPLETED	BY WHEN	RESULT

VISIT MATRIX

Customer	purchasing plan/actual	operations plan/actual	technical plan/actual	research plan/actual	marketing plan/actual	management plan/actual
Supplier						
Account Manager						
Sales Manager						
Distributor Manager						
Marketing						
Technical						
Head Office						
General Management						

OBJECTIVES AND STRATEGIES

LONG-TERM OBJECTIVES

Statement of long-term objectives and period to be achieved:

OBJECTIVES FOR THE PERIOD OF THIS PLAN | RESULT

1
2
3
4
5

BUDGET FOR THE PERIOD

PRODUCT	BUDGET FOR THE PERIOD				ACTUAL FOR THE PERIOD			
	VOL	PRICE	REV	CONT	VOL	PRICE	REV	CONT
1								
2								
3								
4								
TOTAL								

STRATEGIES FOR THE PERIOD

1
2
3
4

Note: VOL = Volume
REV = Revenue
CONT = Contribution to profit

ABRIDGED ACCOUNT PLAN

TERRITORY .... ACCOUNT MANAGER .... DATE ....
PERIOD OF THE PLAN .... CLASSIFICATION ....

ACCOUNT NEEDS
safety, environment, labour, faster throughput, better yield, reliability, back up, training

ACCOUNT SWOT ACTIONS

OPPORTUNITIES TO ADD VALUE

RELATIONSHIP-BUILDING OPPORTUNITIES

OBJECTIVES FOR THE PERIOD

Target volume	Product	Volume	Price	Revenue

OTHER:

ACTIVITY SCHEDULE

ACTION	WHO	BY WHEN	RESULT

NUMBER OF VISITS BY ACCOUNT MANAGER FOR THE PERIOD
PLAN .... ACTUAL ....

ACCOUNT .... TEL .... FAX ....
ACCOUNT MANAGER ....
PERIOD from .... to .... BUDGET $ ..... RESULT $ ....

KEY OBJECTIVES	RESULTS

KEY VALUE ADDED OPPORTUNITIES

ACTIVITY SCHEDULE

WHO	WHAT	BY WHEN	RESULT

ACCOUNT MANAGER VISITS PLANNED ....
ACCOUNT MANAGERS VISITS ACTUAL ....

ACCOUNTABILITY:
PREPARED: SALES MANAGER .... ACCOUNT MANAGER .... DATE ....
COMPLETED: SALES MANAGER .... ACCOUNT MANAGER .... DATE ....

Figure 10: Abridged account plan for an end-user customer—two possible formats

to cover, and have the name of the account manager. As it is to be an accountable document there should also be the provision for the account manager to sign off the plan once it is written, and then to sign it off after the plan has been implemented.

Gather the items from your preparation

It is useful to gather all the key things to be incorporated in the plan before you start. On the first page you should have a heading for each of the main areas from where actions derive. For example, you need to include any items which you need to address as a result of the SWOT. Then you should show those opportunities you have identified you are going to work with, from the value-added search exercise. You will also identify areas of the account profile which are incomplete. You should record these so that during the currency of the plan you remember to address the deficiencies.

Much in selling and account management involves the relationships we establish with the people in our customer's and our own organisation. We need to have several points of contact between both companies. This is sometimes known as multilevel selling, and it recognises that several people within our organisation should establish a relationship at several points within the customer's organisation. From our side this could include the sales manager, marketing people, product managers, internal sales people, technical people, product distribution, finance and the CEO, as well as the account manager. It is the job of the account manager to plan for this to happen and to get the commitment of the people concerned, then to remind them of their commitments and ensure they make the required contacts.

On the other side of the coin, we need to identify the people who are the decision makers and influencers within the customer's organisation, and ensure that we have the right contacts and relationships with those people. Too often companies tend to have contacts with too few of the customer's staff. This leaves the supplier in a vulnerable position if a key person whom they have nurtured leaves or is moved into another position. Account managers will tend to spend most of their time with the purchasing manager, on the basis that he or she is the one who places the orders and with whom they have most contact in running the business on a day to day basis. But sometimes the purchasing manager is only an administrator, implementing a purchasing decision made by someone else in the organisation.

Some multilevel contact can be achieved at the last step, the business review and development meetings. Other contacts can be made on special visits. In any case, before you start writing the plan it is a good idea to identify where there are any weaknesses in the contacts and relationships, and to address them in the plan.

The last useful heading is one where other significant events which could influence mutual business should be recorded. They could include a variety of items such as when the customer is the subject of a takeover bid, or where there is a product complaint with the customer which has not been satisfactorily resolved (in which case fix it, and fix it fast!), or a management reorganisation or restructuring of the customer's business.

At this point a plan is waiting to be born.

Objectives, strategies and activities

In the following chapters we will be looking in detail at what the objectives, strategies and activities might entail for each business type. In this introduction to the account management cycle an overview and definition of terms will be given.

Objectives

These are the goals you want to achieve. There may be long term objectives—those which cannot be achieved in a short time (often called strategic goals). There will also be shorter-range objectives to support the achievement of the longer term ones.

Objectives must be:

* desirable
* achievable
* measurable
* timed.

They may be quantitative, such as a statement about budget sales or contribution, or market share. There might also be qualitative objectives.

At this point in the procedure it is useful to sit back and contemplate exactly what you want to happen at this account. It is critical to make sure that you get the objectives right.

Strategies

These are the methods you will use to get to the objective. They are a statement of 'how' rather than what. The definitions of strategies and objectives are so different that it is surprising they get confused so often. When is an action a goal in itself, and when is it a method of getting to the goal, and therefore a strategy? As long as the key elements of the plan are recorded, and as long as the thinking is sound, perhaps such considerations should best be left to academic debating.

Activities

These are the core of the plan, as they direct time and effort. They are the route map which the account manager uses to manage the business at that account, and in an overall sense his or her time. Activities should follow the strategies, and should be sequenced chronologically so that they are easy to implement. They should also be clear, concise and timed and state who is responsible for them (not always the account manager).

When completed, the activities should lead to the objectives. The whole account management process involves getting these activities right so that the sales people are spending their time doing the right things.

Distributive plans

Plans for non-direct accounts are different in that they are external documents (although you may write an internal plan similar to the direct plan if there are any issues which require it). The plan takes the form of a joint business plan, and will look at what was achieved in the last period and what can be learned from that. An examination of the business by segment should lead to the identification of opportunities for growth (the objective), and strategies for achieving it. These will be overall concepts, such as particular kinds of promotion. The plan should also state who is to be involved in which parts of the plan, and to what extent. In other words, the plan deals with allocation of resources, both people and dollars.

If the plan is being presented to the level where decisions are made on supply, the elements of the deal will be included. This should include everything that you want the other party to commit to. If you do not ask for it, it will be too late afterwards. This means that the plan will comprise both a 'selling in' and a 'selling out' aspect.

The activities are expressed on a quarterly or seasonal basis, translating the strategies and the commitment of resources agreed to in principle into a sequenced list of activities. This list of activities is used by both the account manager and the account to implement the joint plan.

An example of such a plan will be given in Chapter 5.

. . . .

Implementing the plan

It is now up to the account manager to go and implement the plan. If the plans address 70 per cent or 80 per cent of the business the account manager will generate, he or she should spend most of their time in implementing the plans.

The account manager should have a copy of the plans to use as a working document. They should be referred to:

- before every call, in order to prepare and plan for that visit
- weekly or on a monthly basis to help the account manager plan time and make visits to meet the requirements of the plans and the visit schedules determined, and minimise travelling distance in doing so
- at the end of every month to check progress
- together with the account manager's supervisor, usually the sales manager, as part of the management control and review process.

Fundamentally the plan should be implemented and managed by the account manager. The supervisor's function is to support and assist the account manager should they request help, or to manage the account manager.

Productivity and account management

Account management requires more thorough planning than repetitive selling such as retail selling, selling insurance or selling the *Encyclopaedia Britannica*. Most account managers will make fewer calls than sales representatives. The calls they make tend to be longer and more complex, often visiting more than one department in the same visit. They need to invest more time in planning the business and in analysing it, in fact in account managing. They may also spend time in the office managing projects which are part of the account management program. All this is not an excuse for account managers not to think about and manage their own productivity. A very large part of the sales result will depend on the time we spend in front of customers. This time needs to be optimised rather than maximised, in the sense that you can annoy customers if you see them more often than they want or more often than there are things of substance to talk about. There are usually many opportunities, however, for the account manager to broaden the number of contacts within an organisation.

The fact remains, from my experience, that the call rate of account managers, even taking all the planning and support work into account, is generally too low.

Using the plans to manage time

Given that we have determined that the account management job is manageable with current resources, the account manager with all the plans then has to decide what to do next Monday. One of the ways of using these plans is to plan as follows.

71

	Month 1	Month 2	Month 3
Week 1	CN DE AR		BG
Week 2	WL	Easter	
Week 3	Training AR CN		DE
Week 4		Conference	WI
Week 5	CW	FG PC	

From Key Account Plans to a plan for Monday

1 Assign a 2-letter code to each account and plot visits using the Key Account Plans on a 3-month matrix.
2 On a weekly basis plan the next two weeks.

	Week 1			Week 2		
	Plan		Actual	Plan		Actual
	Customer	Contact		Customer	Contact	
Mon						
Tues						
Wed						
Thurs						
Fri						
Unplanned Visits						
	Visits Plan___ Actual___			Visits Plan___ Actual___		

Figure 11: Time management plans

Assign a two-letter code to each of the customers for whom you have written a plan. Then draw up a sheet such as that one in Figure 11 (opposite), preferably for a three-month period, dividing the period into weeks. Block out any dates which are not available due to conferences, public holidays, training courses, sales meetings or whatever.

Go through the plans, entering each of the action items on the calendar using the two-letter symbol. For the start of the week enter it towards the left-hand side of the week box, and for the end of the week on the right-hand side. When you have entered all the action items from the Activities pages of the plans, make sure that they are evenly spread. If they are not, move them around, making sure that any specific deadlines and critical paths are taken into account.

Go back to the plans and look at the number of visits you have identified as necessary, and fill in the balance between the visits you have already recorded and the total number to be made. This also allows you to see whether you are keeping contact with the right frequency. If the plan calls for seven visits in a quarter, you do not want to make those seven visits all in the same month. You need to have some contact through visits, in this case, approximately once every two weeks.

After completing this exercise you can look at each week and see whether the order in which you visit the customers can be changed to minimise driving time. If an account manager spends an average of two hours a day driving, that is 25 per cent of the time that he or she is supposed to work (we all know most account managers work much more than their supposed 35 or 40 hours a week!). Even an hour a day in the car is 12.5 per cent of the allocated time. It is true that car phones make driving time a bit more productive, but their main advantage is in enabling the account manager to spend the day in the field and still be in touch with the office and with customers. This reduces the need for account managers to return to the office.

In working out the order in which you visit customers you may find it better to juggle some of the visits around, maybe even from one week to another. If you look at the plan in chunks of two weeks at a time, you will be able to see fairly easily where the plan calls for you to do a lot of unnecessary backtracking or driving.

There will always be times when the plan has to be interrupted because of some problem or issue to be addressed. This is one of the reasons you should only plan about 70 per cent of your visit time. When things happen which cause you to change your plan you should ask if it is really necessary to change the plan, or if there is some other way of handling the situation. Ask:

> Do I have to do it?
> Do I have to do it right now?
> Can I satisfy the customer or solve the problem using taxis to fetch
> and deliver, or getting internal sales people to help?
> What is the difference between doing it now and tomorrow morning?

Sometimes you will just have to interrupt what you are doing, but on other occasions you may be able to completely satisfy the customer without having to do more than make a couple of phone calls, then return to your original planned visits.

In terms of time management, it is better to try to arrange periods out of the office rather than make a call and then go into the office. This minimises driving distance. If you can arrange three days a week out on visits as a minimum, then you should be able to get through between twelve and twenty calls a week on average. There will be some calls which might take a whole day or half a day, but these will be balanced by those which only take half an hour.

Try to set aside some time for planning. Have a quiet time in the office when you do not take calls or allow interruptions. If this does not work consider doing some of your planning work at home if it is quieter there.

If you are going to come into the office for part of the day, make it the afternoon rather than the morning. In the morning you will tend to get bogged down with enquiries, often trivial, which can stop you from leaving the office when you want to. If you are delayed much after 11 a.m., by the time you reach the customer it is so close to lunch time that you might find the whole morning has been unproductive. If you come in late afternoon, you will have had six hours put to good selling use and can address issues in the office, often after the switchboard has shut down, so that you have fewer interruptions. And you can still get away by 5.30 or 6 p.m.

The final step in time management of the calendar is to transfer two weeks at a time from the three-month matrix to your diary, then make appointments.

. . . .

The business review and development meeting

At this point in the cycle we should have created differentiation, produced results, and undertaken a series of well-considered activities. To complete the cycle we need to review whether the plan has worked. Has it produced the results we expected? This review is not just an internal examination of how the plan went, but in both direct and distributive businesses it should involve the customer, because it is what the customer feels which will determine whether they place more business with us.

Furthermore, it is not just a question of reviewing what happened, but about agreeing with the customer what the implications are for how to approach the business for the next period. The focus must be on what we include in the next plan, learning from the experiences of the last one.

These business review and development meetings (abbreviated to the acronym BRAD meetings) are the events that mark the end of one planning cycle and make the transition to the next. The exact format for these meetings will vary depending on whether you are operating a direct or a distributive selling business. The content and formats for each type of business will be considered under the chapter relating to that type of business.

However there are a few generalisations. The meeting should be held at the end of the planning cycle but enable any implications for the next period to be integrated into the plans. The meeting will vary in the degree of formality. For accounts where you decide to use an abbreviated sheet for the account plan, that is those where there is not much activity and where the business is straightforward, the BRAD may be less formal and involve fewer people from both sides. On the other hand, for a major customer where you have a full account plan there should be some degree of formality. Part of the purpose of the BRAD meeting is to ensure that all decision makers and influencers in the customer organisation are aware of the contribution you make to their business. Ideally you should have all influencers and/or decision makers attend at least one BRAD meeting a year, if not every one.

In businesses such as consumer products sold through the supermarket chains, a process of presentation, negotiation and review is institutionalised. However, even in these cases it is possible to create interest by covering different things in these meetings. For other businesses where the concept is not institutionalised, the more variety and interest you can build in the better the BRAD meetings will work.

Setting up the meeting

The date for the meeting should be set well ahead, perhaps a month or more. The account manager's main contact point in the customer organisation should be converted into a BRAD champion within his or her own organisation. This means that you need to sell the concept very strongly, especially the first time you hold one. It also means that the first one needs to be very good or the customer may not want to invest time in subsequent ones. This is hard because good meetings take practice. For this reason the first

BRADs you undertake should be with 'tame' customers where you already have good relationships and where there are some useful points to review.

The champion should coordinate things from the customer's side, including getting commitment to attend the meeting, and calling the attendees a couple of days before the meeting to make sure that they have not forgotten.

The account manager should propose the agenda, but ask the customer for items to include. (See Figure 12 for a possible agenda.) Both supplier and purchaser should feel joint ownership of the meeting, rather than it being seen as an opportunity for the supplier to do some grandstanding. In fact, it is an opportunity for the supplier to reinforce what they have done for the purchaser, and to underline the differentiation they have created through added value, but this must be done as subtly as possible— as part of a soft sell approach.

The customer's attendees should be encouraged to prepare for the meeting. This rarely happens, but the meetings are much more constructive when the customer's attendees take it seriously enough to get involved. This tends to happen after the first few BRADs have been held, when you have been able to demonstrate the value of open discussions between the trading partners. This is part of this movement from

- introduction
- review of results
  - — recommendation for action
- action items from the last meeting
- review of activities during the period
  - — results
- implications for the future
- trends
  - — technical
  - — market
- any special items
- items requiring action
- new business
- any changes
  - — people
  - — procedures
  - — direction
- summary
- close, set date for next meeting

Figure 12: Possible agenda for BRAD meeting

competitive to cooperative relationships between supplier and purchaser. While there are elements of this relationship that are combative, there has been a tendency in the past to concentrate on these elements. Many buyers are now realising that an open and more cooperative relationship can be more useful to both sides. The BRAD meetings are a step in encouraging this process. Certainly these meetings are generally relaxed, because they are about review and discuss the recommendations for the next period. However, they are not negotiations. As such, they tend to be constructive meetings.

The supplier should prepare well for BRAD meetings. There will be several subjects to be covered. You will need to review their purchases compared to what had been planned or targeted. Make sure you refer to them as 'purchases' rather than 'sales', because that is how the customer sees them, and you should always talk in the customer's language and express things from their point of view. In a meeting with a distributive account it is fine to talk about sales, but make sure that it is clear you are talking about their sales to their customer, not your sales to them. Unless you know what the customer's dollar sales are, it is safer to talk about sales in units.

Handling the BRAD meeting

There is no need to spend time talking about the things that are on target, but some analysis of variances above and below target is warranted. You should also seek the customer's view during the meeting for these variances. Any action that needs to be taken as a result of these variances should be noted. Some discussion of what purchase volumes are likely to be in the next period is also appropriate.

Once the BRAD meetings have been established, there will be action items from the last meeting that need to be reviewed. As these items generally will only involve a few of the people present, these items should be despatched as efficiently and as quickly as possible.

You should review any projects which are under way. This is where you can subtly reinforce the good work you have done by adding value to it. Any action relating to these items should be agreed.

There may be specific items depending on the type of business. These could include product performance, product quality, delivery record or any items that the customer measures as part of their quality programs and which are influenced by supply. In other words, there should be a review of performance against standards that have been agreed to with the customer for judging performance.

There should then be some discussion on trends in the marketplace, both technical and commercial, with views from all sides. There should also be a time for discussing aspects of each organisation that have changed or will change in the next period. These might be requirements from a technical or a product distribution point of view, administration, systems and procedures, people or organisational changes and changes in responsibilities. Any special items nominated by either side will need to be included.

The account manager must ensure that the necessary preparation is done from his or her side. This may mean analysis of figures, and some checking with other people in the company to ensure that everything is running smoothly. This could include anything from making sure that the account is being paid to agreed terms, to making sure that pallets are under control, or that there are no unresolved complaints. The key issue is that the account manager must ensure that the actions called for in the account plan have been carried out.

The account manager should brief those attending from his or her company, particularly on what to say and especially what not to say!

The account manager will chair the meeting, but in such a way that the meeting is seen by both sides as a joint meeting. The time to be allotted will depend on the length of the agenda. It is recommended that you try to complete the meeting within two hours because everyone is busy, and that is about the upper limit of what people are prepared to spend in this type of meeting. If there are any special items that involve only a small number of people, for example the trials of a new product, make sure that if you are bogged down in detail, you agree to set up a special meeting to discuss these issues and that you involve a smaller and more appropriate group of people.

Someone needs to take notes, and record any action agreed to. Sometimes this is done by the chair, but not always. Shortly after the meeting you should issue notes. There may be two types. One is for circulation to both supplier and purchaser attendees. These notes should include any items for action by either side. You may find it useful to record items for your own personal or internal company use, which of course would not be circulated to the attendees from the purchaser.

In starting the meeting the account manager should briefly state the purpose of the meeting, stressing the positive aspects. This might include reference to the fact that the customer invests significant money with the supplier, and that it is therefore important for both sides to be sure that they get the best possible results from this relationship.

The chairperson should make sure that the attendees from the customer are encouraged to participate, and should ask some open questions to get the discussion started. The chairperson must be seen to be fair and even handed. If there are any unexpected problems which are brought up, the chairperson must defuse the situation before the emotional tenor rises too much.

Location and timing

BRAD meetings should be held at a time that best suits the customer, and at different venues. Once a year you may invite the attendees from your customer to dinner or to light refreshments after the meeting. In this case the meeting would need to be held late afternoon. Most meetings will probably be held at the premises of the customer. Try to make sure that you book the best meeting room available, and agree not to answer calls during the meeting. Also check that any equipment you might need is available and working, or take your own.

Make sure that you do not have your own attendees down one side of the table and the customer's team opposite. You should generally try to match attendees from both sides, especially in numbers. You do not want to overwhelm several attendees from the customer with a whole army from your side. The attendees should vary from both sides. Remember that your own sales managers, marketing staff and technical people cannot spend all their working lives attending BRADs, and that both sales managers and sales support have to be selective in the BRADs they attend.

There may be a need to match positions. You will find it much easier to get their CEO along if you have some high-powered people from your side, including possibly your own CEO.

. . . .

Completing the account management cycle

The BRAD meeting is the last step in the cycle. From these meetings you may identify more ways where you can add value, more information as input to your SWOT, and more information for the account profile. There may be implications for the marketing department to take into account, in writing, their marketing plans for the next period. This transfer of information completes the cycle.

The internal review

Whilst it is not part of the account management cycle activities with the customer, the internal review nonetheless is a critical step. There is a need to make sure that the whole account management program is on target. Such a review is not simply a review of the progress towards meeting your objectives for all the major accounts, it is also a question of fine-tuning the process itself. I find that for most clients the account management system as they adopt it is an evolutionary process. After they have worked with it for a time, they modify elements to fit their business better. This is to be encouraged—as long as the key elements are retained. One of my clients, in an attempt to get the whole account plan on a computer and in a defined available space, missed out the section on setting objectives. How can you have a valid plan if you have no place to state your objectives?

The internal review should be done twice a year, at the end of one planning cycle and just as the second planning cycle begins. In reality however, I also suggest that you should not have all your plans in a direct business starting and finishing at the same time. Otherwise there is a burden not only in getting all the plans written at the same time, but also in conducting the BRADs. In this case you will have staggered plans, and the timing of the review is perhaps less important. Maybe it is best to hold the reviews twice a year, six months apart, at a time which is convenient to get people together without disrupting the business.

Both sales and marketing should be present, as well as any other functions (such as technical or customer support who are involved with these accounts). There should be a clear format, and the account managers need to prepare beforehand. The process should be streamlined as much as possible so that it does not become a repetitive and boring exercise.

At these internal review meetings there should be a review of the execution and results of plans for the key accounts. You should not spend a lot of time on plans which are on track. In reviewing plans which are not on track, you need to understand why they have varied, and agree on action to get them on track.

Part of the reason for having these reviews is to reinforce the company's commitment to the process. The fact that an account manager has to brief colleagues and managers on what has happened with his or her key accounts is as good as incentive as any to make sure their 'house' is in order.

The account management cycle and negotiation

Because in the case of distributive businesses the account plan becomes the document for the presentation of what will hopefully become a negotiated commitment between supplier and reseller/retailer/dealer, negotiations will take place as part of the cycle of account management. The ideal situation is that prior to the commencement of the year (financial or calendar, depending on the convention of the industry where you operate) you should make a presentation for how you and the reseller will work together for the next year. This will include the outline of the commercial arrangements and the types of activities of a selling-out nature that both parties, together or separately, will undertake.

On a quarterly basis, before the next period starts, the detail of the activities will be noted down, with dates and specific action. The main negotiations for the year will have already happened, so these quarterly discussions should be fine-tuning the details. There may be some discussion and negotiation on some of the points.

The method of operation for the different types of distributive businesses will be discussed in Part 2.

In the case of direct selling the time to negotiate is much more variable. In some cases there are contracts that could stretch for three or more years. Even so, it is critical to keep the account management cycle rotating. It is desirable to have some stability in your business by locking down business through contracts, as long as they are flexible enough to allow for enough price adjustment to keep both sides satisfied.

In a less rigidly structured operation you may negotiate whenever an order needs to be placed (usually the case in selling capital items or products or services that are not regular consumables) or, in the case of consumable products for which orders are placed on a regular basis, the status quo may be maintained until a competitor makes an offer and the customer is asking you to react. This can happen at any time.

You are clearly in a much better position to negotiate if the account management cycle has rotated a few times, because you will have demonstrated your ability to add value to the customer's business through the account management program.

However, as we have already mentioned in this chapter, the account manager must be able to sell the whole package of what you provide, and to be able to get the added value reflected in the quality of the commercial arrangements you enter into.

Handling multisites and multi-SBU contacts

There can be two types of complication in account management. They are more of an issue in direct selling, but there are some similar issues in distribution selling.

The first complication arises when you are selling to a customer who may have several points at which sales contact is required—either several operating sites, or even a Head Office and regional or state offices. We need to ensure, especially when these sites are in different cities or even states, that we coordinate our activities and our approach. Apart from any other consideration, the customer is likely to coordinate information from their side, and we cannot afford to have a different approach, different policies or, worse, different prices across the same customer.

The second complication occurs when there are sales people from more than one strategic business unit (SBU) or division of the same corporation selling to the same customer. In this case the customer would usually prefer to see the corporation as one entity, but the SBUs are often reluctant to agree to appoint one account manager to look after the whole account—unless of course that account manager belongs to *their* SBU.

Handling multisites

There is no simple way to handle multisites. The only approach I have found to work is what I call a bottom-up, top-down approach. Information and consideration of what should happen at a particular site is prepared first, and then it is passed up to the person who is the account manager for the Head Office entity. That person has the benefit of seeing the issues at all the other sites. He or she then can write the plan for how you manage the Head Office or main site, taking into account all of the issues at all the other sites. This plan is then passed back to the account managers for each site, and they then write their site account plan to be consistent with the Head Office or main site plan.

If there are also state offices which intervene (as might be the case in a large A direct account or some of the distribution chains), the process has to be done in two steps. Again the information is fed up to a state level and then up to the national level. The national plan is written first, then the state plans and then the site plans.

Each site manager should provide:

- a site account profile
- a site SWOT
- a site value-added search
- recommended site objectives, both target sales and other objectives.

The overall objectives for the customer are set at the Head Office or main site level, and this can have implications for the plans at all the other sites. It may be that it is not in the best interests of the company to agree to all the recommended site objectives. If, for example, there is a limit to the national share of business a given customer will allow you to have, then you would prefer to 'take what you can' in the locations where the business is more profitable. A major consideration may be freight if you have capital city freight equalised pricing.

The best way to handle such multisite accounts is to get everyone together to do the planning in the same room at the same time. It may cost a little money to do this, but you should get your people together for internal reviews periodically anyway. And for the really large A accounts, where multisites are most likely to occur, the business is large enough and important enough to justify the expense.

When several SBUs sell to the same customer

Key account management logic dictates that one person would be the account manager for the customer overall. But life is never as easy as that. What happens when there is more than one SBU with total profit accountability selling to the same customer? Businesses are becoming more and more global, and many multinationals run their business so that their reporting worldwide takes precedence over the local company. When this happens, the SBU responds to the requirements of the world business in Frankfurt, London, Tokyo or New York, and is less likely to worry about the impact of what they do on their fellow SBUs who have different reporting lines. This is especially true if Multinational Australia Pty Ltd loses its power. This is a real-life situation in many multinationals.

Imagine that there are three SBUs within Corporation X, selling to a customer. Out of the total business Corporation X does with the customer, SBU A has 35 per cent, SBU B has 60 per cent and SBU C has 5 per cent. Assume that SBU C has a product complaint in which it is not really clear whether the supplier is liable or not. In such cases a commercial decision is often made. SBU C looks at the business, decides that it is very small, and decides not to accept the complaint. The customer tells the account managers of SBU A and SBU B that unless this matter is resolved to their satisfaction they will take business away from them. They both protest that it is outside their jurisdiction. Unless SBU C can be persuaded to see reason, there is not much SBU A and B can do, and both those account managers and the customer feel utterly frustrated. What to do?

83

The best solution here is to have a key account management group which sits outside the SBUs and is responsible to the main corporation, and which represents all the SBUs at the large customers. They may rely on technical and marketing support from the SBUs, but they are the overall account manager with the fundamental responsibility for the total customer. They would need to plan negotiations carefully, and they may need to involve people from the SBUs.

There are a few companies—unfortunately very few—who have decided to operate this way. Most find that the profit accountability they have is such that they insist on having sales under their own authority completely. So how can such situations best be handled?

Again, there is no simple solution. What I propose requires the agreement of the SBUs to cooperate, should there be conflict. The basic philosophy is to agree to put the needs of the corporation before those of the SBU. On the face of it, this is common sense, but when the SBU is accountable for profit there may still be a reluctance to agree to it.

Taking the above example of Corporation X, I suggest that there be one account manager from one of the SBUs who is considered the Account Manager Leader (AML). This account manager would have the following responsibilities and authority:

- in the event of a conflict in how the account is managed between two SBUs, the AML should try to reach resolution between the SBUs
- if this fails, the AML has the right to be heard by all the SBUs, and at the most senior levels if necessary
- the AML does not have any business authority over the other SBUs
- the AML must make sure that all account managers from all the SBUs involved at that account compare their account plans before they are signed off by the SBU
- the AML will ensure a free interchange of information (such as the account profile)
- if the customer has an issue which they want to take up at a more corporate level, they will direct themselves to the AML
- the AML will be known to the customer as the Corporate Account Manager Leader, while also understanding that that person does not have business responsibility outside their own SBU.

In our example we could make the account manager from SBU B the AML, as they have more business at that account. If that SBU should predominate, in most cases the other SBUs may object to that as a policy. In that case you can look at the customers concerned and split the responsibilities between the SBUs. Alternatively, you can rotate the responsibility, say every year or two, at every customer between the SBUs.

This approach is not perfect, but it can be made to work. Common sense needs to prevail.

. . . .

Summary

In this chapter we have talked about the concept of the account management cycle as a structured way to manage your key accounts. This forms a series of sequenced events that you should repeat every few months. Many people question how it relates to or should be adapted to their particular business. In subsequent chapters that deal with consumer business through chains, other distributive businesses and selling direct to accounts, we will provide specific guidelines on how the account management cycle should work in different types of business.

4

Creating the right support infrastructure

Account management does not just happen. To manage customers in a professional and structured way a company needs to ensure that the right support systems and infrastructure exist. They can be divided into two main categories: those concerned with allowing the account manager to get on with the job of account management and not waste time chasing information or problem solving, and the provision of information necessary to manage the business.

Account manager efficiency

We have already discussed the fact that the sales-call productivity of account managers tends to be low. This is serious, because good account managers are hard to find. To be a good account manager you need a wide portfolio of skills. These include:

- selling
- negotiation
- analysis
- planning

- interpersonal
- organisational
- financial and business
- technical
- communication.

We cannot afford highly skilled and qualified people to waste their time doing the sort of things machines or less skilled and lower paid people could do for them. Good account managers tend to be well paid. On a return on investment (ROI) basis account managers need to spend their time doing the things that they are good at and for which they are being paid.

Part of this is having the right information available for customers so that enquiries can be answered fast and correctly, and part of it is having the right internal sales support to take the routine items off the account manager's hands. The account manager should never have to spend significant time chasing up deliveries, complaints, accounting errors, administrative confusion (pallet returns is a classic), stock availability and so on. These items should be available at the push of a button, or there should be enough internal sales staff to handle it.

This is easier said than done, and it requires considerable investment in information technology to ensure it happens smoothly. One of the problems in the past was that the EDP (electronic data processing) department had experts in mainframe computers that dealt mainly with things like payroll, salaries, inventory, invoicing and credit and receivables. The sales figures were generated almost as a side-effect of the credit and invoicing procedures, so the reports rarely gave the sales people the information they needed in the format they wanted. In fact, many sales reports were so large that a few months' figures could almost fill a Compactus, and sales staff built muscles carrying them around.

An attempt to change this was blocked by either the inexperience of the EDP people in anything other than the current operations of the mainframe, or by the estimated costs in changing anything on the mainframe. Often the non-experts suspected that they were being misled by a reluctant EDP department, where the real issue was that EDP did not want to change anything.

This has changed since the advent of very powerful PCs. There is more flexibility, easier access to computer terminals by a wider range of people, better ability to network through the company system, and a breed of people, in what has changed from EDP to IT (information technology), who know something about PCs.

The role of internal sales staff

Internal sales staff are often called 'order-entry clerks' rather than sales people. This is a mistake, because if you tell people that they are order-entry clerks, they will identify with orders and invoices rather than sales and customers. Position titles can also determine the reporting channels within the company. Order-entry clerks are likely to report through administration and finance. Internal sales staff will logically report through sales. Internal-support sales staff should report through sales and sales managers, as part of the concept that if we want to deliver customer service, we must organise ourselves round the customer, not the administration. This is a serious point and one that is often ignored by companies, even those who pride themselves on a strong customer-service tradition. If you want to provide customer service you must put the timely satisfaction of the customer before the needs of your own systems and procedures.

This may require some empowerment of junior people in the organisation to help satisfy the customer. This requires both courage and patience from managers, and staff training. Mistakes will be made but people learn from them.

If you are going to rely on internal sales staff to contribute to this process, then you must involve them more in the business, so that they have the right approach, background and knowledge as well as experience to make the right decisions.

Ideally the same sales person should handle a particular customer base, although this is not easy when you have centralised ordering, or several internal sales people who handle telephone calls as they come in. It may be useful to have the internal sales people teamed up with one or two external sales people, so that they can work as a team.

The internal sales people often have more frequent contact with customers than the account managers. They get to know the customer's purchasing people and often a good work relationship is established that should be fostered. The internal sales people should go out with the account manager from time to time, so that they can get to know their contacts personally. Involve the internal sales people in your sales meetings and even in the account management process, through assisting in the planning process. The more you involve the internal sales people in the business, the more interesting their jobs will be and the less likely it is that they will leave.

We all know that when a good internal sales person leaves there is a large gap to fill in the short-term by taking people off the road to assist.

Entering orders into a computer is a boring job that does not encourage people to think about what they are doing, but just to process work in a mechanical way. Being an internal sales person is varied, more interesting and more demanding, and encourages the person to think about what they are doing, and take whatever action is necessary to provide customer service and satisfaction. (This is not to say that internal sales people should be given autonomy, but it means allowing them some authority to be flexible within certain guidelines. If they understand what the business objectives and plans are, they will learn where the limits are.)

Every encouragement should be given to open and frequent communication on day-to-day business between account managers and internal sales staff, so the internal sales people will provide the sort of support which helps make the account manager more efficient, productive and effective.

. . . .

Information the account manager may need

88

There is information the account manager needs to run the business on a day-to-day basis, and information required for analysis and planning. There is information that has to be accessed from areas that are controlled by others, such as delivery records, sales figures, receivables etc., and information the account manager will keep, such as account profiles and account plans.

The starting point is to be absolutely clear what information is important in running the account management program, then defining the best way for it to be collected and presented for use by account managers. There may need to be some compromise in areas where the information is generated also for other people or by other people.

Areas that become particularly important are those which customers are controlling for their own purposes, often as a result of their implementing a quality program. It is quite common for customers to present suppliers with an analysis of orders placed and actual delivery against requested delivery. The supplier should not rely entirely on the customer's assessment, but should have a system of their own to double check.

Account profitability analysis

Account profitability analysis is another very important tool. Not only does such an analysis tell you where you are making your profit, but by making comparisons you can see why some customers are more profitable than others. This could be because of freight costs, packaging, special products or selected products for which insufficient price premium is obtained, or because the price is lower, or because you sell a mix of products with less contribution. There may be more support dollars allocated through special assistance, local promotions, or poorly negotiated cooperative advertising or allowances and rebates. (See Table 4 for a format for account profitability analysis.)

Once you can see where you are making profit and how, then you have a formula for success. For those accounts where profitability is low, you have a diagnostic to see why, and you can take the necessary action to redress the situation. You can even use the poor profitability at these accounts as a negotiating ploy. For example, a supplier was being put under pressure to lower price. The supplier showed the customer the profitability analysis, which proved they were actually making a loss on parts of the business. The purchaser backed off.

How businesses make profit

Part of the problem is that retailers and resellers tend to believe that because manufacturers make higher gross margins, they have an almost inexhaustible ability to give more money. The argument is that if the retailer/reseller makes only 10 per cent gross profit and the manufacturer makes 25–60 per cent, this is unfair, and the manufacturer should even it up a bit. This is an argument used against suppliers to any distributive business every day, either bluntly or subtly.

But the argument is flawed. The key criterion for a business is the return on investment, not the gross profit.

where R = net profit before tax
S = sales revenue
I = investment in fixed assets and working capital
ROI = R/I
= R/S × S/I

In manufacturing industries the I figure is very high. There are large fixed assets through plant, equipment and buildings. There are also high working capital needs through the provision of credit to customers, and through inventory, covering raw materials, work in progress and finished goods. If the figure I is very high, then to reach an acceptable ROI the R figure must also be high. In other words, manufacturers need high margins to compensate for the fact that they turn their investment over so slowly.

Retailers and resellers have less money tied up in fixed assets. They try to minimise their receivables and keep the lowest inventory possible to satisfy their customers, whilst demanding fast supply from suppliers to ensure they can offer delivery to their customers without having to keep the stock themselves. Supermarket chains can often put money out on the short term money market because they have cash in from their customers before they have to pay their suppliers.

Table 3 provides a comparative overview.

Table 3: How different businesses make money			
Type	Manufacturer	Wholesaler	Retailer
I	large	small	medium
R/S	9	1.5	3
S/I	2	12	6
R/I	18%	18%	18%

Key issues for manufacturers:
* control fixed costs
* conserve working capital
* inventory and credit
* volume sales
* maintain margins

Key issues for wholesalers:
* ROI/space
* fast stockturn
* fast delivery
* high volume
* maintain margins
* money in versus money out

Key issues for retailers
* ROI/shelf
* range
* margins
* volume
* inventory to support sales

Using the account profitability analysis

The key issue is that identifying account profitability is very important. Such analysis should be used to identify target markets and target customers. A model for working out account profitability is shown in Table 4. Some assumptions may need to be made when things cannot be measured directly, for example, few companies are geared up to know what their freight costs are for each order. This means that extra costs for rushed deliveries rarely get allocated to the account. The best many

Table 4: Account profitablilty model				
	1995	*1996*	*1997*	*1998*
Invoiced sales				
– discounts				
– rebates				
= Net sales revenue				
– Cost of goods[a]				
– Packaging				
– Freight[b]				
– Credit[c]				
– Marketing support[d]				
= Gross contribution				
– Invoicing costs[e]				
– Sales force costs[e]				
– Sales support costs[e]				
– Technical support[e]				
= Net contribution				

[a] Usually based on standard costs.
[b] If you can measure actual freight costs, use them, if not, work out averages for that city, inner or outer suburbs.
[c] Take average payment days over 365 × corporate overdraft rate × annual purchases.
[d] Such as promotions, promotional allowances, special project or export incentives.
[e] Work out total costs of the facility, and then a cost per invoice, per visit etc, and multiply by the number of visits, invoices etc.

companies can manage is to average delivery costs for one state or city relative to another. Technical and sales support costs can be calculated by knowing the average cost for a sales call and the number of calls made to the account. In the technical area it can happen that we over invest resources with some customers who are usually the ones who do not have good resources themselves and who may not even be key accounts. We need to recognise this, and maybe even limit the amount of free service we provide if it is restricting our ability to implement technical programs at key accounts. Such considerations should drive where technical service spends its time.

If a product is selected, or is in any way different from a standard product, there should be some way of reflecting a higher cost. Failure to do this is ignoring the facts.

· ·

The role of the computer in account management

The information technology industry moves so fast that almost anything I say in this section will be out of date before it is printed. Only a few years ago the main focus of information was the mainframe. At least as far as sales and marketing are concerned, that has changed totally, with the focus now being the PC and the laptop.

The issue of obtaining information in the format that the account manager can use is still valid. But the more important issue is putting the whole account management program on computer.

Most of the steps, but not all, in the account management cycle are better handled on the computer. It is neater, safer, has easier access to a wider variety of people, is easier to manage and to cross reference. It means that the account manager can take the whole system with him or her on the laptop. They take the office with them wherever they go, and this means that there is really no excuse for dead time. Even if a customer keeps you waiting, you can do some work, or fill in gaps when you arrive early for an appointment. It just makes so much more plain common sense than having the whole system on lots of bits of paper.

Account profiles are the most obvious first candidate to be put on a database. Keeping them on paper is laborious, inflexible and outmoded. It is however useful to get right on paper first the formats that you finally decide to work with. It is easier to change formats on paper than on a database. Get the right six boxes we referred to in Chapter 3, and then set the menu prompts.

I have several clients who like to put their account SWOT and Value Added Search on computer, but frankly I do not advocate it. I suspect that some of the account managers of these clients just like to play with computers! Both the account SWOT and the Value Added Search are brain work. The formats are there just as prompts. If you put them on the computer they become more of a form-filling exercise than ever, and that is what we should try to get away from. In this section what we want people to do is to think about the account, and their business there. Having to enter everything on a computer can impede this process as it can be a mechanical interruption to thought.

I recommend that the account SWOT and the Value Added Search be done 'manually'. But the outcomes from each of these exercises should be recorded on the computer as part of the second page of the full account plan in 'Items from the preparation', as 'Action items from the SWOT' and 'Priorities from Value Added Search'.

The account plan should also be on the computer. Not only is it easier to manage and for others to have access to, but it also makes it easier for you to look at the action items in different ways.

For example, when you are following the logical flow from an objective to strategies and down to the action items, it is easier to write them in that form. But the way you carry out actions is to look at what needs to be done in chronological order. You need to know what you have to do in total with this account in the next month. The computer allows you to look at the actions in subject order and in sequenced order. You can in fact transfer them to a diary format, which is the computer's way of performing the manual manipulation shown in Figure 11.

You can then use the computer as your contact record, measuring also the number of visits you make compared with the plan. You can add your comments as an alternative to writing visit reports. The account manager then has virtually the whole customer planning, implementation and reporting needs together.

Which software?

The importance of establishing software to handle sales planning and information systems is demonstrated to me by the fact that nearly all of my clients who are part of a multinational are taking a worldwide approach. The parent company is investing in the development of a worldwide company information system, usually which is intended to be used by all divisions or operating units and in all countries. Sometimes they buy a commercial package and then have it modified, sometimes they develop a system from the ground up. This of course reduces the market for anyone considering developing a commercial package to be sold as a standard program. And the specific requirements of customers in the combination of information they need differ to the point that a standard program would still require modification. As a result, there is a paucity of suitable off-the-shelf software ready to install and use without customising.

Some of my clients have been trying to hang files on their mainframe, but it is a relatively expensive and cumbersome exercise. Others have used programs like Tracker, which is really a contact management program, and does not in its present form do everything an account manager would want.

Many people are finding that the global systems their parent companies are producing are too general, too inflexible and do not have the facility to handle the complex information the account manager needs. Many are suitable for sales representatives, but not for account managers.

As a result there are a few different approaches being used. One is to take the company global system and to supplement it using word-processing documents. Another is to use Microsoft Access. Others prefer Lotus Notes.

The main general technical requirement of all software setups is to ensure that every time their account manager logs on with their laptop, the system recognises that there have been changes and automatically updates the main file. This allows easy access by other interested parties of the up-to-date status, and is a useful backup.

Other useful software

In the distributive businesses large dollars are 'invested' (often just given away) in promotional activities. This will be discussed in more detail in the relevant chapters. However, there are some very specific programs available to help account managers manage items like promotional funds and promotional programs, and determine their contribution to profit or loss. A good example of such a program is Promax and Proscan (available from The Professional Assignments Group in Sydney). Promax also generates sales budgets at the customer product level. The supermarket area has far more information available than any other. Warehouse Withdrawal data is a basic tool of the trade, and Apollo shelf management software is critical for any company wanting to discuss shelf layout and category management issues with customers. It is also possible to buy scan data from Coles (Univers), and sample scan data from most of the other chains. These considerations will be discussed more in Part 3, but suffice it to say that far more data is being generated in this area than either the chains or the suppliers can use effectively. Between withdrawals, scan and DPP and planograms by store, there is sufficient data for chains, with assistance from suppliers, to more effectively micromarket products. In fact this is not happening effectively, largely because of data overload and an inability to analyse it and come up with solutions cost-effectively.

Especially for those selling to distributive businesses, the presentation document, the account plan or joint business plan, must be put together professionally, because it is an external document to be presented to the customer. There is usually some similarity between plans and it can therefore be useful to have a broad format, which can then be changed to meet the needs of each account plan. Where there is analysis of figures leading to identification of opportunities, the use of visual information like pie charts and bar charts is almost necessary.

All this suggests that these account plans or presentations should be constructed using an appropriate PC package. Good word processing packages come close to giving you desktop publishing facility—especially if the hard copy is printed out on a high quality printer. Once a format has been devised for account profiles, account plans and presentations, the account manager should be the one to create the documents, rather than have a secretary type it from a written scrawl by the account manager.

Customer service

There is nothing more frustrating, or unnecessary, than when the sales force has done everything right but the relationship with the customer is ruined or strained because someone else has slipped up. Customer service is about how everyone in the company treats the customer or performs any task which is likely to affect the customer, and in most companies that ought to include nearly everyone and everything. The clerk who makes an incorrect computer entry can damage relationships just as much as the delivery truck driver who abuses a customer, or the telephonist who keeps a customer hanging on the line, or the operator who produces poor quality goods.

Part of the infrastructure to make account management work involves getting customer service right.

Establish a culture

Unless the management talks about it, sets standards, provides the skills, measures it and reinforces it, the chances are that it will be a short-lived fad. Customer service involves everyone, and is an attitude and a culture. My favourite writer on this subject is Jan Carlzon, who became the youngest appointment to CEO of an international airline carrier when he was appointed CEO of Scandinavian Airlines System. He wrote a book called *Moments of Truth* published by Harper & Row. In this book he talks about the fact that every time there is contact between your organisation and a customer, at any point or level, where the customer is able to make a judgement about your company, it is a 'moment of truth'. Each person must learn how to manage every moment of truth to make sure that the customer is left with the best possible impression of your company.

All these people have some contact with customers
- sales personnel
- marketing personnel
- technical personnel
- upper management
- receptionist
- telephonist
- delivery drivers
- secretaries
- credit control and accounts personnel
- anyone who might pick up a telephone and find a customer on the other end.

You need to decide how each group of people should manage the customer contact. Standards should be drawn up and training given. Then you should measure the results through some form of survey, if possible. For example, ICI some years ago decided that they were not very good at answering telephones. They implemented a program that involved everyone in the company who might speak on a telephone, and gave standards and training. Periodically a phantom caller would call random numbers to see how well the program was operating. The results were published on every noticeboard, comparing the performances of all the ICI Groups. The difference was amazing, and ICI became one of the best organisations to deal with on the phone.

Follow-up for satisfaction

One of the most impressive things you can do to show customers that you care is to make a follow-up call, personally or by telephone. This is useful when there has been something out of the ordinary, such as a new product they have tried or a rushed delivery. The fact that you have followed through enough to want to call and make sure that everything was fine, impresses customers. It reinforces what you are doing for them and if there is a problem it allows you to do something about it before it affects your relationship.

. . . .

Summary

For account management to work well you need to give considerable thought to the infrastructure to support it. This is not just nuts and bolts issues like equipment and systems, but involves making sure you have a responsive customer centred organisation too.

Selling Through a Distribution Network

12

Selling
Through a
Distribution
Network

5

Account management, distributors and outlets

. . . .
Definition

The general and common elements of account management were dealt with in Part 1. In Parts 2, 3, and 4 we will look more specifically at how the overall approach can be applied to the three main types of business. These are selling through distribution networks, selling through the supermarket chains as a special case of the first one, and selling to those accounts which use the product and or services themselves.

Part 2 discusses selling through distribution channels other than the supermarket chains. Supermarket chains will be dealt with separately from other distributive businesses because there is a particular jargon and certain information available which is not available in other businesses, and a way of operating which is specific to the chains. Part 3 is really about selling to companies like Coles, Franklins and Woolworths. Where would pharmacy chains like Amcal or hardware chains like Mitre 10 or BBC Hardware fit? Is there a difference between selling to wholly-owned chains like BBC, and to franchises such as Mitre 10? The answer of course must be 'yes'. In the case of selling to a wholly-owned chain, including the supermarkets, there is far less ability to influence what happens on a store-by-store basis, because this tends to be centrally controlled by the head office. Part 3 makes suitable reading if you are selling to wholly-owned chains of a substantial nature whatever type of chain, grocery, hardware, variety or pharmacy.

Part 2 looks at what can be achieved in an account management sense on an individual outlet level, as well as aspects of how you can structure account management at the level of head office or of smaller conglomerates or small chains. Parts 2 and 3 give a comprehensive perspective.

Why distribution?

The main reason companies sell through a distribution network is that they perceive it as the best way to reach a large and diverse clientele. There is a range of outlets who tend to specialise in certain types of products. These could include:

- consumer products
- hardware products
- pharmacy
- food service
- health and beauty
- clothes
- shoes
- manchester
- electrical goods
- building supplies
- agricultural supplies
- furniture
- vehicles
- stationery
- computers and communications
- fabrics
- carpets
- specialised suppliers of technical products
- travel.

The principle is that the supplier is able to do two things by using a distribution network. First, get physical product distribution at locations where the customers know they can access the products, and second have an army of sales people selling the products to potential consumers. The degree to which the latter happens depends on the type of product and the distribution network. In the case of supermarket chains, or any self-service store, there is little or no selling on behalf of the outlet. The customer just comes in and chooses the product. Whether the customers buy will depend on how well the product is advertised through the media or in the store, whether the customer can find it, and what the price is relative to other stores. This is why issues like cooperative advertising, special promotions, positioning and the number of facings are so important in retail selling of consumer goods, especially in the grocery business.

But in any other distributive businesses the outlet sales people influence what the customer buys by doing a very clear selling job. We might describe the activities concerned with getting commitment to physical distribution, getting outlets to stock the product, as 'selling in'. This is traditionally the activity which gets most attention from sales people from supplier companies. However, it is probably more important to ensure that the activities required to 'sell out' the products from the outlet to the final consumer, are undertaken. Otherwise, your products may sit on the shelves of the outlet, but they may stay there while the sales people from the outlet are actively promoting the products from your competitor. Yours may be sold only if someone specifically comes in and asks for it.

One of the key differences in general between the approach to Part 2 and Part 3 businesses is if your products will be actively sold and promoted, or whether it is a self-service situation with little or no expectation of sales support.

In a supermarket the most you could expect is for store staff to tell customers whether they stock a certain line and where it is located. On the other hand, in many other outlets you would expect the store sales people to advise customers which is the best product to meet their needs. In the supermarket success is about merchandising, and in the case of non-self-service stores there should be a large component of personal in-store selling.

The types of selling-out activities through non-chain outlets are more varied, and there is more scope in terms of account managing at the store level. In the case of the chains, what happens at head office provides much more scope for creativity, whereas at the store level there will generally be fewer opportunities for different selling out activities, and those which do exist will be mainly merchandising issues.

. . . .

The distribution decision

If you have a large customer base or potential customer base and a limited sales force, the chances are that you will have chosen to sell through a distribution network of resellers/retailers/dealers (outlets). You may do something like Amway, where you create a multilevel marketing organisation which relies on personal selling by a large number of people arranged in a hierarchy. At the customer interface, selling is door-to-door or through small groups of people, whom the sales person invites to their home or another location.

You might have a tele- or mail-ordering organisation where you advertise through TV, brochures mailed to potential customers or through some other organisation (credit cards, airlines, magazine subscriptions) then send the goods direct to the customer, with payment often by credit cards. In the USA there are now TV channels which specialise in selling merchandise. The internet has also entered the scene.

If you have chosen to sell through a distribution network, the first major question you will have to address is which distributors/resellers/retailers dealers to work with. Should you try to get distribution through every outlet who could sell your product (which is how the grocery business in Australia works), or should you have a restricted distribution through only some of the potential outlets?

Open versus closed distribution

If your products are sold primarily through outlets where the key issue is merchandising rather than personal in-store selling, you might take the view that the more outlets which stock your product, the better. This is certainly the approach with the grocery business and the supermarkets. There is a point of view which says that even in cases such as these, there is some advantage to both the supplier and the supermarket in a degree of exclusivity. It revolves around the strength of the brand name. If your brand is strong enough that people will go to a specific store to buy it there is some real advantage to the outlet in being able to offer it, especially where their competitors do not. It will create store traffic for other items. As long as the brand loyalty is strong enough the sales will be the same in volume irrespective of the number of outlets, and it should be more cost-effective to work with fewer chains and stores. This is why in some countries there are chains which offer some brands and not others. That does not seem to be the way things are done in the supermarket business in Australia because there is so much emphasis in promotion on price. Even so, brand loyalty is underestimated by both suppliers and by retailers.

This chapter is not primarily about the supermarket business, but the arguments about distribution are just the same in the non-supermarket business.

Open distribution, so that everyone is encouraged to stock the product, means that:

- you require more sales support staff to visit all the outlets
- there is likely to be more stock at the points where sales are made
- outlets will tend to compete with each other on your product and drop margins so that the product becomes less attractive to sell
- outlets will have less loyalty to your product since you have less loyalty to them

- outlets are more likely to sell products from other suppliers which will compete with yours
- you will find it harder to get the outlet to promote your product over others
- the outlet will tend to play off one supplier against another, promising to support the one which offers the best deals
- the poor service provided by some outlets may have a negative effect on your product
- there is likely to be better potential reach to the customer base, but less interest in promoting your product over others.

If you have a selected or restricted distribution:

- the outlet has less competition on your brand and is not going to have its margins pressured by other outlets discounting the same product
- fewer sales staff are required to visit the outlets, or each sales person can spend more time with the outlet concentrating on selling out activities
- the outlet is more likely to actively promote your product
- the outlet will be less likely to promote products competing with yours (but may still do so)
- a method of directing or attracting customers to the outlets which stock your product must be found
- you can build the image of your product by selling only through outlets of a certain standard
- there is poorer reach to potential customers
- there is likely to be more active selling of your product by the outlet.

If you decide that you have more to gain by getting the highest possible reach, either because yours are impulse items or you have not sufficient brand loyalty to avoid switch selling, the distribution decision is easy. You go for as many outlets as you can.

If your products are technical in nature, end users can be identified so that specific targeted selling can take place. You are generally better off to have a closed distribution network of a smaller number of dedicated and competent resellers who are prepared to get behind your product, and who make a good margin on selling it.

If you are going to have a selected distribution network, the problem is much more complex. You have to decide which outlets you want to work with.

Deciding which trading partners you want

The question of which organisations you want to work with can be complicated. The ideal situation is to achieve geographic reach with an outlet which is competent and motivated to actively promote and sell your products in each area where you seek to sell. Years ago most outlets were independently owned and operated, but now in almost any kind of retail or outlet business there are groups of outlets which operate together in some way. They are owned by one owner, or they are franchised, or they have formed some kind of association. In each case there is in effect a central buying organisation which, through the volume of its purchases, can obtain special deals from suppliers to the mutual benefit of supplier and reseller.

Such groups can never be ignored by the supplier because they do represent a significant volume. Account management must plan both to deal with the central organisation and the individual outlets. This is even more true when the individual outlets are not owned by the central organisation. Both levels of account management will be discussed in Part 2.

With most groups you will find that you would not want to work with all of the outlets associated with a particular group. There will certainly be the top few with whom you would have chosen to work anyway, but there will often be some with whom you would have chosen not to work. The problem is that if you have an arrangement with the organisation, they will not normally enter into one that excludes some of their associates/affiliates. The supplier needs to establish with the organisation that there will be priority given to only certain outlets. This may mean that not every outlet stocks your goods, and it could mean that you will not provide support to every outlet. The difficulty comes when in a particular area, suburb or country town there is an independent outlet which exactly meets what you would want from an outlet, but in that area there is also an outlet associated with an organisation with which you work, but which in your view is not a very effective outlet. You probably cannot prevent this associated outlet offering your product, and they will also inevitably have access to the special deals you have made with the central organisation. The only way you can try to push the business towards the independent outlet you want to work with is by the amount of local sales support and promotion you give them, but this may lead you to a degree of conflict with the organisation whose outlet you are tending to ignore. There is no easy answer to this. The more you can develop a close and mature relationship with the 'head office' organisation, the better are the chances that you can reach some satisfactory arrangement for both sides.

Conflict of interests in the field

The situation becomes even more complicated when there are two or more group organisations with which you are working, and you have an outlet associated with each one in a particular area. This leads to exactly the sort of thing you are trying to avoid by having a selected distribution, namely the fact that outlets will compete with each other on your product. Some of this is inevitable, and it has to be managed on a case by case basis.

The main reason that you want to avoid too many outlets offering your product is that they will tend to lower the margins, which means that they will be less interested in promoting the products because they make less gross profit out of it. At the same time outlets will put pressure on you to lower your price to them so that they regain their lost margin (this never works: if you lower your price someone will use this lower price to try and buy volume against other outlets, and you end up back where you started).

If a business is dominated by a few large organisations, they tend to use their strength to try to control the supplier's business. Experience shows that such organisations start to demand discounts and special deals, often under the guise of money for promotion. In this sense there starts to be some similarity with the way the supermarkets operate. The rebates demanded have become so high in some industries that suppliers are desperately trying to find an alternative method of distribution.

There have been cases where the share of a supplier's business, which a particular organisation represents, has risen as high as 40 per cent. The danger is that organisation feels they are in such a dominant position that they can dictate policy to the supplier and hold them to ransom on price. It is very dangerous for any supplier to let their business be dominated in such a way. If you find that 10 per cent of your business is represented by one organisation, you should make a specific attempt, if you can, to limit growth in such accounts and develop more business through others. This is not easy, since often the organisation which absorbs that extent of your business has done so because they are good at retailing in that business.

What typically happens is that dominant organisations start to complain about margins and will tell you that to avoid pressure on your own margins, the best thing you can do is to give them your product on an exclusive basis. They are confident of their ability to move the volume, yet with no competition there will be good margins for both sides. This is only a step away from getting you to abandon any market position you might have in those businesses where the supplier also has a relationship with the end user. This is typical of businesses selling consumables like chemicals, especially where there is a technical content to the business. If you perceive that it is important in any way for you to have some contact with the end-user base, never back off too far from contact with end users. Suppliers of products like cars, computers and software, agricultural products and so on, need to make sure they can identify their end users, otherwise they will be stuck with the distribution network they have, because if they change it they will not know where to look for their customers. The supplier must retain adequate control over the market.

Distributors and agents

One way you can try to prevent price erosion is to control prices at the outlet level. If you sell the product to an outlet, you cannot do this, as it is strictly against the law (*Restrictive Trade Practices Act*). But if your distribution network are distributors or agents, the situation changes, and the distributor or agent does not buy the product from the supplier. The supplier pays the distributor or agent a commission or a fee for stocking and selling the product. The supplier retains title to the product and the customer or end user is invoiced for the goods or services by the supplier. This means that the invoice should be an invoice on the supplier's paper and the supplier carries the risk, provides the credit facility and is paid the money. The distributor or agent may perform some of these steps for the supplier (like invoicing and collecting money), but in the eyes of the law it is a transaction between the supplier and the end user, for which the intermediary is paid a commission or fee.

This can work quite well where the business is selling product to the same customer time and time again. Not only is it important from a sales point of view for the supplier to know who the customers are and to have some sort of contact with them, but it may also be important in a marketing sense. The marketing department can devise better promotional programs if it has access to the end users.

There are higher operating costs associated with this kind of operation and there is more risk of bad debt. However, you maintain more control of the end user, are less vulnerable to increasing pressure from the buying groups, and are better able to have a marketing program which is independent of the distribution network.

In some businesses there are two levels of distribution, where the supplier sells to a wholesaler or distributor, who then sells to a reseller. In some cases these resellers may be owned by the distributor, and in others may be independent. If you make the wholesaler the agent, you only control pricing to the reseller, not to the end user. As it is the reseller or retailer who actually makes the sale to the end user, unless there is sufficient margin at their level, there will still be the problem that the reseller will not be motivated to sell your product. There have been cases where this kind of system operates and where the supplier has decided to cut out the wholesaler and deal directly with the reseller.

This can work when the majority of the resellers you want to work with are independent of the wholesaler or buying group, otherwise you may end up losing some of the resellers you really need to sell your products. This was a hot topic in the area of selling agricultural chemicals a few years ago. Du Pont in Western Australia implemented a pilot scheme to invoice the farmer and make the reseller the distributor. This allowed them to set prices to the farmer, and to guarantee the reseller a margin. What it risked was upsetting the head office entities.

One other possible strategy is to forward integrate so that you own and control part of the distribution network. While this puts you in competition with your own customers, it sometimes works quite well because you can establish price levels in the marketplace so that the benchmark is at a higher retailing margin than would otherwise be the case.

. . . .

A distribution plan

There are two levels at which distribution planning should be done. There is the marketing level where the considerations are the issues of how open the distribution network should be, and what types of organisation you want to act as outlets. Such a plan should also address issues of whether the outlets should be resellers or whether they should be agents or distributors.

Then you have to decide if you are going to restrict distribution, and how you are going to do it, whether through the amount of support you provide in store through your own sales force, and, hence, selling out activities, or through some form of accreditation and advertising your product as being available from and backed at accredit ed resellers. If you can gain an agreement that only certain outlets of buying groups will sell your products, then so much the better, although in most cases the groups will be reluctant to agree to that.

This distribution plan is most important and should involve the sales and the marketing people.

Once the distribution strategy has been defined, the sales people should nominate how that should be implemented in their own areas, which will normally be geographic. This takes into account the abilities of the individual outlets. Any conflict between the needs of a given area and the interests of the company state-wide or nationally will need to be resolved. A given local area may have to be sacrificed in the interests of the larger picture.

These two processes define the groups which have to be dealt with on a head office basis, and the key stores which are to be included in the key account management program. Again some sort of Pareto principle will be operating. At the local level there will be more changes in the trading partners we want to work with than in the more strategic distribution decisions at a macro or head office level, in the sense that outlets will open and close and people will change. In franchises and associations there will be businesses which change hands. This means that at the local level of a territory (the geographic area for which a sales person is responsible),

107

distribution should be looked at once a year, preferably before you start the annual account management presentations and negotiations.

At this point you will have identified which are the groups you want to work with, with the 'head office account management' job to be done there, and you will also have defined the outlets which are priorities, both independent and associated with or belonging to the defined groups. These are the key accounts and they are the candidates for your account managing.

. . . .

Who is your customer?

There is a tendency for suppliers to refer to the end user as the customer, and, in a sense, the end user is the customer of the supplier. The supplier certainly has some legal obligations to the end user with respect to product performance and warranty agreements. The end user is also the person to whom much of the media advertising will be oriented. The end users and potential end users should be quantified and understood. In businesses where end users and potential end users are not easily identifiable by any other means, market research plays an important role not just to identify who the potential customers are and how many there are, but what their needs are and how they are likely to make purchasing decisions. Marketing can then make decisions on media advertising and promotional programs.

The end user is very much the customer in a marketing sense, but there are other definitions of customer. From a sales point of view we could say that the customer is the one who is invoiced, on the basis that that is the one who buys the goods or services from you. In this case the distribution network is the customer, either the wholesaler or head-office entity of a group, or when you invoice the stores they are the customer.

The point about asking who the customer is relates to where the sales force spends their time and how they look upon the distribution network at various levels, how they interact with them, and how they look at the end user.

In businesses where the end user walks into the store there is no easy way of predicting who exactly an end user is or might be. Both local promotion by the outlet and the media advertising by the supplier will be aimed at getting potential end users to come to their outlet. In this case the supplier will generally not have any contact with the end user at the time the selling is being done or the purchasing decision is being made. The sales force will inevitably spend most of their time with the distribution network. They will see the outlets as their 'customers', the people they sell to.

But there are other business where the sales people of the supplier have a significant amount of contact with the end user, for example in food service. This is where food or other consumer products are sold to institutions such as hospitals, prisons, or hospitality outlets such as hotels, clubs, cafes or restaurants. Although the end user buys the product from a wholesaler, who specialises in food service products, the end user is invoiced by the wholesaler, gets delivery from the wholesaler and pays the wholesaler, whilst the wholesaler almost never does any selling. The sales people of the supplier visit the end users, often taking orders which they then pass on to the wholesaler. The supplier does the selling to the end user, who then buys it through the wholesaler, who is really acting simply as a stockist. We hope that the margins the wholesaler makes are consistent with their involvement in getting the business!

When the outlet can identify its customers

There are businesses, however, where the supplier's sales people and the sales people from the distribution network might be overtly selling to the end user. A classic example, which applies to many other businesses too, would be in selling agricultural chemicals to farmers through a distribution network of resellers. Traditionally it was the supplier's sales people who did much of the selling to the farmer, by what is called canvassing and is really on-farm selling. It was not unknown for sales people from the supplier to take an order from the farmer, then pass it on to the reseller of the farmer's choice. In these cases there is a real confusion on who the customer of the supplier's sales people is. The more established sales people will still see the end user as their customer. However, as products move to more 'me-too' types of product as patents expire and products move to commodities, there is less margin for either the reseller or the supplier. Suppliers can no longer afford large sales forces whose job is to sell to a very large end-user base. Inevitably in businesses such as this, there is a need to refocus the efforts of the sales force away from selling direct to the end user, towards selling through the distribution network. This means that the account manager's job becomes largely one of working with the distribution network to make sure that they are able to sell the products effectively to the end user. This may mean that there are joint visits made together with the supplier's sales person and the reseller's sales person to the end user, but this should be primarily as a training role for the sales people of the reseller. There may be joint selling missions to very large end users, and perhaps support to the reseller in problem solving.

This implies that the outlets have their own external sales people who visit their customer base, and this is the case in many distributive businesses. There is some potential conflict here, because there almost seems to be some dual ownership of the end user. The resellers may sell the end user a variety of products from a number of different suppliers and will guard that relationship with what he or she correctly sees as their customer, the end user. The supplier may take the view that to the extent that the end user buys product made and backed by them, the end user is their customer too. This needs to be resolved in the minds of both the supplier and the distribution network.

Firstly, the end user is very much the customer of the outlet. In fact, a loyal customer base is one of their most valuable assets, and the supplier must realise this, accept it, and conduct themselves in such a way that the relationship between the outlet and the end user is not prejudiced. At the same time the outlet must accept that there is some relationship between the supplier and the end user. The supplier must know where the market is, and how to best promote their products to it.

The conclusion must be that there is joint ownership of the end user by distribution and the supplier, because both have a relationship with, and obligations to the end user. Both of them also depend on the end user to

110

make a profit. Furthermore, the supplier and distribution have the same interests unless the outlet wants to sell the end user a product which competes with your own. If there is a case to be made that the competitor's product better meets the needs of the end user, then the supplier is best advised to be philosophical about it and accept that they cannot win every round. Otherwise the supplier may need to re-examine whether they have the right outlet representing their interests in that area.

Account management should lead to the sort of relationship where both the supplier and distribution see that the best way for them to approach the marketplace is through a cooperative effort. Both have some ownership over the end user. Both parties act understanding this and respecting it. The outlet and the supplier are so dependent on each other for success that it is hard to see why they spend so much energy on the aspects of their relationship where compromise may be required, and less on the major areas where cooperation will lead to success for both. This requires trust and stability in the relationship, and is part of account management.

. . . .

The territory plan

We have talked about distribution planning at two levels: the marketing plan which seeks to set the overall strategy for distribution, and a plan for each area or territory which takes those principles or guidelines and identifies the organisations and outlets with whom you will work on a priority basis in that area.

Part of that answer will depend on how effective you feel the current distribution is, and to what extent there are opportunities which you have not realised. The account manager or territory manager needs to understand the marketplace in his or her area, meaning the size and shares of the various suppliers and outlets into the market and the potential business. This unrealised potential is very important, because it defines an opportunity both for the supplier and for distribution. Some businesses have data available from government statistics or privately produced figures. For example, Solutions in Sydney specialise in collecting and generating for clients specific information on the market. In other businesses there is market research data available, but sometimes you have to look at the demographics of the area and make some assumptions from what you know in general about the market.

There should be an overall territory or area objective, which needs to be broken down into the key outlets which you expect to generate the sales. In some businesses there will be differences between outlets in terms of the market segments they cater to. Equally there will be different markets for your products, depending on how the local market is made up. This might also vary with demographics. The account manager needs to match the market segment opportunities with the specialisations of the various outlets. There may be one outlet in an area which caters for a certain type of customer, and another outlet which tends to attract another type of clientele; the chances are that these two outlets would not conflict with each other, and the sorts of promotional programs which would be successful may be very different for the two situations. These factors should all be taken into account when putting together the distribution plan or territory plan for the area.

A final comment on this subject is that in looking at the expected results from a given area you could do it either bottom up or top down. Either look at the whole area and determine the business you should be able to get, then apportion it by outlet as the basis for a target for each outlet, or look at what you think you can get by each outlet, then build that up into the large picture.

There is some preference for doing it top down. If you do it bottom up you may double count business, which more than one outlet claims or expects, in which case the targets will be too high, or there might be business out there which you never plan to address, because it is not being considered by any of the outlets with which you are planning. Defining the total current and potential business for the area lets you set targets not just for volume and share, but also for market penetration. Comparisons with other areas then become useful. If you have different penetration figures in different areas you must ask why, and what you are doing right in the areas where you are successful.

111

Top-down analysis might also suggest where you have not got enough coverage through distribution, because it looks at the total market rather than the market of the people through whom you work.

· · · · · · · · · · · · · · · · · · ·

Account management through distribution

This book is primarily about a systematic approach to managing key accounts, called account management. Once the initial steps have been taken to decide which key groups and outlets you wish to work, it is time to look at the principles discussed in the first part of the book, and see how they might operate with distributive businesses. The thrust of account management is to manage the distribution network so that you get distribution through the outlets you want on terms and conditions which are acceptable to both sides, and then agree on whatever action is necessary by both the supplier and distribution to get the product to sell out to the end users.

If the outlet is independent, you will have to include both selling in and selling out aspects. If the outlet is fully owned by the head office, the selling in will be done at the head-office level. If the outlet is associated or franchised, there will be a selling in job to be done at the head office, then this will need to be reinforced through more selling at the outlet level. This only affects the construction of the presentation and what is negotiated at each level. The process of account management will be the same at the outlet level in all these cases.

How distribution makes its money

Before we talk specifically about the account management cycle in distributive businesses, it is worth reflecting on how distributive businesses make their money. The reason for this is that the principle of account management is that if we can show how our customer can earn or save money we will have a good argument for them to buy from us. The relationship of the outlet to the product is different from the end user. The end user wants to gain some effect from the product or service, which should meet a specific need. The benefits of the product, which result from the product features, will meet an end user's need. The reseller or outlet only cares about this insofar as the end user continues to believe that the product will meet their needs. The reseller simply wants to make money out of buying and selling the product. For example, if an end user needs to feel more attractive and decides that by using a certain perfume they will be more attractive, then purchasing the perfume will meet the perceived need of the end user. Whether it makes the end user more attractive or not is of no interest or concern to the reseller, as long as the end user is satisfied and keeps buying the product. The interest to the reseller in the product working is only insofar as it gives the end user satisfaction. I have a friend who has a retail outlet selling terracotta, whose best-selling products are those he would never consider buying himself. The fact that others are prepared to, however, is the only thing he cares about.

So, distribution makes its money from buying and selling. This sounds very obvious, yet far too many sales people talk to outlets about the product as if they were selling it to the end user. The end user may want to know what it will do in a product performance sense. The outlet only wants to know how many they can sell and what sort of margin they can make on it. If selling is about satisfying customer needs, then selling to distribution involves recognising that their need is to make money out of buying and selling. They will be more interested to hear that you believe they will be able to sell 1000 items this year at a gross profit of $20 each, than knowing that it has a hydraulic, laser activated coupling mechanism. That might be a useful piece of information when they sell it to the end user, but in itself it is not likely to influence whether they are going to stock and promote the product.

This difference in what the product means to the different levels in the selling process is important, especially when there is confusion in the supplier's sales people on who their customer is. They should see the distribution network as their customer, and sell to them on the basis of what they can make out of selling the product. They then need to give the outlet the product knowledge, including the product features and benefits, to enable the outlet to sell the product to the end user.

Stores and ROII per linear metre

Fundamentally the outlet has access to certain funds which they invest in stock which they sell to their customers, and on which they make money. The amount of money they have to invest in stock is finite, as is the space to store the product. If they want to look at how efficiently the money they invest in stock is being used, they must do it on an ROI basis. The return they are going to get for the investment they make in the stock is sometimes expressed as ROII, or return on inventory investment. This must take into account both the volume sales and the margins they make. If they are particularly short of space, the volume the product takes up on the shelf is important too. A product which has a higher margin is better for the outlet for a given volume of sales, than one with lower margin. If two products have the same volume and margin characteristics but one requires less investment in stock than the other to support the same sales, it is a better product. If you have equal performers under all these criteria, but one product takes up less room than the other, then that is the better product. The outlet can use the space saved to stock something else on which they can make a profit.

The ultimate criterion could be considered as ROII per cubic metre or per linear metre of shelf space. There is no easy way of determining the actual profit from a product, in the sense that it is very hard to apportion fixed costs. In the grocery business there has been an attempt to do this by calculating what are known as direct product costs, then calculating direct product profitability (DPP). What this exercise seeks to do is to apportion many of the assumed fixed costs of the business, such as transporting the goods around the store, storing them, putting them up on the shelves and packing them in bags at the checkout, so that these costs in effect become variable costs of that product.

In all other businesses there is no alternative to measuring contribution, including margin and rebates multiplied by volume sales. This gives the 'R' figure, the return, or in this case the contribution. Then the inventory

investment is the value at their purchase price of the average amount of inventory the outlet carries to support sales.

Considerations such as these identify the best products for the outlet to sell, but outlets will not set a standard below which they will not stock products. There are other considerations to take into account. For example, there will be products which may not perform very well, but which are 'service lines'. Customers will come in and ask for these products, and will expect the outlet to sell them. These tend to be products which are strong brand names, a stock item for that business or industry, or products which are heavily advertised in the media.

There may be cases where an outlet may agree to stock certain products from a supplier even though they do not perform well, in the interests of maintaining a good relationship with the supplier on other parts of the supplier's range which perform very well. The outlet will want to pick the best-performing products out of the ranges of their suppliers. There is no supplier which has a full set of good products which will perform well for the outlet; there will always be weaker products which the supplier will try to push along with the strong lines. Just as it is in the interests of the outlet to pick and choose products from the supplier's range, what the supplier should do is to package the whole range so that the outlet has to take the weaker ones if they want to get the stronger ones. This is usually the subject of negotiated agreement, and is one area where the interests of the outlet and the supplier may be in conflict. Such is business and distribution and suppliers have to learn to reach a satisfactory compromise.

Choosing dancing partners

The insightful distribution company will recognise that rather than be a 'prostitute' for a few cents margin, buying wherever they get the cheapest price, there is an advantage to be gained from a stable relationship with a relatively small number of suppliers. In the same way that the suppliers have a strategy for distribution which defines the people with whom they want to work, so should distribution have a policy which defines the key suppliers with whom they want to work. This decision will be influenced by the ROII performance of their products, but will look at other issues too.

- How stable are they?
- How good are they at developing the market?
- Are they likely to develop new products?
- Do they advertise their products in the media?
- Are they prepared to do local promotions?
- How flexible are they?
- Will their sales people help sell the products out?
- How competent are their sales people?
- How easy are they to deal with as a supplier?
- What degree of competition is there with other suppliers with whom they want to work?
- Are they trustworthy?
- Do they back their products in the field?
- How well managed are they as a company?
- Are they dedicated to the business?
- Are they Australian?
- Do you like them as a company and as people?

115

Deciding to work together has been described very aptly as 'choosing dancing partners', and it is very important from the points of view of both the supplier and distribution. We can also see it in a sense as a marriage. There will always be times when the outlet may want to sell the products of another supplier, because in the short term they can make a quick buck out of doing so. As long as their partner, the supplier, does not find out or does not complain, then they can have their cake and eat it. However, if the supplier does find out, they can always make the point that such actions are not in the interests of the overall relationship. This is not a question of legalities: demanding loyalty is not the sort of thing which the *Trade Practices Act* looks kindly on. However, if the outlet values the relationship with the supplier there is danger in continuing to sell the products of another supplier, if there is a chance that they may lose the relationship with the original supplier and hence those products. These things have to be worked out in the relationship, just like life itself. Account management should lead to a situation where the supplier becomes more desirable as a trading partner and, therefore, enhances the value of the supplier in the outlet's eyes. If a supplier wants to make themselves a more desirable partner to distribution, all they have to do is go through the preceding list and make sure they perform well on those criteria.

. . . .

The account management cycle

The marketing plan

We have already discussed one aspect of the marketing planning, that of a distribution policy. Several other dimensions of the marketing plan will have an impact on account management. The main one is promotional programs, either media advertising or promotions which are designed for use in-store or on a local basis. The marketing department should always talk with sales before deciding in-store promotional programs, to make sure that they are the sorts of things which will be sales multipliers.

In the next chapter we will talk a bit more about the approach to the marketing dollar, and whether it is better to invest heavily in media advertising, or provide funds for local promotions to be managed by the sales force as part of the account management program. For the time being, let us accept that sales needs to understand clearly what the marketing program is and how to get the best out of it.

Communication on such items works much better when there is a determined cycle of events, for example on a quarterly basis. At the end of Q1 sales and marketing meet and sales presents a review of highlights of the last quarter's trading, results and comments on the effectiveness of any marketing programs, usually promotions. Marketing presents to sales the plan for Q3, and any fine-tuning to the plan for Q2, which was presented to sales and agreed at the end of the previous quarter, Q4. The sales force also need to have an agreed mechanism for communicating the key elements of these meetings, on the assumption that not all the sales force will be involved in the quarterly meetings with marketing.

The account profile

Information on the business needs to be kept at two levels. We have discussed the need to have information on the marketplace collected by area or territory. The same principles apply, as we discussed in the case of account profiles in Part 1: we know quite a lot about the market, but it may not be recorded anywhere. The marketing department may be able to provide information to assist the account manager or territory manager in putting together this information for that particular area. Write down what you know first, then gradually build the database. Keep the information on territories in the same format, and put it on database which can be accessed by marketing. These are some of the things you may need to know about the business in an area, and, therefore, may be headings for collection of information.

By product or product group, for each major market segment note the:
- existing market size
- potential market size
- volumes and shares of the key suppliers split down by retail outlet and groups.

At the account level the sorts of things you need to know are:
- ownership of the outlet, associations and affiliations
- the people, including their effectiveness in selling and their product knowledge
- how the business operates and whether it is well managed
- the objectives of the owners, personally and for the business
- how the decision makers decide on supply
- their natural client base, either demographically or by end user
- their retailing philosophy, especially on pricing
- which other suppliers they represent
- your ranking in their business as a supplier, volume and margin
- volumes, shares and penetration in their natural sales area or territory (are they getting their fair share of business and how they are doing relative to others in the marketplace).

The extent to which you can find out the information on the market will depend very much on the type of business you are in. The desirability of knowing such detail will also vary. In some businesses, such as chemicals, you really need to understand penetration and shares. In other businesses it is more important to know what type of clientele they service and what the local demographics are, because then you can decide which products to promote through which outlets and how best to promote to them.

SWOT analysis—focusing options

SWOT analysis is a flexible tool. In distribution it could be looked at on any of three levels, whichever analysis seems to be useful.

You can look at it on the basis of the territory: where do you stand in an overall sense in the territory compared to competitors? This is almost a marketing dimension, and is useful in deciding your distribution policy.

You can also look at it with a focus on strengths in the immediate area together with a particular outlet. This is again looking at the market place.

Or you can do it with a focus on how a particular distributor sees you, how you compare against other suppliers in their eyes. This is useful when the distributor sells products which compete with yours.

Value-added search and profit growth opportunities

Because the distribution network makes money from buying and selling the product, added value or opportunity for them focuses on improving their ROII per cubic metre of shelf space, rather than what the product can do itself. This means identifying where are the opportunities for the outlet to sell more volume or get better margins, for the optimum investment in inventory to support the sales. In many cases such results are exactly what the supplier wants to achieve too.

The difficulty is not so much in selling the idea of where the opportunities for both supplier and distribution are, but in agreeing who should do what about them! Even so it may require some selling by the supplier to persuade the outlet that the market really does exist, and that the opportunities are real. This is where solid facts on the market are invaluable.

Some care must be exercised, because not all growth for outlets is in the interests of the supplier. If, for example, the outlet were to target business in the supplier's products currently sold through another key outlet of the supplier, the supplier is no better off. In fact they may find themselves under pressure to assist the other outlet who is losing the business. Usually such attacks by one outlet on another are mounted on the basis of price, and the outlet losing the business will accuse you of supporting the attacking outlet, and demand that you lower your price so that they can maintain the business they originally had at the margin they had.

Not all outlets will be looking for growth, some may be content to just keep the business they have. The problem is that if you try to stand still in business, you will find that you advance or drop back, usually the latter. Your best key outlets are going to be those who want to build on the business they currently have, and get more. Otherwise they are likely to

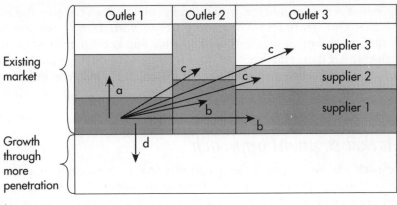

Notes:
a Increases share at an outlet
b The outlet takes your business from
   other outlets
c The outlet takes business of other suppliers
   from other outlets
d New growth from more market penetration

d is best
a is fine, if it is not done on price
c is fine, if it is done on service
b is bad for you

119

Figure 13: Growth share gains through distribution

decline, even if that is not their plan. It is generally true to say that the key accounts will be attracted by seeing how they can hold onto what they have and then have growth as well.

Growth strategies

In looking at opportunities for growth in an area there are several strategies (see Figure 13, above). The best growth is further market penetration because it is not disruptive to the existing status quo. No-one loses business. Other acceptable growth strategies are when one outlet gains business from another on the basis of service they provide to the end user, especially if the business taken is from another supplier operating through a different outlet. It is generally less attractive to the supplier if one outlet just takes business in a product from another outlet. However, if this supports a move to tighten distribution it can be useful to the supplier. Supplier growth, when the outlet gives the supplier a share of the business previously given to the competition, is great from the supplier's point of view.

A counterproductive situation is when one outlet attempts to gain business with the supplier's products by offering them at a lower price against the supplier's products sold through other outlets, or against competitors' products sold through other outlets. Lowering prices is a retrograde step, which tends to advantage only the end user.

Identification of opportunities depends on knowledge of the market. Is this outlet selling as much as you would expect—given the size, the area and the demographics? Are there parts of your range they are not promoting, and missing sales, based on what you know in the rest of your business? Are there end users out there who could be buying your product and are not? Has this outlet got the right share of the business in the area for the size of its operation?

Market segment approach

For each market segment the account manager must analyse present performance of his or her company through the various outlets against the performance of competitors, compared with the potential market. This allows identification of growth opportunities, where you can add value to your company as a supplier in the eyes of distribution and at the same time boost your own volumes.

Inventory is another area for consideration. Is the outlet missing out on sales because they do not have sufficient stock, or do they tend to overstock? Do they manage their inventory so that they have a proper stocking and ordering procedure, with managed upper and lower levels? This is best managed through computerised invoicing, which automatically adjusts stock and alerts the outlet when more stock needs to be ordered. Is the stock operated on a FIFO (First In First Out) basis, so that the outlet does not end up with stock which is old and in poor condition? There may be opportunities for the supplier to help the outlet better manage inventory and reduce its costs while maintaining the necessary stock to support sales.

With large ticket items, the drain on cash flow resources in having stock on the floor can be considerable. In the vehicle industry there are finance arrangements called floor plans which are often operated through finance organisations that often are the same organisations whose retail product the dealership will sell when arranging finance to the end customer. There are other providers of floor-plan financing through companies such as Bridge Wholesale Acceptance Corporation BWAC, whereby an outlet can finance floor stock in a wide variety of capital items to ease cash flow requirements, and to have the stock on the floor so that end users can look at it, handle it, see how it works or even try it out. This is important because experience shows that the outlet with visible product is much more likely to make the sale. Furthermore, once people have made a purchasing decision, they generally want to take delivery of the goods as soon as possible. The outlet who can supply out of stock has a distinct advantage.

Some suppliers of large ticket items will make an arrangement with finance houses as part of their marketing program and will even subsidise the costs involved in providing floor-plan finance, because they understand the importance of having stock out in the field.

Another aspect of contribution to profit is the question of whether the outlet is selling at a margin that will give them the best overall profit? This question of margins is so important that it should be given separate consideration.

Margins and pricing for outlets

We talked earlier in this chapter about the different figures by which distributive businesses and manufacturers achieve ROI. This showed that manufacturers need much higher margins than distribution to make the same ROI, because they have more money tied up in the company in fixed assets and working capital.

This means that most outlets work on much smaller margins than manufacturers, but make them much more often. They can have quite a satisfactory business at margins lower than those of manufacturers, but the effect on their profit by dropping price is far more dramatic.

For example, assume there is an outlet selling a product at $100, making 10 per cent gross profit. A customer comes in and says 'You know that I am a good and loyal customer of yours. You have always provided me good service, good advice and you have always backed the products I have bought from you. I am about to buy 100 of these things which you are selling at $100 each. You need to know, however, that the guy down the road is selling exactly the same thing at $97 each. From your point of view it is only a tiny three per cent difference, just three dollars per item— three out of a hundred. Because I am such a good and loyal customer of yours, I have come to tell you that if you are prepared to meet this price of $97 each, I will buy the hundred items from you.'

If you accept the proposal to sell at $97 instead of $100, how many more of these items do you need to sell to make the same gross profit as you would have done on the original sale? The answer is that by dropping your price 3 per cent, you will have to increase your volume 43 per cent to make the same gross profit and nowadays there is rarely another 43 per cent around to grab.

This is how you work it out.

If the gross profit you make selling the product at $100 is 10 per cent, then you make $10 on each item you sell. This means they cost you $90.

Retail price: $100
Cost price: $ 90
Gross profit $ 10

If the order covers 100 items, then at full selling price of $100 you will

121

make a total gross profit of 100 × $10 = $1000. If you drop your price to meet the competition and sell at only $97 each, this is what happens:

Retail price: $97
Cost price: $90
Gross profit: $ 7

This means that whereas you made $10 each time you sold one thing at $100, now you only make $7 per thing. If your target is to make the same gross profit as the original case, which we have calculated as $1000, then the number of items you need to sell to make $1000 if you only make $7 per thing, is 1000 divided by 7, and the answer is 143. In other words you have to sell 43 per cent more volume to make up for the loss of margin, if you want to make the same gross profit.

Obviously, when the margins are lower this effect is far more noticeable.

Here are a couple more facts:

In the case of a gross profit of 10 per cent, you would actually make more money by putting your price up 5 per cent, even if you lost 30 per cent of your volume. The lesson from this is simply that retailers and wholesalers must get the highest possible margin they can. The supplier might take the view that distribution margins are nothing to do with them, but this is not quite the case. If the retail margins are too low outlets will not want to sell those products. Equally, if the outlets have rebates paid by the supplier on volume sales, there is a tendency for an individual outlet to boost their sales volume by dropping their price in order to get the volume rebate. In this case the supplier is encouraging the problem. There may also be a price positioning that you want in the marketplace relative to other products. Since the supplier cannot manipulate prices at the retail level but can only make a suggestion through a recommended retail price, there is a chance that pricing too high could discourage sales, and pricing too low could prejudice the price positioning in the marketplace and affect other suppliers in the area. You may not want your product to be identified with price discounting, because the product is designed to appeal to the end user through status or quality.

The first thing the supplier should do is to explain the price positioning strategy to distribution, then give the recommended retail price. This price will usually allow the retailer an adequate margin. The supplier should then show the retailer the impact of discounting the price on his bottom line using the calculation above, but with actual figures.

Keeping distribution selective will also help in maintaining retail margins.

Having said all this, there will always be someone who will seek to quit stock, create cash flow, gain share or have a 'loss leader' to create traffic, and will drop the price. What should the outlet do when a competing outlet drops price?

We have said that it is better to drop volume rather than margin up to a certain level. What is that level, and how do you know how to react initially?

There are many studies that look at whether the end user buys on price. My experience working with clients in a wide range of industries, is that each client claims that their business is different, and their customers really do buy on price. This falls into the same category as the fact that 90 per cent of drivers believe they are better than average. All the studies I have seen suggest that around 15 per cent of purchasers buy on price across a wide range of industries and situations, meaning that 85 per cent do not. Many readers will state that their business really is different; even if it were true, if those 15 per cent account for 85 per cent of the business it still leaves you with an enormous problem.

Suppliers believe their customers buy on price, because that is what the customer tells them. The customer has absolutely nothing to lose by doing so. Let us assume that you provide a very good back-up as an outlet, stock the full range, have stock on the shelves, well merchandised and easy to access. Your sales staff are competent, polite and friendly, and they know the products well. Your prices are reasonable, not discounted but not excessive. The chances are that you are the outlet where the customer would rather shop. So when the customer says to you that your prices are too dear, they are saying that their ideal would be to buy from you but at the price of another outlet who does not offer any of the elements of service you do. If you drop your price, then the customer has achieved the ideal. Usually the consumer will expect to pay a bit more for service, and would prefer to pay more to get service.

The best thing the outlet could have said to the customer who came in and asked to buy at $97 was something like this:

'I am glad to hear that you have appreciated our service all this time. In fact we work hard at it, and it is true that we take care to advise our customers well. We take the time and trouble to understand the products we sell, and we back up every one of them, as you know. But we would not be able to do this if we had to sell at the low prices some of our competitors, who do not offer these services, sometimes give. In fact we might not even be in business if we sold at those prices. There is not very much margin in retailing today, and we need every bit of it if we are to deliver the sort of service the customer expects. I cannot meet the price you mention, but what I will do if you place your order with us is guarantee the same service we have always offered you, and just to show my good faith, I will give you a "whatsit" free of charge.' (The whatsit would have cost you maybe $20.)

Service for a price

The principle for the outlets is that they should provide the service to end users, and make theirs the outlet where customers prefer to buy. If challenged on price, justify the prices by the service you provide, and if you feel you need to make some gesture to allow the customer to save face and feel that they have made a point, then make some sort of gesture by a small reduction in price or by some merchandise that the customer will find useful and will value.

The chances are that if you force the customer to make a decision between you and the cheapie, they will choose you or at least 85 per cent will choose you, and 15 per cent will choose the cheapie. This is an act of faith that most outlets are nervous in making. This is after all about differentiation again. The better outlets differentiate themselves on service they provide, giving added value to the customer, and charge slightly higher prices. The worst thing you can do is let the minority of customers who shop on price set the price levels for the whole business. For example, some years ago a farmer in Western Australia bought an extruder that made Type 50 agricultural high density polyethylene pipe. His overhead was next to nothing, the extruder small and old, and he just added what he thought was a fair margin. This put his price well below that of the big players like Vinidex, Humes and James Hardie. They all panicked. To meet these prices they were going to have to drop below costs. But this farmer with his little operation could only supply 3 per cent of the market at full production, so they should have just let him be rather than drop their prices to his level.

As a supplier you should encourage the outlets to adopt this strategy. Provide a superior service, charge a little bit more, and make sure that the outlet staff can handle the price question when it comes up. Remember that when you look at grocery retailing even though the major chains promote themselves largely on price, we all know that the largest ones are not in fact the cheapest. If everyone shopped on price and nothing else, then they would be.

Your own experience will probably show that you are more likely to have changed your purchasing habits from retailers for other than price reasons in most cases. Research shows that far more sales are lost by poor service than by anything else. One of the most valuable assets an outlet has is its own staff. If staff are rude and lazy, gossip to each other instead of attending customers, are off-hand and lacking in interest, it will make the customer want to go to another outlet next time. If the staff are friendly, interested, solicitous, well-informed on the products and try to assess the customer's needs before making a recommendation, the chances are the customer will feel comfortable shopping there, will return and even recommend that store to others.

These considerations are interesting to the supplier and to account management for these reasons:

- they should drive the identification of the key outlets you want to deal with
- you do not want to be associated with price cutters unless you are prepared to be subjected to price pressures yourself
- your positioning is such that you want your product to be identified with quality and service
- you should be helping the outlets adopt and achieve this goal through your assistance in the account management program.

. . . .

The joint business plan

We now come to the central part of the whole process. We have discussed many of the issues and looked at a few philosophical questions. Now let us look at the practical issue of how the plan should be constructed.

The main difference between account management for direct and distributive accounts is in this plan (illustrated in Figure 14). For distributive accounts the plan is an external document that you are going to present to the outlet or the head office of the buying group, and you are going to reach a negotiated agreement to it. There may be an annual plan that looks at the basis on which you will do business and the principles of how you will operate. This would then be fine-tuned on a quarterly basis to include the details of various activities. The annual plan will be about selling in, the deal and rebates, the terms and conditions, and it will include some activities which will be about selling out. These may be local promotions and they may be about specific selling out activities. These will be talked about in general in the annual plan.

When it comes to the quarterly plan, there may be some last minute details on aspects of the selling in, but most of the plan will be in locking down the detail of exact dates for selling out activities. The exact format of these plans will vary with the industry and business you are in, and the amount of information you have to identify opportunities for growth.

The front page should look clean and smart, and have the logos and names of both the trading partners. The outlet's name should be at the top and the supplier's at the bottom. It should state the period the plan covers. Ideally you should try to estimate some desirable result that you can demonstrate is an achievable goal. Here are a few end results that you could use:

- '$50 000 Profit Growth Plan for Outlet X'
- '20 per cent volume increase over last year'
- 'A Plan for Outlet X to achieve $500 000 sales in 1998 of Supplier Y's products'
- 'How Outlet X can contribute $220 000 to profit in 1998.'

The outlet may be sceptical about how it is possible, but they will be interested enough to hear you out. The initial result must be both desirable and achievable. You can make the figures sound better by expressing them over a year. If the raw dollars are not large on your range of products you could express increases as a percentage. You must make it clear that this is an estimate, a plan to reach a goal, and that you are not in a position to guarantee the result. You should be sure that the estimated result can be achieved, because if you create an expectation which is not achieved, you will lose credibility and possibly damage your relationship.

In any part of the plan where you refer to estimated profit, gross profit or contribution, you must make a statement that makes it clear that you are not trying to manipulate or fix prices or margins. This could be '* based on the average margins that you achieved in 1998', or '* based on a common industry margin of 10 per cent for calculation purposes only'.

The next part of the plan demonstrates where the opportunity exists. This is a result of the analysis you will have done. Any detailed figures on markets and market research should be in an appendix for the outlet to examine if they wish, not in the body of the presentation.

126

You will normally find it easier to take the major market segments and look at the opportunity for each segment. Always try to talk from the outlet's point of view and use segments which they use or at least can identify with. As far as you can, make the plan fit with the way they organise and look at their business.

For each segment you can look at performance for the previous year, expressing it as sales or purchases. You might look at shares, volumes, penetration, performance relative to other similar areas or situations. From this estimated opportunity, you can set targets or goals. For each opportunity you must have some plan on how you are going to achieve the result, either through promotional activities or selling activities.

It is also a good idea to address how you plan to maintain the business the outlet currently has. In businesses where the outlet sells products to consumers year after year, this is particularly important. The extent to which you can plan a campaign for external selling to the end user, other than waiting for the customer to come into the outlet, depends on whether these end users can be identified and whether the outlet has an external sales force.

Where the end users can be identified it is possible to plan more specific selling out activities, such as personal selling, direct mail or meetings. In such cases it is even more important to have a plan to ensure that the loyal user base is encouraged to continue to buy your product through that outlet. These activities should all be seen as cooperative, with both the supplier and the outlet participating.

Review of 1997

Highlights:

1 Purchases from East Coast Company exceeded $300 000 for the first time. This is higher than the turnover for similar stores in similar areas.
2 Good sales through the trade in conjunction with the Smith's lines.
3 The new plastic pack was a good seller.
4 Special Combi pack increased sales of Z190.
5 Printed $20 vouchers was a good promotion to non-trade customers.
6 Free advice weekend brought in traffic.
7 Local advertising did not work as well as expected. It needs to be more targeted.

Opportunities for 1998

1 Build on the existing trade business in the area, with some special promotions and trade nights.
2 There is still only estimated 55% penetration in the area. We need to increase penetration, with a target of 65% for 1998.
3 There is also the potential for East Coast Trading to gain business from Country Traders, who sell competitive products, on the basis of better service.

Objectives and Strategy by market segment

Trade
1997 volume $130 000 of purchases.
Target 1998 $150 000 of purchases.
This will be possible due to:
- increased primary installations starts in the area
- a small but positive growth in the economy

A JOINT

BUSINESS PLAN

FOR

EAST COAST TRADERS

WANDEROO

AND

PRODUX LTD

FOR 1998

Figure 14a: The joint business plan—sample 1

Product

We will continue to promote the plastic pack. The Combi package will be offered again.

Pricing

Pricing to East Coast Trading will be at current ruling levels, with a 3% discount for purchases from Produx of more than $75 000 in any quarter, and paid on total purchases. The thrust in the market will be to gain share on the basis of service and promotion.

Summary of East Coast Traders financial gains:

Total 1997 volume purchases $300 000
Target 1998 volume purchases **$348 000**

The key activities to support this will be:

- Trade nights (two in the year), with BBQ
- Mailing flyers with council plan approvals
- Agreeing a sales story to promote to the trade, and provision of sales material to help
- Mail outs to those customers who bought in the last 3 years, aiming at a retro updating
- Direct joint selling to any large new developments
- Continue to companion sell with the Smith's product

Independents

Estimated 1997 volume of purchases $84 000

Target 1998 volume of $93 000 of purchases

Features:

Environmental campaign summer and winter.

Strong POS for both campaigns.

Local advertising ($2000 *to be invested, Produx will pay 50% and will provide the bromides*).

Education weekend, with Produx staff to provide free consultancy advice to customers.

Staff training by our account manager before both campaigns.

Mail out for the winter campaign, concentrating on prime installations.

Refer enquiries to 3 selected customers from the trade with whom we worked last year.

Provide free supply and installation as a prize to the Wenderoo Rotary annual picnic. Produx will provide the product, and East Coast Traders will arrange and pay for the fitting.

Replacement Market

Estimated 1997 volume of purchases $84 000

Target 1998 volume of purchases $105 000
This is the area where there is plenty of opportunity for more market penetration.

Key Activities:

- Find out where the original installations were from council
- Mail out to all such installations
- Selective telephone follow up for large installations

ongoing activities

AM/ECT	Selective telephone selling to large installations
AM/ECT	Joint selling to any approved significant developments
ECT	Refer enquiries to one of the 3 selected fitters
ECT	Check council approvals and mail out within 3 weeks

ACTIVITY SCHEDULE FOR JANUARY TO JUNE 1997

WHO	WHAT	BY WHEN
AM/ECT	Approach council to try to get flyers included in council approvals of plans	18/1
AM/ECT	Design and print flyers - Produx to provide flyer on Z190, ECT to write a covering letter	1/2
AM/ECT	Arrange prize of Enviromax for Rotary picnic on 25/3	10/2
AM/ECT	Hold Trade night and BBQ showing video film, and presentation, including promotional material to help the Trade sell the product	
AM/ECT	Attend Rotary picnic	15/3
AM/ECT	Training night on winter campaign	25/3
AM/ECT	Identify original VWB installations from council records	15/4
AM/ECT	Local advertisement in Wanderoo Weekly using environmental message to be prepared. Split costs, Produx to provide bromides, & ECT to arrange	23/4
AM/ECT	Free consultancy weekend in store	1/5
ECT	Identify retrofit potential customers who bought since 1995, mail brochure and covering letter	6&7/5 / 1/6
AM/ECT	Review results for first half and fine tune plans for second half	20/6

A 1997/8 Highlights

1
2
3
4
5
6

B Opportunities and main thrusts for 1998/9

1
2
3
4
5

C Selling out activities and promotion

(If there is a customer loyalty program of some sort, you may want to include it here.)

EAST COAST COMMERCIAL SUPPLIES

AND

PRODUX INTERNATIONAL

JOINT BUSINESS PLAN

FOR

**JULY 1998 TO JUNE 1999
SALES INCREASE
ESTIMATED AT $80 000**

Figure 14b: The joint business plan—sample 2

E Produx International support

Promotional material, training, technical back up, delivery service

1
2
3
4

F East Coast Commercial Supplies support to the business

Inventory levels, promotion, merchandising, selling

1
2
3
4

G Trading terms

Payment terms, rebates, delivery, etc.

H Summary gains for East Coast Commercial Supplies

Main segments	1997/8				1998/9			
	$ Purchases		Gross profit		$ Purchases		Gross profit*	
	Actual	Target	Actual	Target	% Inc.	Target	Estimate	% Inc.
1								
2								
3								
4								
5								
6								
TOTAL								

* In all cases estimates of gross profit are based upon your advice on the average margins you make, and do not imply any suggested pricing by Produx International.

EAST COAST COMMERCIAL SUPPLIES SUMMARY RESULT

An estimated increase for 1998/9 over last year of

$$$$ in sales revenue or % %

$$$ in gross profit, or % %

D 1996/7 Business by segment

(I) Segment 1

Main products	1997/8			1998/9		
	$ Purchases		Gross profit	$ Purchases		Gross profit
	Actual	Target	Actual	Target		Estimate*
1						
2						
3						
4						
5						
6						
TOTAL						

Key opportunities for growth

1
2
3

Selling out activities to support the segment

1
2
3

(II) Segment 2

Main products	1997/8			1998/9		
	$ Purchases		Gross profit	$ Purchases		Gross profit
	Actual	Target	Actual	Target		Estimate
1						
2						
3						
4						
5						
6						
TOTAL						

Key opportunities for growth

1
2
3

Selling out activities to support the segment

1
2
3

132

EAST COAST COMMERCIAL SUPPLIES

AND

PRODUX INTERNATIONAL

JOINT BUSINESS PLAN

FOR
JANUARY 1998 TO DECEMBER 1998
SALES INCREASE
ESTIMATED AT $40 000

Figure 14c: The joint business plan—sample 3

F Activity plan for January–June 1998			
Activity	Who	By when	Result

F Activity plan for January–June 1998

Activity	Who	By when	Result

A Key opportunities by industry segment for 1998

1 Industry segment opportunity:
  Selling out activities:
  Target key growth end users:

2 Industry segment opportunity:
  Selling out activities:
  Target key growth end users:

3 Industry segment opportunity:
  Selling out activities:
  Target key growth end users:

B Produx International support

C East Coast Commercial Supplies support

D Customer loyalty program

E Summary gains for East Coast Commercial Supplies

Product category	1996/7			1997/8	
	$ Purchases Actual	$ Purchases Target	Gross profit Actual	$ Purchases Target % Inc	Gross profit* Estimate % Inc
1					
2					
3					
4					
5					
6					
Subtotal					
CUSTOMER LOYALTY $					
TOTAL RESULT					

GROWTH OVER PREVIOUS YEAR: $_____

* In all cases estimates of gross profit are based upon your advice on the average margins you make, and do not imply any suggested pricing by Produx International.

An estimated increase for 1997/8 over last year of $$$$$$$

Here is a list of some of the things you can do:

For an identifiable customer base:
- personal selling at the end user's premises
- mail outs
- telephone selling campaigns
- end user meetings
- demonstrations by invitation
- visits to successful past users
- early order and other special promotions
- frequent buyer programs (this helps identify the large end users)
- previews of new products
- technical evenings
- discussion groups.

When you rely on attracting people into the store:
- local advertising
- mail drops
- special advice days—an expert in the store this week
- in-store days
- merchandising material
- brochures
- special promotions
- use the windows to advertise
- promotions linked with companion products
- local sponsorships
- draws for a prize
- tagged media advertising
- catalogues
- seasonal specials
- product demonstrations.

For each market segment or group of products you will need to select the appropriate activities to achieve the result you are estimating. The account manager must prove that this market exists, which is why supporting data should be included in an appendix. If you fail to convince the outlet the opportunity really exists you will not get their commitment to the plan. Why should they chase ghost markets? The more you can incorporate figures on the market which the outlet has supplied, the more likely the outlet will be to agree. The figures you use should be pooled from the supplier and outlet.

There are some outlets who are reluctant to share information of this sort with the supplier. This is a very narrow outlook. The more you can gain the confidence of the outlet through account management, the more likely they will be to share information with you. You must stress the benefits of deciding where the market is and what to do about it. Once you have shown the usefulness of pooling information in terms of directing effort and producing results, it should be easier on subsequent occasions.

For the annual plan you will be suggesting which overall activities need to be undertaken, who should be involved and how the investment should be shared. This might include, for example, local advertising to be shared 50/50 between supplier and outlet, bromides to be supplied by the supplier and all arrangements made by the outlet, with a maximum contribution for that type of promotion of $1000 for the year. When you come to the level of the quarterly plans, you would set dates and agree exactly what has to be done and who will do it. These should be sequenced chronologically, including all the steps, and involve both the account manager and other supplier staff, as well as personnel from the outlet. The activities should be clear, specific, timed and measurable, as well as state who is responsible.

A flow chart emphasising the cyclical nature of running a joint business plan is provided in Figure 15.

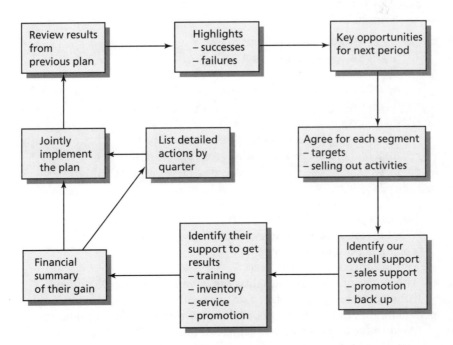

Figure 15: The flow of the joint business plan

The training role of account managers

Some of the activities may revolve around your helping the outlet staff to provide service and sell your products. This could require product training or even training in how to sell. You might put together what I call 'Easy Sell' cards—plastic laminated cards which tell the outlet sales people the main features and benefits of the product, and how to answer the most common questions and objections. You can include on these cards anything which will make it easier for the outlet's sales people to sell your products. You can tailor such cards to campaigns, include the elements of special promotions, or use them in training sessions with the outlet's sales people.

In Chapter 7 there are some comments about training of external outlet sales people, and also about internal sales staff. It needs to be said here however that switch selling is a key issue in the retail business. Outlet sales people have an extraordinary ability to influence the product customers end up buying. If the customer does not specifically ask for a product by name or brand, the sales person can make a strong recommendation for the product they prefer to sell, and most of the time the buyer will follow that recommendation.

Some of the reasons a sales person might recommend a particular product might be:

- they know the product well
- they find it easy to sell
- they have tried the product and like it
- they think it is the best product for the customer
- they make more margin on it
- there is some incentive on selling that product
- they like the account manager from that supplier
- instructions have been given to push that product.

The sales person simply has to say:
'What I would recommend is…'
'The most popular product is…'
'We find this one sells the best…'
'This one is of very good quality; we haven't had a single return…'
If the customer does in fact ask for another product, the retail sales person might ask a question about the customer's needs, and then say:
'We do have that product available, but have you thought about the…?'
Then they make a few benefit statements such as:
'We get far fewer problems with this one…'
'We find our customers prefer this one…'
'This one is much better value for money'

'This one has better performance'

'We have had a few problems with that other one lately'

It is a brave buyer who, faced with all that, says, 'Well I want it anyway!'

If there is a chance to switch sell, either for you or against you, you need to try and establish a policy with the outlet which promotes your product in preference, and make sure that the sales people themselves are informed of that decision. Then provide some training in how to switch sell to your products—using some 'scripts' if it helps—and then doing some role plays. As a generalisation we spend some time training distributor sales people on product, but nowhere near enough time on how best to sell our products.

Remember that, when you are not there, there are sales people from all the other suppliers trying to persuade the outlet to sell their products rather than yours. Even if these products do not compete with yours, if those products divert the time of the sales people in the outlet from selling your products, you could be losing out. You want to establish relationships with the sales people of the outlet so that they, like you, know how to sell your products and are motivated to sell them.

We could almost make the analogy of a sales manager selling through a sales force. The sales people of the outlet are doing the selling to the end user on your behalf, the supplier. They are like your extended de facto sales force. However, they have many other sales managers vying for their time and effort. If you can help them to sell and motivate them to sell, the chances are they will tend to put more effort into your products than those of their other suppliers.

137

This is one of the reasons that the account manager should spend time with the outlet and their people. The account manager needs to see the outlet as his or her customer.

These activities of outlet staff training should be included in the plan.

Getting agreement to share the load

For each segment of the business you will have established a goal, hopefully showing growth in at least some of the segments. You will have defined the activities necessary to achieve them and suggested how those activities and the resources to make them happen should be allocated between the supplier and the outlet. There may be some argument over who should do the work and pay for any items like local advertising, customer evenings and special promotions. This is where the plan requires negotiation. If there is a chance you may need to negotiate on any aspects of the plan, such as people or dollar resources, when you write the initial plan you should ask the outlet to commit to a little bit more than you expect them to, and you should offer a little bit less than you are prepared to. This means that when you have to negotiate, you have room to move without conceding more than you wanted to. You also allow the outlet to feel that they have extracted more from you, which is likely to leave them feeling more satisfied with the arrangement.

Rebates and targets

If there is a rebate system which depends on the achievement of agreed targets, there will be some argument over what those targets should be. The outlet will try and talk them down and the supplier will talk them up. For this reason alone it is better to try and find an alternative way for providing rebates, if you have to provide them. Many suppliers are making rebates contingent on some form of accreditation or selling out activities which the outlet will participate in. This rewards the activities which are most likely to lead to the right results for both parties. The point of volume rebates is that the supplier does not have to pay them unless the outlet provides enough business for the supplier to be able to 'afford' to pay them. It is payment for results. The problem is that if sales are down, the outlet may start to price below cost towards the end of the period to try to build up the volume, which may be counterproductive in the marketplace. One method of avoiding this problem is for the supplier not to declare exactly what the rebate will be at the end of the year, but to announce it only after the results have been achieved. This requires a lot of faith from the outlets, and generally has not worked.

Equally the outlet may just simply miss out, which will leave a bad feeling. If the supplier pays for the activities, there is a risk that the volume sales may still not be achieved but the supplier still has to pay the outlet for performing the activities. In the long term, carrying that risk is a better deal for the supplier, if it leads to better relationships and more dedicated outlets. There is always risk in business. The advertising agency gets paid for a job done, not on the results obtained from the advertising program. I feel it is better to avoid volume rebates altogether, but if you feel you cannot, at least make a part of the payment contingent on outlet activities rather than just on volume sales. Distributors really do not like volume dependent rebates, because they feel that it entails too much risk for them.

When you come to the financial summary page, if you get agreement to the targets (you should have a goal even if there is no rebate dependent on it) for the various segments of the business, you should not have too many more problems in reaching agreement on the whole plan.

. . . .
Head office plans

Most of what has been said in the previous section has been about plans at the outlet level. At the buying-group level the plan should follow a similar format, but should define the opportunities for the whole group. This may not be able to be expressed in the same detail as by outlet, but should reflect the sum of what you believe can be achieved by outlet. This suggests that the work on the account plans for the outlets should be done first, so that the plan for the group can be built up. The presentation to the head office should, however, take place first, and when agreement has been reached, how you are going to work together with each outlet can be presented to the outlets individually.

In the case of head office, where the outlets are owned by the organisation, you may be restricted in what you say to the outlets by the agreement you make with it, especially if the outlets have certain policies. In the case of franchises and even more so in simple associations, the head-office entity will be less likely to intervene in how the outlets operate and, therefore, in the detail of the plans.

The total head-office result will include the expected results from the key outlets. The totally owned chains will be more concerned with this, whereas the ones where the outlets are more independent will be less interested in the detail. They will simply want to be assured that the overall figures you are suggesting are realistic. The latter group will see their role primarily as using their combined purchasing power to get better prices and a commitment from the supplier to invest more money in promotions and specials. They will claim that they cannot commit to selling out activities, since the outlets are independent businesses. Unless you are careful, you may end up making concessions simply to get group distribution, and then not getting any commitment to selling out activities. An agreement that special prices and promotional funds are available only on performance of certain activities can be very useful. Try to make the arrangements dependent on the performance of individual outlets. Do not even accept that all outlets should be treated in the same way by you, the supplier. You can hardly stop them getting the same price, but you can direct any activity designed to create sales towards specific outlets.

Head offices will often seek not to pass all the benefit they negotiate to the outlets. In the case of wholly owned outlets there is little you can do about this, even though it is very frustrating not to be able to tell an outlet that you have made considerable concessions to the organisation which they never see the benefit of at store level. This is another reason why you should avoid conceding on straight price, but be prepared to invest money in sales creation activities, otherwise you transfer money from your bottom line to theirs, and often get no recognition for it other than an agreement to stock your products.

One of the difficulties is that not enough retailers really understand how to make money out of retailing. You should stress to every level in the distribution organisation the money they make out of selling your products. Their business is buying and selling at a profit, so they should be focusing on ROII from trading, not wasting more money from suppliers. Their primary business is trading, and that is where they have to develop their expertise if they are going to have a healthy business in the long term. The more you can stress this the better.

Because head offices of franchises and associated companies in a buying group will generally not pass everything they get in negotiations back to the outlets, funding their own existence out of head-office rebates, you are in effect paying them to run an organisation that has the primary purpose of getting money out of you. You may take the view that you cannot avoid it because they have the power to take your product off the list of available products, but do not forget that their business is to buy and sell product. They need to buy. Such considerations are about power and negotiation: the stronger your brand, the more the end user will ask for it and the stronger your position. Because the head office will want to pick from your range, you must package the whole thing so that you pull through the weak products with the strong.

The way you structure your presentations and especially the deal will have some influence over negotiations. Keep showing them the money they make out of trading so that the argument over the deal becomes less important.

Ask for everything you want

It is important to include in these plans anything you want the other party to do. There should be statements on stocks (you want to make sure they have enough at any given time), on merchandising material, including its use and care, payment terms, any administration issue, responsibility for complaints and how they should be handled, and anything where the outlet or head office could do things in a way which would make your life easier and save you money, resources or time. You may stipulate certain information you would like them to start keeping, which is usually also in their own interests. There are many cases where the end user is identifiable and buys products on a regular basis, but the outlets do not even keep information on who their loyal end users are or what they buy. This makes it very hard for a mailing campaign to ensure you retain these end users' business, or to direct mail, or invite specific end users to meetings to introduce new products, or for any kind of special promotion. Such laggards must be encouraged to establish a database on their customers and what they buy. For example, the local car dealership where I have my car serviced not only calls me sometimes after I have had the car serviced to ask me if I am satisfied with the work they did, but invites me to preview and test drive any new models they think might be of interest. They cannot guarantee I will buy the next car from them, but they are certainly sitting in the box seat, and will probably lose my business only if they decide they do not want it. In other words, they will always get the last chance.

Information on the business is critical for targeting sales effort. Establishing a database may be one thing you might try to get agreed as part of the plan, and making accreditation and special pricing, rebates or promotions contingent upon it is a good way of persuading your trading partners. The information must be shared with you on a confidential basis so that together you can plan the business.

If you do not ask for all of these items now, it will be too late. The worst thing that can happen is that they do not agree to it, in which case you are no worse off than if you do not ask for it. Experience shows that you will in fact get agreement to most of the items you ask for, especially when many of them such as information, stock control, care of goods and education of staff are very much in their interests as well as yours.

Possible formats of account plans are given in Figure 14.

Getting commitment to the plans

The first time you present plans, especially to an independent outlet, they may not understand that they are to be taken as a serious commitment. If you get agreement too easily you should suspect that your trading partner has not really thought about it, or your plan is brilliant and you may be providing more of the resources than you should be. It will become clearer to your trading partner how seriously you take these plans when you implement them.

If there are changes which need to be made to the plan, make them and get a copy of the new plan to the other party as soon as possible. Ideally these plans should be signed, because they then seem to be a bit more formal and both sides will take them more seriously. An alternative is to send a letter with the plan, stating that it is your understanding that the plan represents an agreement of both parties to carry out the actions described.

You should ensure that the outlet or head office not only has a copy of the plan, but that those people within their organisation, who are to be involved in the plan and its activities, are informed of its contents. The person responsible for activities within the outlet, usually the store or outlet manager, should keep the plan. You would also encourage them to manage the plan, and to make sure that actions happen even when you are not there. This is perhaps a vain hope, which is why the account manager should visit the outlet regularly with the plan, and review progress with the outlet manager.

Implementing the plans

These plans are the route map for the account manager to manage their time and the business. The account manager should refer to them before each call, take them on each call, and review them on a regular basis, at least at the end of the month, to make sure that all the things which need to happen are happening.

In the calls on the outlet and the head office, the account manager should get the plan out and encourage the contact to do the same. This will lead to much more effective calls and less wasted time for both the outlet and the supplier. The outlet will see the account manager and the company as much more professional.

Managing the plans becomes easier if there is an activity list in chronological order for each plan. The account manager can use the plans to plan down from three months to a week and a day.

The plans can form the basis of an appraisal system, where the account manager is judged on the quality of the plans and how well he or she has implemented them and obtained the planned results. In this case the account manager and the sales manager do not actually sign off the plans in the same way that they can with plans for direct accounts, which remain internal documents, but they can sign off on the totality of the plans.

Plans and your own agenda

Because these account plans are external documents that are presented to your trading partners, and agreement is reached on the content, then used on a daily basis in the mutual management of the business, you cannot include any items that you do not wish to share with the outlet or head office. These might be to do with personal relationships, with addressing a weakness at a particular account, or even the fact that there are gaps in what you know about this organisation. They may refer to specific events such as an unresolved complaint, or the fact that they do not pay their bills on time.

If there are such items, you should have a one-sheet plan which you keep separate from the account plan, mainly to avoid embarrassment. This is an internal document and addresses your own agenda with the outlet, and should under no circumstances ever be seen by them. It might be safest to keep it in the computer and not to print any hard copies from it. The plan should be simple, have only one or two items on it, and might look something like the format in Figure 16.

ACCOUNT .... TEL .... FAX ....
ACCOUNT MANAGER ....
PERIOD from ...... to .... BUDGET $ .... RESULT $ ....

KEY OBJECTIVES	RESULTS

KEY ISSUES TO BE ADDRESSED

143

ACTIVITY SCHEDULE

WHO	WHAT	BY WHEN	RESULT

ACCOUNT MANAGER VISITS PLANNED ....
ACCOUNT MANAGERS VISITS ACTUAL ....
ACCOUNTABILITY:
PREPARED: SALES MANAGER ...... ACCOUNT MANAGER ...... DATE .....
COMPLETED: SALES MANAGER ... ACCOUNT MANAGER ...... DATE .....

Figure 16: Internal account plan for distribution

A high degree of flexibility in these brief plans is required since the issues on your own agenda will vary widely. Make sure that action items are measurable, clearly stated, have a time for completion and state who is responsible.

. . . .
Business review and development meetings

Each plan should be reviewed with the trading partner at the end of the period. This means that there will be quarterly BRADs and annual BRADs. The annual BRAD may also incorporate the quarterly one for the last quarter, so that there will still be four meetings a year, although the annual one will be significantly more important and longer.

The quarterly BRADs can be held at the same time as you present and fine-tune the next quarter's plan. Sometimes it is better to have three months' lag, so that at the end of Quarter 1 you review what happened in that quarter, fine-tune the plan for Q2 that you had agreed three months earlier, and present for agreement the plan for Q3. Whether you choose to review and present at the same meeting depends on the degree of negotiation you expect for the future quarterly plans. Generally, if you have agreed on an annual approach, the quarterly plans will be straightforward. In this case you are better off to have the two meetings in one.

You will review by segment what happened in the previous quarter, what worked and what did not and why, what both parties can learn from that, and what implications if any it has for the plans already cast for the next quarter and the rest of the year. Then you will examine what the plan called for in or the next quarter(s), and reach agreement by segment as you go through, using the review directly as the input for any changes to the plans.

One of the problems is that of timing. You do not want to hold your annual BRAD at the same meeting as the presentation and negotiation for the next year, but it is clearly much better to have the review before the presentation of next year's arrangements. Unless the BRADs are all held in the last few days of one year and the presentation made in the first few of the next, which is impractical, there is going to be a problem. One way around it is to do the review first but to review results examining the previous twelve months. For example, you could hold your annual BRAD late October, covering the twelve months finishing 30 September. Then in

November or early December you could present your plans for the twelve months starting 1 January.

There is some advantage in having a different schedule for the various outlets and group head offices, as it is hard to get through all the reviews and the annual presentations when they are bunched into a few weeks. If you can have some accounts on a calendar year and others on a financial year it helps. However, the guiding principle should always be to try to make the schedule fit the customer's needs and way of doing things. If they want to work round their financial year which runs from April to March, then you should try to do so.

In other businesses there will be seasonal considerations. This is true with any seasonal product from travel and seasonal foods or clothes, to agricultural chemicals and seeds.

The quarterly BRADs are often relatively informal meetings with only the account manager and the main normal contact from the account present. They should be formal to the extent that an appointment should be made and that both the account manager and the contact should spend time preparing for the meeting and thinking through the issues, especially what seemed to work and what did not, but the meeting may not have a formal agenda.

The annual BRAD should be more formal, and may involve other people from both sides. In the case of an outlet, it may just involve the manager from the outlet, but could involve the account manager and maybe the sales manager from the supplier. In the case of a large outlet, the owner as well as the manager might be involved. If there are section heads, the appropriate ones should be there too. In the case of a head office marketing people and operational people as well as management might be involved.

The main thrust of BRAD meetings must be to identify more opportunities and to agree on what was learned from the last period which can be used for the next. It is a chance for the supplier to talk about their plans for the next year, including marketing programs, promotions and so on. It might include a section on new products. The outlet or head office would be expected to share with the supplier their objectives and plans in overview for the next year. Both should give their views of the marketplace and business trends.

The supplier is then in a good position to write the plans for the next year. There will be few surprises, and many of the major issues may have been discussed and even agreed at the prior BRAD meeting. Once the account management process has been operating a while, the negotiation of the annual arrangement will become easier.

. . . .
Summary

This chapter has discussed how the account management cycle might operate for distributive businesses other than the special case of supermarket chains. Within this definition there are many different types of business. Readers must think about the points which have been made and decide how they would best apply to their situation. The exact way the process will operate will vary and the design of the plans and other formats need to be tailored to each industry. Use the formats shown as a starting point for designing your own. Extract what is right for you, and be prepared to let go those parts which are not. The more you can stamp your own company culture on the process, the more you will have created something that will work well for you.

6

The marketing dollar and the distribution network

. . . .

Introduction

Traditionally in distributive businesses when we talked about promotion it referred to media advertising. The way the supplier impacted on the end users to buy the supplier's goods was through some form of media advertising. The supermarket chains started to change this thinking, by introducing the concept of cooperative advertising, where the supplier spends (invests?) money in advertising goods with a particular chain. These became known as promotional funds, and started to cover things like paying the supermarket chain to use a gondola end at the end of a shopping aisle. The concept of promotion became confused with the notion that the chains could get money for their 'real estate', and provide some extra contribution to their bottom line.

Nowadays the money which suppliers invest with their trading partners directly is often as much as their total media budget, or the money they spend on media advertising. There are even specialists within some suppliers to the supermarket chains who look after the decisions on dollars invested directly with the chains. They are called 'trade marketing', and address the marketing and promotional aspects of dealing with the trade rather than consumers. The traditional marketing department addresses how the supplier relates to and markets to the end user, and trade marketing looks at how the supplier interacts with the distribution network. Non-supermarket distribution is heading in the same direction.

. . . .
Media advertising versus cooperative promotions

In non-supermarket businesses the question of promotional funds invested with distribution is becoming an issue. Some of the organisations or groups would like to follow the supermarkets. Others want the suppliers to assist them in promoting their organisations. Others want to hijack some of the funds which are currently being invested by suppliers in media advertising, and divert them into specific promotions through their organisation. They would even like in some cases to just get their hands on the money, then promote the supplier's products in whichever way they see fit. This is particularly dangerous, because the supplier loses control of how their own products are going to be promoted.

There is much suspicion among suppliers because of some of these factors when distribution talks about cooperative promotional funds. They fear it is a ploy to grab money from them to subsidise distributors promotion of their own organisation, and that they will never get their return on investment. The fear may be justified, but that does not mean that the idea is altogether bad.

Most sales people wonder whether their company gets a good return on media advertising. We hope that the marketing people worry about this too, but suspect that not enough hard analysis is done to answer the question. The marketing people continue to push for their advertising budget, and their advertising agencies tell them they need to do more advertising to be in the race. The marketing people often see a large part of their job as coordinating the advertising campaign.

. . . .
Local promotions versus state or national promotions

We know that advertising works, but we do not know how much is enough and to what extent it works. An intriguing thought is that in distributive businesses, such as the ones covered in this section, that is everything except supermarket chains, the company might get a better return on its promotional dollar by investing less in media advertising and more in local promotions allied to the activities of certain key outlets.

This immediately creates a problem. The marketing people have control of promotion as one of the four 'Ps'. They obtain and manage promotional funds, but if you were to do local promotions at the store level, i.e. local advertising, mail drops, mail outs, demonstrations and in-store days, it would be administered by the sales department as part of the account management process. This means that marketing would lose some control, and indeed some of the dollar responsibility. (If you are unfortunate enough to work for a company which subscribes to the Hay scheme, there is a chance that the reduction in dollar responsibility by transferring control to sales could drop a marketing person's points such that the job merits a lower grading, and the midpoint for salary assessment would drop too. In other words, it really could hit the marketing people right in the pocket, apart from any personal considerations of status.)

Marketing people argue that promotion is all about marketing, and sales people are not competent to get involved. They see promotion as their area of authority and will be reluctant to let it go.

There is a parallel here to other marketing dimensions such as price. There is no reason why the marketing people cannot set a policy on types of advertising and promotion for sales people to choose from, with limits set. Marketing can control the content by issuing examples of pro forma copy, or insisting on checking copy, or even setting down rules for the production of material, but this does not mean that they cannot let the management of promotion at the local and the store level out of their hands. Only the local sales people can know enough about the outlet, their business and the local demographics, to make the right promotional decisions.

There are many businesses which would get a better return on the promotional dollar by diverting a percentage to local promotions handled through the account management process by the account managers. The marketing plan would define the menu of promotional activities for particular market segments and for certain demographics. There should be a budget for each area or territory which the account manager should manage, with guidance from the sales manager. In many companies there are small budgets for promotional activities which the sales people administer, but they are usually of the order of a few hundred or a couple of thousand dollars, but I am suggesting a change in the way the company looks at promotion, and the recognition that 20 or 30 per cent or more of current promotional funds be diverted into local promotions.

149

Conventional promotional activities include:
- local newspapers
- sponsorship of local clubs and organisations

- mail outs
- mail drops
- end user meetings
- demonstrations
- product tastings
- raffles and draws
- spot prizes
- catalogues
- local radio.

The more creative and original the ideas the better. Whatever process you have for managing such a concept should encourage people to be creative, and as long as it seems to be a reasonable idea there should be a preparedness to give it a go. That way you can show distribution that you are prepared to try something new.

It is also a good idea to get the outlet or group to participate financially and physically in these programs. If the promotion is going to boost sales for them as well as for us the supplier, there is every reason why they should contribute. A 50/50 basis is reasonable for most activities, and the workload in arranging the details and holding the promotion should also be shared.

The whole thrust of the programs should be that both parties will be investing money only in those activities which both agree have a good chance of multiplying sales. It is important to establish these principles at the outset, before distribution gets any ideas about making the project an attempt to transfer money from your bottom line to theirs.

. . . .

Know which promotional methods work

You should analyse your results from the promotions, looking at incremental sales. This may not always be easy to measure, but the more data you keep on promotions the more you will be able to build up a trend which will tell you what gives the best return on the promotional investment.

One area for investment which you should be wary of is the group catalogue. This is where suppliers pay for their products to be included in the outlet's catalogue, which is usually then delivered by mail drop or some form of mail out. Clients who participate in these catalogues, because they want to keep good relationships with distribution rather than for the extra sales they believe will be created, are convinced that not only does the chain cover its costs for the catalogue, but in some cases makes a profit. This sort of approach is close to that warned about above. Try not to over invest in promotions like these. That is not to say that catalogues are not useful in creating extra sales. They probably do work, but watch the amount you contribute.

There is some truth to the statement that sales people do not understand as much about promotion as marketing people, therefore managing local promotions through the account management process can also be a learning opportunity. In order to get account managers to think through what they are trying to achieve it can be useful to get them to fill out an application for these local funds. The concept could be that they have a budget, but they still need to justify each expenditure to get access to it. It is almost as if it is kept in trust for them by the sales manager, or a product manager.

The application form would be composed of a number of questions which the account manager would need to answer before the funds are thawed.

151

Questions could include:
- the outlet or group of outlets
- type of promotional activity (clear description)
- suggested copy of any text
- cost of the activity (with breakdown)
- target market
- current level of sales through this outlet
- estimated increase in sales volume, and the contribution from those sales
- cost of our share of the promotion
- the outlet's contribution to costs
- the outlet's estimated return through improved contribution
- activities we will perform to support the promotion (including our attendance in store).

This should be submitted and agreed. There should be another part of the form for analysis after the promotion, which looks at actual figures. This should include costs of the promotion, resources and, most importantly, estimated increase in sales volume and contribution. There should be room to make comments about the promotion, i.e. aspects of it which worked well, and anything we should take note of for future promotions. There should be a summary assessment of whether it is the sort of promotion we should repeat.

. . . .

Entertainment

Many suppliers have found that some investment in entertainment of personnel from distribution has shown a good return. This includes things like taking people from distribution to events like the football or major sporting events such as the Grand Prix. Whether you do this will depend on the culture of your company and its policies on such entertaining. This should not be confused with promotional activities, and should come out of a separate budget, as they are separate activities even if the desired result of more sales is the same. Entertainment is exactly that, and usually it is geared towards people from distribution. Promotional activities are directed towards the end user, working through distribution. Promotional activities create sales directly at the end-user level. Entertainment creates relationships which lead eventually to better work relationships and more sales. Such expenses need to be dealt with differently from promotion at least for tax reasons.

152

Any prizes like a weekend away for two for the outlet which achieves the best result, should also come out of a separate cost centre from promotion. Any incentive for distribution personnel needs to be handled carefully. There are some head offices of chains, especially the ones who own the outlet, who will not allow such things, saying that they cannot have their own policies on what they sell and when overturned by incentives offered by suppliers. The argument is that the chain may want to promote something, but a supplier of a different product offers incentives to outlet staff to sell something else. Never offer incentives to outlets belonging to a chain unless you have cleared it first through head office.

Incentives can work well if they are seen to be fair, reward effort and lead to a worthwhile prize. Campaigns should run over a short time, and be consistent with agreed objectives for the period. If there is any doubt about an incentive meeting these criteria, do not do it. The fact is that more incentives do not work than do work, and the ones that do not work often create bad feeling.

. . . .

Literature and point of sale

The most important thing to be said about literature is to make sure that you are clear about its purpose. Is it to be used by distribution with consumers, or by account managers with the distribution network? Is it designed to inform people about the product or how to use it, or is it intended only to create awareness?

Too much money is spent on literature without consideration given to this issue. The result is that the literature is neither one thing nor the other, and neither the sales people nor the distribution people know how to get the best from it. Most literature is stuck into a rack, looks untidy, is often faded and detracts from rather than adds to the image of the supplying company. Account managers need to make sure they understand the best way to use the literature and train the store staff how to use it.

What has been said about literature is true about point-of-sale material in general. The marketing people should consult with sales before they commit dollars to producing POS. It should be acceptable in the store (pharmacies are already cluttered, so you need robust and small POS there), and have a theme which means something, or a message which helps sell the product in some way.

An innovative method was used by the Gallagher sales force in New Zealand, selling electric fencing through agricultural resellers. They painted the wall around their displays in store the distinctive orange colour of their own logo. It was apparently very successful.

It is worthwhile impressing on outlet staff that literature is expensive to produce, and so is point-of-sale material. It should therefore be well looked after and used in the prescribed way to get the best out of it.

153

7

Selling technically complex products through distribution

. . . .

Introduction

There is a separate chapter on selling technically complex products because the skill required to sell them is different, and when the selling is done through a distribution network it needs some special treatment. When the products are complex, the end user requires more information to make a decision. They do not always have this information, and if the issues are complex enough the end user is often not in a good position to evaluate what the sales person is saying. If the goods and their application are technically complex it requires knowledge and skill to sell them.

These are the processes in selling technical products
• open the call—establish some rapport
• assess customer needs through questioning
• decide on the right product to meet the customer's needs
• sell the benefits of that product against the defined customer needs
• have evidence that what you say is true
• handle any objections
• close the sale.

These steps need to occur whether the sale is made by the outlet's store sales staff, or whether it is made at visits by any external sales staff from the outlet. For the supplier's sales people it is straightforward in the sense that you are selling your own product range against the product ranges of the competitors, but for the outlet it is more complex. They have to decide which products from which suppliers they are going to stock and sell. They may not be in a position to offer the end user a variety of purchasing options for a particular need, but in most cases they will. The question then arises of choosing the ones they will promote. The answer to that should be the one that most completely meets the end user's needs and, everything else being equal, the one which provides the outlet with the best margin.

Sometimes there are shades of grey. The outlet may perceive that one product will do the job, it may not be quite as good as another, but they make more margin on it, or have a much better relationship with the supplier, so they will promote that product.

Every supplier will be putting forward the reasons why their product is better, and even the outlets may sometimes have difficulty in judging which products really are the best. They will consciously or unconsciously monitor the reaction of their own customers, the end users. In many cases it is easier to wait for the end user to ask for a product and then sell it to them, but the outlet which really wants to offer a good customer service will take the trouble to make sure that the product the end user is asking for really is the right one for his needs.

To be able to do this the sales people from the outlet need to have a good product knowledge across a wide range of different products. Not only do they need to know one range of products well, they need to know several ranges well, and that is not easy.

. . . .

Helping the outlet to sell your products

Human nature being what it is, most people will take the easiest course of action. They will sell the products which are easiest to sell, and will work hardest for the people they like and who support them. The message in that for you the supplier is that the stronger relationships you can establish with the sales people from the outlets the better. The easier you can make it for them to sell your products, the more likely it is they will sell them.

This means that the sales people from the supplier must spend time with the sales people from the outlets. They must train them in the products and particularly their application. They also need to train them how to sell the products.

For outlets with an external sales force the best way to train them is for the sales people from the supplier to go out with the sales people from the outlet on joint selling and training missions. In some industries, as discussed previously, the sales people from the supplier have gone out selling to the end users. Frequently they have made these visits on their own, and they have picked up orders which they have delivered to the reseller of the end user's choice. This is not a productive way for the supplier's sales people to spend their time. They may pick up orders, but their prime objective must be to provide the outlet with the capability to do the selling themselves. There are too many end users out there for the supplier sales people to do the selling. Their job is to create sales through the distribution network. The focus must be on equipping the sales people from the outlet to be able to sell, rather than doing the selling themselves. There is an analogy with the job of sales manager being to create sales through the sales people who work for him or her, not to do the selling him or herself.

When the sales people from the supplier visit customers with the sales people from the outlet, much of this training can take place, not just during calls but also in the car as they are driving. The sales person from the supplier should not do all of the selling; the sales person from the outlet should do some of the selling so that the supplier's sales person can help them learn. There is a belief, held by some sales managers too, that all the 'teacher' has to do is to show how to make the sale, and the other person will learn from watching. This is only true in a very limited way. Watching how others sell can be useful for people with very little selling experience in the initial stages of acquiring selling skills, but by far the most powerful way of helping people learn how to sell is to let them do the selling, and then to talk about it afterwards. This requires some skill in the trainer. It is better to allow the outlet's sales person, who did the selling to assess their own performance than to have the supplier sales person literally tell them what they did wrong. The sales person from the supplier has to be diplomatic and gentle in helping outlet sales people to learn, because they do not report to them. They do not even work for the same organisation. Some of the phrases which can be useful for the supplier sales person to use in debriefing after a sales call are:

- How did you feel it went?
- Any thoughts on how it could have been improved?
- Where do you think it seemed to go wrong?
- Where do you think you lost him?
- What I find works for me is…
- The way I look at it is…
- It seems to me that an important point is…
- What I recommend is that you…
- You might find it works better if you…

The first questions are about getting the outlet sales person to think about what happened and what they did in the call. The second type of statements are more concerned with the supplier sales person giving the outlet sales person some gentle advice and coaching, without being brutal, and allowing the outlet sales person to save face.

The key issues are product knowledge and product comparisons. The main point is what the product does for the end user, and how that compares with other purchasing options the end user has, either from the same outlet (competitors' products to the supplier) or from other outlets. It makes life much simpler if the outlet sells only your own products, rather than also selling products which compete with yours. This is a consideration when deciding which outlets you will select to represent you, as described in Chapter 5.

Whatever the situation, product knowledge should concentrate on application and performance of products relative to the other options. Easy Sell cards are particularly useful with technically complex products. There will certainly be technical manuals and so on provided by the supplier, but there is so much information in these that the outlet will find them too difficult to refer to.

An Easy Sell card could have some of these headings, with a concise few lines under each one:

* key customer needs we can satisfy
* features and benefits of the product
* key points on application
* most commonly asked questions
* objections and how to handle them
* product comparisons.

Your promotional and/or technical sales brochures may also be useful in both selling and training others how to sell. Make sure that the outlet sales people know how to get the best out of using these brochures with their customers. It should involve more than handing the customer the brochure. The outlet sales person could perhaps highlight with a marker pen the key benefits to the customer as a result of their discussion, and mark the recommended product (see Chapter 6).

It is a good idea to hold formalised product training sessions with the outlet, if possible involving all their people, internal and external sales staff and the management. These sessions can be held early in the morning before business starts or after the end of the trading day. You the supplier may wish to encourage people to come along to these sessions by providing some cheese and beer afterwards.

Such sessions should always concentrate on the key issues and on product knowledge as it applies to selling the product. Select products which are topical, or those for which you are going to have a particular promotion. If you are having some competition from another product in the marketplace, you might handle how you can best sell your product against the competition. Make the sessions relatively brief—an hour or so is usually acceptable to outlet staff as long as it is not every week.

Outlet internal sales staff

Although the sort of on-the-job training with external sales people from the outlet is possibly the best training you can do, you should not neglect the internal sales staff of your outlets. Many outlets will not have any external sales people and will rely on their store sales people.

Many store sales people see their job as primarily selling the customer what they ask for. There are, however, significant opportunities for these sales people to perform a far more overt and valuable role.

There is the question of making sure that the customer really is buying what they need; there may be other products on the market which you sell and which they are not aware of, and which would meet their needs much better. This is being seen to give the customer the right advice and caring about them. It is also a question of protecting the interests of the outlet. The outlet should be dedicated to making sure that the customer really does buy the best product for their needs, otherwise they may hold you responsible for not keeping them advised of better options.

There may also be opportunities for companion sales. Do you have the equipment to apply it? Do you have enough disks? Do you have somewhere to store it? Other consumables? and so on. By knowing how the product is used and what else is involved, the sales person can quite often sell the customer more than they were going to buy, but products which they very much need.

Furthermore there is the question of switch selling. If a customer asks for product X, the outlet person may be able to change the customer's intention so that they buy product Y. If it is important for you to be able to switch sell at the point of purchase, make sure that the outlet sales people know how to do it. You can even do a few role plays with them on an informal basis so that they gain skills and confidence in doing it.

. . . .

Technical advice, responsibility and complaints

One area of concern is when part of the technical advice is on product application. If the end user has a problem because the product was not used correctly, whose fault is it? It could be the fault of the end user for not following instructions, or the outlet for not giving the right instructions, or even the sales person from the supplier for not making sure that the outlet knows what advice to give to the end user. Normally there will be application advice on the label of the product and in brochures. These must be brought to the attention of the customer.

If the sales people from the outlet give the customer any specific advice, they would be well advised to note in a diary exactly what they said. If the sales people from the outlet are in any doubt whatsoever, they should contact the supplier's sales person and get their advice. The sales people from the supplier should also make sure they note any advice given to a customer.

When giving end users technical advice, or when there are very large orders, the assistance of the supplier sales people in selling to the end user is most desirable.

In most cases providing advice will not be a problem, but from time to time there will be complaints about the performance of the product. It is important for both the supplier and the outlet to recognise that they have a responsibility and a vested interest in resolving the complaint. If the end user is not satisfied, both the outlet and the supplier lose a customer. There can be a situation where as soon as there is a complaint, the outlet wants to wash their hands of the whole thing and treat it as if it is a problem between the supplier and the end user. This is naive and wrong. To start off with, the end user bought it from the outlet and could well be expected to purchase more items from the outlet. They will talk to other people about their experience, especially if it is bad, and the outlet is likely to be as damned as the supplier if the matter is not handled correctly.

You as the supplier should develop with the outlet a procedure for handling complaints. There are two important things. The first is to show the customer that you care and that something is being done about it. Most people who have a complaint get quite upset if it is not handled correctly right at the start. The second point is that you need, as soon as possible, to get all the information to judge the complaint. The information required should be listed so that the outlet can start things moving, even if the sales person from the supplier cannot get there immediately.

You must ensure that you have procedures which lead to the resolution of complaints as fast as possible. This is easier if there is a clear complaint procedure within the supplier organisation, and when this procedure is handled by an independent body, rather than someone in sales or operations. If the culture of the organisation is such that complaint means 'duck for cover and protect yourself by whatever means', then you will not learn much from complaints, with the result that they are likely to continue to happen. If you have a culture which says that complaints may happen from time to time and that they are an opportunity to find a way of avoiding them in the future, you have a better chance of fixing any problems for good. There will be occasions when the end user will fabricate a complaint for various reasons, or has used the product incorrectly through their own ineptitude. These situations need to be identified. But otherwise the prime aim of both the outlet and the supplier is to keep the customer happy, and do so quickly.

. . . .
Summary

Technical products give more of an opportunity for both supplier and outlet to differentiate themselves from other suppliers. The challenge for the supplier is to equip the distribution network with the knowledge, skills and attitudes to be able to differentiate themselves in the marketplace through the quality of technical advice and service they can offer, and through the quality of their technical selling skills.

Selling Consumer Products Through Supermarket Chains

8

The challenges of dealing with supermarket chains

. . . .

Introduction

Why separate selling to supermarket chains which sell consumer products from the previous section on distributive businesses? The reason is mainly that there is a specific method of operation which has evolved, with some specific jargon and some very specific problems for suppliers. Part 3 then refers specifically to supermarket chains, but it should also be read by anyone selling to the head offices of groups and organisations owned, affiliated or associated in areas of business other than grocery, as it may give you some ideas that you can adopt in your own business. But it can also show you how these chains could operate if they chose to, and warn you of some of the danger signs and pitfalls so that you can learn from the errors of others.

Selling to Australian supermarket chains

This suggests that the situation in the grocery supermarket area is bad. In fact most or maybe all suppliers to Australian supermarket chains would say that the amount of money they waste to keep products on shelves is frightening. The transfer of cash from suppliers to the chains in Australia would have to amount to billions of dollars over the years. This money is not invested in sales creation activities, irrespective of what they are called. For the most part it supplements the inability of the large chains to make enough money out of their real job of retailing.

The reasons are well known by anyone operating in the supermarket area. In each state the business is dominated by a small handful of chains. There is no state where less than 70 per cent of the supermarket business is made up by more than three chains. Most of them operate nationally, which means that these few chains control the supermarket business, giving them enormous power. If you as a supplier are in, then you are guaranteed the best possible chance of having your products sold. But if you are locked out, there is an enormous gap in your distribution which could cost you badly in lost volume.

The supermarket industry in Australia is price driven. Although there have been some attempts recently to advertise service and range, most advertising is on the basis of price. In fact this seems to be a problem not just of the grocery trade, but with many aspects of Australian business life. This may be because at the time of our strongest economic development and growth, after the Second World War, there was little marketing expertise. As a result we tended to sell everything on the basis of price. We ended up with some poor quality products and very little concept of service. One particularly noticeable example was plastic housewares. The products made in Australia some years ago were cheap and unattractive, yet in Italy, France and the USA there were some very smart products available, certainly at a higher price but with much more appeal. The manufacturer and retailer were making a better margin and the consumer paid a bit more but for a product which they were satisfied with. Plastic kitchenware in those countries never had the sort of negative aspect it did in Australia ten or fifteen years ago, so their plastics industries in that segment were more vibrant than the Australian one.

This price obsession may be the reason that today in Australia there are few supermarkets of the quality of Tesco and Sainsbury in the UK, or Pick and Pay in South Africa, Migros in Switzerland, Euromarché in France, or the chains in the USA. Price is such an issue that there can only be very few percentage points between those who are considered the price setters and the higher end of the market. This means that the lowest priced supermarkets and the standards of their store become the benchmark. A few percentage points above this does not allow for the 'lifestyle' types of store you can find in other countries.

How the chains boosted their profits

As the supermarkets sought to compete heavily on price and attract traffic through specials, the chains had to find ways to bolster their poor retail trading margins. The way they did this was to use their dominance in the marketplace to force money at the head office level out of suppliers, which has not necessarily been to anyone's advantage, although the retailing chains produce financial results which are comparable to those in other countries. By far the most profitable part of the grocery business today is in fresh food and those chains which have fresh food can use the higher margins to put pressure on the other chains by discounting the dry goods.

The consumer in Australia does enjoy cheap groceries by world standards, but such comparisons are not always useful. Part of the reason for our cheaper groceries is a decline in the Australian dollar, so that most of the effect comes from exchange rates. The real pressure has been put on the suppliers, and they are generally making less satisfactory margins than their counterparts in other countries. This gives rise to amalgamations, mergers or takeovers.

165

How they changed their demands

The situation today is that for years the supermarket chains have developed ways of getting money out of suppliers at head-office level. They have changed how they ask for this money, because if they were to ask for it in one lump sum or as one single rebate, the supplier would refuse. The list of ways supermarket chains get money from suppliers seems almost endless, and certainly is creative.

These are some of the well-known ways supermarkets get money from suppliers:
- national terms (rebate)
- preferred supplier rebate
- ullage
- cooperative advertising
- case deals
- new line fees
- special promotions

- loss of profits (on things like bonus packs)
- price reductions to meet competition
- one-in-one-out policy on distribution
- store opening contributions.

These costs can sometimes be as high as the media advertising budget, and are handled separately through a trade marketing department. They have pretty much become part of the way things are done, and those selling to the supermarket chains have to accept much of this transfer of funds as a fact of life. There will already be an adjustment in invoice prices to counter some of the money conceded at head office level.

The key issues are:
- to try to make sure that there is no more degradation through more rebates of whatever kind
- to make sure that you get value for money for promotions you do invest in
- if possible, to reduce some of the elements or dimensions of the rebate
- reduce the amount of rebate under some of the headings.

This means either not to pay new-line fees, or to pay less than you are asked for. Agree on less money guaranteed for cooperative advertising, or at least make sure that those cooperative funds are invested in promotions which will actually create more sales.

The issue is that the power for many years had been seen to be all in the hands of the chains. If they de-list you, you have a real volume problem. This threat is what led suppliers down this slippery slope. However, there have been cases where some suppliers with powerful brand names, after an examination of their account profitability, told certain chains that they were going to call a halt on the funds they were providing. It seems to have worked for those suppliers who had the power in their brand and the courage to say 'no'. But not always!

· ·

Information potential

The technology of retailing has been changing. The use of computers allows far more information on the supermarket business to be generated —and in many ways it has been overkill.

166

For years, warehouse withdrawal data has been used by account managers to show where they are missing out and where the supermarkets themselves could have been missing out. They have been used to show that home brands are overexposed and performing poorly. They have been used to show how good one supplier is and how poor another is. They are used to justify taking products off shelves and putting others on. They have been a very powerful weapon in the hands of the people who are best at extracting information from the masses of data, analysing it, and presenting it as part of a sales argument.

But warehouse withdrawals was just a start. They only tell you what was taken out of central warehouses. There is a time lag which means that the specific effect of more instant things like promotions and price cuts were harder to assess, and the results were generalised across a number of stores possibly in quite different areas with different demographics. Scanning was the next breakthrough. It allowed in principle the identification of sales and changes on a store-by-store basis over periods as short as a few hours. You could tell exactly how much of which product had been sold in a given time, because it measured what went through the till.

This allowed in principle the identification of which products sell better in which stores. Then it became theoretically possible to measure the effect of promotions, case offs, different pricing, changing position on shelf, increasing or decreasing facings on shelf and company block versus product block. The answers to many merchandising questions were finally within everyone's grasp. Each store could stock the products, which really worked for that particular store, rather than have a fixed planogram for every store.

This thought was encouraged by the development of shelf-management software programs. Appollo became the standard for the industry. There are others, but once both Coles and Woolworths bought Appollo, the die was cast. Using this software, a shelf layout can be changed without having to go to a physical mock-up and physically put the items on shelf to see what fits and what does not. By making certain assumptions about the effect on sales of making shelf changes, you can enter margins and calculate expected changes in contribution to profit for different shelf layouts. There was a problem that these assumptions really were assumptions, and for the most part were untested because to understand an effect you needed to control all the other variables. If you wanted to see the effect on sales of reducing facings from three to two, you needed to compare sales of the two situations for two similar periods when nothing else had changed. Before scan data was introduced that was almost impossible. The only way you could have done it was to have changed from three to two facings in every store and then take long enough periods, so that the warehouse withdrawal data would not be distorted by the lag.

167

Direct product profitability

With scan data it became possible in theory at least to carry out a few experiments to see whether the assumptions on merchandising were in fact correct. A further refinement became possible with the advent of direct product profitability. If you look at product performance only on the basis of the gross margin on shelf, you will get an incorrect view. You should add in some allocation for the moneys which are paid at head office level. Although the margin on shelf in Australia may be lower than in other countries, the amount supermarkets receive at head office in other countries is much lower. If you add up both sources, you will end up with similar results, so there needs to be an allocation against the product of these moneys. There are plenty of other costs which had always been lumped together as overhead because they could not be separated and allocated. These included costs of receiving goods, transporting them round the central warehouse, taking them out of the warehouse, delivering them to the store, putting them in the stock area, keeping them there, then putting them on the shelf and finally being packed in a plastic bag at the checkout. If you take two products with the same margin, for example a 2 litre soft drink and a toothbrush, it must be clear that the costs to the supermarket in performing those activities described above must be much higher for the 2 litre soft drink than the toothbrush, because of its weight and its size.

Direct product profitability provides a method for measuring the costs associated with the above activities, so that they can be attributed directly to the products rather than just lumped together in overhead.

There is a prescribed method developed by FMC (Food Marketing Corporation) in the USA for measuring the direct product costs. This is a costly and lengthy procedure, and should allow retailers to have a much better idea where and how they make their profit. To get the best out of the process a planogram would be devised to cater for the individuality of the business at each store, so that there would either be individual planograms for each store or at least a series of different ones, one for each group of stores with similar attributes. To manage that effectively would have required an enormous amount of work at the store level, either by head office staff allocated to get the right planogram by store, or by the store manager. It is asking too much of store managers in an environment when chains are trying to cut down staff at the store level in order to cut costs, to perform this task. It also begs the question of the skill level required to extract meaningful information from all the data, analyse it and then put together a planogram. In fact there has been a trend towards more centralisation rather than less, no doubt driven by the need to keep operating costs down. Even the state organisations of some chains have fallen by the way, and business is being conducted nationally through one national head office.

Even so, starting in the late 1980s the large chains selected as partners a leader from the major sections of the store, and offered them the chance to work alongside the chains in establishing direct product costs. This was to allow the spreading of the costs and, in particular, the workload in getting DPP up and running. At the same time it offered those select suppliers the chance to establish a more cooperative working relationship with the trade, and to get to know them better. There appeared to be a tacit understanding that while they were working together there would be less harassment on items such as terms, co-op and the like.

. . . .

Micromarketing

What happens from now on is yet to be written. The economy in Australia has shifted the focus to be changed to cutting operating costs. The vision of micromarketing has not happened, and appears unlikely to. The predictions that we would see less range for some of the larger high DPC and low DPP items has not come to pass. Neither have we seen the emergence of stores which specialise in certain areas of the market, such as the American bulk barn type of store, and the more 'boutique' types of supermarket.

The fact is that DPP has been placed so far on the back burner that its name is almost never mentioned. Certainly planograms are nowadays a standard, but any thought of looking at the DPCs and therefore the DPP as a basis for these planograms has disappeared. Part of the problem is the lack of skill at the store level to use such information on a micro basis. In fact the tendency is again for more and more centralisation, and less autonomy for store managers.

. . . .

Category management

Whereas the trade used to be organised functionally, with a manager for promotions, one for planograms and another in charge of buying, there have been some changes for the better. The problem with the functional organisation was that if you have a package which talks about terms, range, positioning, facings and co-op, which is the way the business should be looked at, because they all interact, you would need to have several managers agree to the proposal before it was accepted. Furthermore, the functional managers had such a broad product spread that they did not have a deep knowledge of any product area. This can be important in making decisions on promotions, special pricing and merchandising issues. It allowed the chains to fragment the decision, so that it was hard for an account manager to get anyone who would give an answer on a proposal straightaway. Decisions within the chain were made at meetings—where conventionally there are no suppliers present—called the Buying Committee. The best an account manager could hope for in most cases was that his or her contact would promise support in the meeting. Inevitably by the time it came back from the committee there were more demands on the supplier.

The change to category management was a real opportunity for the suppliers to establish better relationships with the trade, and for a more cooperative approach to getting the best out of retailing for both the retailer and the supplier. Despite some brave attempts by suppliers to achieve this, there have not really been any significant changes because the chains are still trying to get as much money as possible out of the suppliers.

It is true that there have been some benefits in category management. Discussions do centre around categories, and both the trade and the suppliers are more competent to have meaningful discussions on the business. But any hopes that it might lead to more cooperative relationships where the trade and the suppliers would 'work together to build the category' have come to nothing.

Part of the difficulty in predicting the future is that as chief executives of the chains change, there will be a different focus in the business. For example, Coles may go through a very centralised phase with cost cutting as a major strategy, which is certainly a long way from micromarketing and merchandising.

. . . .

Summary

Suppliers need to try to present their propositions to stress the profit made from better retailing and trading practices, and to minimise the pressure on them to pass money over the counter at the head office level. The next chapter will talk about some of these specific points, and suggest how the presentations to head office can be constructed to help. There are also certain actions which can be taken at store level to support this push.

9

Terms, co-op and deal and getting it right

Introduction

We have looked at some of the background to the situation which exists today for suppliers selling to supermarket chains. There are really two issues in this business. One is to get distribution without bleeding to death, and the other is to have the chains agree, at head office or at store level, on promotion and merchandising decisions which will help the products sell out and not cost the supplier a fortune.

Assessing the current damage

A good starting point is to make a list of what you currently concede to each chain to whom you sell. The first items you will write down will be the major ones mentioned in the last chapter, the rebates and deals, the co-op, the case offs, loss of profits, the new line fees and so on. But there are also more subtle things you concede too. Include items which are not necessarily part of the formal agreement, but which cost you money anyway:
• late payments

- investment buying
- non-return of pallets
- deductions off your invoices
- non-compliance with agreements.

There may be specific things you do in your industry:

- demonstrations
- samples
- bonus packs
- tastings
- recipes.

List the ways of spending or investing money. It is quite common for this list to reach fifty items. There is some useful analysis you can do with this list. Remember that not all these items will be seen as having the same value by the supplier and the chain, so you should look at the value to the chains and the costs to the supplier. Some, like rebates, will be identical, a straight transfer of funds from the supplier to the retailer, but there are others which will have a value greater than the cost. Those items which are of higher value to them and of lower cost to you are the priorities of concessions you make when it comes down to the negotiation stage.

If you identify any concessions you make or they take, which are of more cost to you than the value to the supplier; you should make a note to withdraw them if you can. They are not going to work well for you.

Write a list of all the things you would like back from the trade. Include any concessions they make. In some ways of course this list is the mirror image of the previous one, but if there are things the supplier could do for you, which would make your life easier, or which would save you money these are high priorities for you to gain their agreement. These changes may not cost them anything, but just require them to do things in a different way. You may even find on the list items which are in their interests as well as your own.

My experience of literally hundreds of account managers in the grocery business performing this exercise is that although it is slow to start, when they get into it they come up with lists that are longer than the first one, which makes them feel much better.

The same sort of analysis can be done on this list as the previous one. Look at the cost of the concession to the chains and its value to you, and prioritise those items which cost them little and are of most value to you, and give less priority to those items which are of less value to you and greater cost to them.

The first thing the account manager should do with these two lists is to resolve to shorten the first and to get agreement for some of the items on the second. For several of these items on the second list it can just be a question of asking for them, especially those which cost little or are in the trade's interests too.

The fact that other suppliers do or do not provide items on the list is irrelevant. Each supplier has a range of products which will contribute to the chain's business in a different way. There is nothing which says that all suppliers should operate on the same basis. The trade may say it, but you do not have to accept it. You must try and focus their attention on the trading side of their business and concentrate on the activities which will enhance it. This principle should also guide the selection of concessions you will want to work with. Whatever money you do invest with the trade should be geared towards creating a better result for both sides.

. . . .

Changing the way things are done

Many tired and battered account managers reading this will be war weary and thinking that things cannot be changed. This is not true. There have been many cases where suppliers have pursued this philosophy and have been able to agree trading relationships which are more advantageous to them.

173

The extent to which they can be changed will depend on the strength of your brand. If you work for a company which has a very strong brand leader, especially one which is advertised in the media, despite what the trade tells you they are unlikely to delete it. There have been occasions where the trade has delisted such products, but the stand lasted less than a week and the supplier got back in more or less on their terms. You certainly need to try and package weak lines along with the strong ones, otherwise they will pick the best parts of your range and not give you distribution on the rest.

The weak position the suppliers have let themselves be beaten into has been a miscalculation of power. The suppliers have believed that the threat of delisting has forced them to concede to the trade. Once you the supplier have developed the mindset which says that things can be changed if you have the resolve to do it, then you can start looking at the details of how and where.

. . . .

Merchandising aspects

You need to know the merchandising criteria which favour your products. This could perhaps vary from store to store, but we have established that micromarketing and micromerchandising is not about to happen right now if ever.

Which is the right section for your products? There are cases where the supermarket insists on a classification which you know is wrong. People just do not look for your product in that section. Know where you want your products to appear, what is the best shelf position, and the next best place. Also know which is the worst shelf position, so that you can avoid it. There are assumptions on this subject. As was said in the last chapter, it would have been excellent if these assumptions could have been tested using scan data. You can in fact buy scan data from Coles, but it is grouped together for several large stores, and is not, therefore, really very much help.

Be prepared to question shelf position assumptions, which generally say that eye level is best and top shelf for large items is bad. The worst place is the bottom shelf or anywhere likely to be hidden by a bin, and the first section from an end is not good. These assumptions may not be true for you.

Far more important is what effect the other products in that section have on your sales. If yours is not a large moving product, but you find that being positioned near a non-competing complementary product helps your sales and does not detract from theirs, that is a good position on shelf. Everyone wins.

You need to know whether company block, where you have all your range together, works better for you than product blocks where your baked beans are with all the baked beans, your peas are with the other peas, and so on.

There is no guarantee that you will get exactly the shelf positions you want, but at least if you know what you want there is a better chance you will get some of it. These are items you can put in your proposals to even up the score, and to make a few demands to counter any demands which might be made on you. This implies that you abandon the concept of giving in, but start to negotiate and swap concessions. Never be prepared to give anything to the trade without getting something back in return.

Facings

Facings are another important issue. You will find that generally facings are not in proportion to sales or potential. You need to understand the effect of facings on your sales. Since it is hard to find this out from the chains, try to establish a relationship with a good independent retail store which has scanning, then give them some incentive to change a few issues like section, shelf position and facings, and measure the effects in that store. The danger is that there will always be different answers for different stores, but to take the results from one good retail store and apply them to the chains is a much better solution than simply guessing or recycling folklore, which is what tends to happen now.

In the chains, most home brands are overexposed relative to their market shares. You do not know the margins the trade makes on these home brands relative to the brand leaders, but since the home brands are less expensive on shelf you can be sure that the margins are not very much larger than on the brand items, especially if you take the head office rebates into account. This suggests that for most chains the home brand is not a very good performer on ROII per linear metre. By checking into the warehouse withdrawal data you can discover sales volumes, then make some analysis and come up with alternative suggestions for the section.

The battle for facings and position is continuous and while you are trying to improve the shelf merchandising of your products, someone else in the section, maybe not even necessarily a direct product competitor, will be making an attempt to get your product off the shelf altogether or at least to reduced facings.

The degree to which elements of shelf management can be influenced at the store level has changed. Some chains have turned a blind eye to local store managers changing the planogram to meet local needs, as long as the overall store results were good. But others always have had, and still have, a strict centralised approach to planograms, which leaves very little room to influence things at store level. Even in a very centralised climate such as what we seem to have at the moment, especially with 'sameness' being the order of the day, there are still useful activities to perform at the store level of supermarket chains. We will discuss this later in the chapter.

175

The fact remains that these considerations have to be handled at the head office level and should be addressed in your presentations and negotiations.

. . . .

In-store promotion

The supermarket business works on the basis of attracting people into the store, then merchandising the stock to maximise the use of shelf space. The supplier attempts to influence the consumer to buy their product through media advertising, and their sales will be assisted by an advantageous position and facings in store.

Then someone thought up in-store promotion of goods, which involved both the store and the supplier participating in the program to sell more through special promotions. The store would attract people in through the promotion, who would buy that product and at the same time buy other products. The supplier would increase sales through a share increase against the suppliers who were not promoting. The details of the first promotion of this sort are unknown, but it was probably extremely successful. The problem today is that there is so much of this promotion that the supplier gets no overall benefit from it. The chain manages to grab money by renting out their store 'real estate', and the consumer may get some benefit, although some of the costs in these promotions must be passed on to the consumer.

Co-op

Today these promotions are not cooperative, and they in many cases do not multiply sales. The way it works nowadays is that as part of the agreed terms under which the supplier and the chain do business, an agreement is made to invest a certain amount of money in promotions. This is often a large sum of money which is calculated on a percentage of sales by the supplier—perhaps yet another case where people seem to think that sales creates advertising, rather than the other way round! However, the issue is that the dollars that suppliers commit to promotions is enormous. Even worse, in some cases, the trade tells the supplier what promotions they are going to get. There is a cost structure for these promotions. For example a gondola end at the bottom of the aisle can cost upwards of $25 000 for a state for a week, depending on whether it is the end of a busy aisle or not. The supplier is expected to drop price on the product so that the chain can make a special out of it. Normally these promotions last a week, but the chains will expect to have access to the lower price the week before and the week of the promotion; in theory so that they can get the stock in, but some chains even get agreement to the price cut the week after. This allows them to do what is called 'investment buying' where they buy stock at the lower price some of which gets sold at the normal price. Some chains have offered to stop investment buying in exchange for an extra rebate!

There are less expensive forms of promoting in-store, such as bins placed around the store for which the supplier pays, and 'shelf talkers', which are stickers or tags advertising that product; tagged something like a 'week value opportunity', which is supposed to attract the shopper to the product and create more sales.

There are also theme specials, for example, for Christmas, Easter or school holidays. The chains will usually try to get the suppliers to agree to these special themes in addition to funds already agreed. The story usually is accompanied by statements about how that supplier's competitors are very interested in participating, and unless the supplier wants to be left out of this amazing opportunity they had better make a commitment right now. It is a classic game of upping the ante, of addiction in one of its most expensive forms.

Price specials

These promotions are invariably price promotions, which is part of the generalised approach to marketing by Australian supermarket chains. The fact is that not all products react to price cuts. They certainly do not react to the same price cuts. There is evidence to suggest that good brand names not only do not react very well to price cuts, but they can be counter-productive because the loyal customers lose some respect for the brand

and brand loyalty decreases. Usually the chain expects the supplier to fund the price decrease so the chain expects a guaranteed margin. There have even been cases where a supplier has agreed to a price cut on a promotion only to find that the chain has pocketed some of the cut and not passed it all on to the consumer—the chain using the supplier's money to enhance their margin.

Handling co-op

The supplier's aim in this promotion area should be to limit the amount of money they agree to spend for a given period to what they consider 'reasonable'. This should be no more than last period, and if possible less. The supplier then needs to negotiate what they are going to get for their money.

Firstly the supplier needs to make sure that the funds remain under their control, and not let the trade decide which promotions to select. The selection of promotions will depend on what sort of promotions seem to work for the supplier's company and products. Not all products in your range should be promoted in the same way, and some maybe not at all. The supplier will also be negotiating what they get for their money in terms of the cost of each promotion. There are different prices for the same gondola end for different people depending on their ability to negotiate overall arrangements. Get away from 'per cent of sales' agreements.

You the supplier do not want competitive products to be on promotion at the same time. Seasonal factors and coinciding with TV and other media campaigns can be important. Timing can be an important issue.

You also need to make sure the trade does not do any investment buying. This means limiting the period for the buy for the case deal, so that the trade cannot investment buy, and gain an agreement that any price cut on the case price is reflected on shelf. You then need to check at store level that this is what happened.

Measuring promotional effectiveness

There are excellent tools available for planning and managing promotional campaigns. If you want to build an information base on what type of promotions work and which ones do not, you have to find some method of measuring their effectiveness. Many companies would take the view that they have to spend this money, so why bother quantifying results? If you do have to spend the money, the more sales multiplication effect you get from it the better. If you can show that there are some promotions which work better for both the supplier and the trade, then

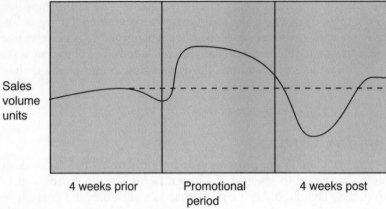

4 weeks prior   Promotional   4 weeks post
period

Figure 17: Sales volumes and promotions

you can often get more of these promotions. If you never measure it, then no-one will know or care.

    Measuring whether a promotion is effective, is not just a question of looking at how much extra you sold during the promotion. There may be consumers who simply stock up when your product is on special, and instead of buying two weeks requirements they will buy four. This means that you can expect to see a drop below the normal rate over the next few weeks. You may even find that there is no net increase in volume, and that the only thing which has happened is that the consumer has bought four weeks' supply at the discounted price. The consumer will be happy, the chain has made their full margin and received a fortune for their real estate and even received their money early. The one who is hurting is you the supplier. There are impulse items, like snack foods, where a promotion can temporarily or even, if you can get new users and convert them, permanently increase the market, but there are others such as toilet paper where usage will be fairly constant.

    In measuring promotional effectiveness, you should set certain standards for the promotion. The only one you can use is ROI: the return, in terms of incremental contribution to profit against the cost of the promotion. To measure the incremental sales is a question of establishing a benchmark of 'normal' sales, which is not always easy because there are few periods of normal sales for some of the fast moving goods that are heavily promoted. Normally you would look at sales for four weeks before the promotion period, then the week before, the week of, and the two weeks after, and the four weeks after that. What you will probably see looks like Figure 17 (above). There will be a level prior to the promotion, an increase during the promotion, and a dip afterwards. Sometimes you are lucky enough to find that the level to which the sales level returns is a bit higher than the level before the promotion. These have been good promotions which are giving you a lasting effect.

In measuring what has happened, you need to also take into account the case deal, because this means that you are getting less contribution to profit for the same volume. Some promotions are so bad that even if you measure the total rather than the incremental sales during a promotion, suppliers can lose money!

If you are going to set financial standards for performance you have to use your actual costs, usually standard costs, or you have to set some arbitrary figure below which you will not go; this figure being higher than your standard costs. You then need to take into account the net contribution, given that the supplier usually provides a case off discount.

Calculating promotional return on investment

There are many ways you could work this out, but here is an example of a common standard for the industry. Let us assume that you normally sell a case at $20, and that in a normal period you would sell 1000 cases. You have a promotion, and in that period you sell 2000 cases. You fund a $3 per case price reduction and the promotion costs you $3000. Was it any good as a promotion?

You can work out some kind of answer at the most simplistic level, which says:

Deal $3 per case,
Co-op per case $1.50 per case
You sold 2000 cases
Cost was $4.50 per case
As a percentage of normal price $4.5/20 = 22.5$ per cent
As a percentage of price net of the case deal, $4.5/17 = 26$ per cent cost

You can set standards and then measure against these standards.

There is a further refinement which says that you would have sold 1000 cases anyway in that period so that the incremental sales were only 1000 cases. Then you spread the costs over a smaller figure.

The deal per incremental case becomes $6, because you gave the deal over 2000 cases at $3 per case. The co-op per incremental case becomes $3 per case, being $3000 over the incremental 1000 cases. This gives a cost of $9 per incremental case or 45 per cent cost on normal price, and 53 per cent on the net price. Clearly this is not looking so good.

If you want to take into account that there was a drop in sales for the next period, so that the adjusted incremental effect over the whole period was actually only 500 cases, the news is even more depressing. The deal, per real incremental case, becomes $12. The co-op per real incremental case becomes $6. The cost becomes 90 per cent of normal price and 106 per cent on net price. If the standard or manufacturing cost of this product is $10 per case, you have a better picture. It means that the extra contribution to profit you achieved as a result of this promotion was $10 per case on 500 cases, or $5000. The trouble is that you spent $3 a case on 2000 cases for the deal and $3000 for the promotion. In other words, it cost you $9000 for this promotion for a net gain of only $5000. You made a loss of $4000.

You may claim that this is unrealistic because if you do not promote you will lose sales, and that if your competition had promoted during that period and you had not you could well have lost half your business, which would have cost you more. This may be true. The fact is that these promotions become integrated into the way the business operates. You cannot get off the treadmill of promotions, but you can certainly start measuring the result of them. These results can help you plan for the promotions that do work, provide direction for promotions to seek with the trade, and serve as a negotiation point when it comes to haggling over the promotional program.

You can calculate break-even volumes, set cost standards, measure your performance and mount your arguments to the trade accordingly. The best program for this is Promax, for planning budgeting and measurement purposes, from the Professional Assignments Group, Sydney. It is easy to use and operate on a PC. Their excellent book *Profitable Trading with Australian Grocery Chains* is available through AIM or direct from PAG.

Compliance with agreed promotional programs

There are a couple of other things you should watch in promotions. The first is that the promotions you agree to and pay for, actually happen in each store. This is a policing role. You want to make sure the promotion starts when it is supposed to, that it is ticketed in the agreed manner, that it is on the aisle end agreed, and that there is plenty of stock to support it. Make sure that there are no competing promotions, and that any other conditions you specified and have agreed to have been implemented.

The account manager must ensure that there is good communication to the field staff of in-store sales people or merchandisers of the exact details of the promotion, so they know the details you want checked.

If there is non-compliance, the account manager should be informed so that the company can get some compensation, usually in terms of a discount or free extra promotion. However the chain will tell the supplier that they have to fund the case deal on this extra promotion.

Many of these promotions are very poorly merchandised. There may be stacks with no pricing on them, or products on display from the supplier paying for the end, but with products from other suppliers on the same display. (Joint displays of companion products can work very well, especially for the smaller suppliers, but only according to an agreed arrangement.) There may be untidy stacks, or stacks which are not well stocked, or they could even be out of stock. Point-of-sale material supplied by the supplier is either in poor condition because of ill treatment in the store, or sometimes is not used at all.

What we have discussed so far in this chapter are special ways that the supermarket business operates. The principles of account management do not change—the thing which is different is the nature of the agreements made.

. . . .

Marketing direction

There could be two types of marketing direction to take into account: consumer marketing and trade marketing. The former is about how you the supplier are going to promote products to the consumer. It should provide direction on which are the priority products, and there will often be something about new products. Trade marketing will have some statements about the way the supplier should structure their business with the trade, and have guidelines on how much they are prepared to invest with the trade and in what ways. Your company may, for example, decide not to pay anything for preferred supplier status, but may allow some discount for prompt payment. There will be standards set for promotional effectiveness, as discussed in the last section. Trade marketing should also specify the merchandising elements which favour your company products.

The account manager needs to make sure that these are understood. There should be a formal mechanism for communicating these plans between sales and marketing. Just as in the case of other businesses there needs to be two-way communication, with sales briefing the marketing department on trends, and what seems to be working and what does not. There needs to be agreement between sales and marketing on what is realistically achievable.

It is worthwhile pointing out that although there are state and national organisations for most of the chains, it is a good idea to have some central control over what you do in individual states. This is because what you do in Hobart today with a particular chain will be known by tomorrow in the state offices of that chain in Perth, Brisbane, Adelaide, Melbourne and Sydney. You can get caught out if an enthusiastic account manager in one state gives away too much.

. . . .
Account profiles

You need to know about both head office and the stores. The in-store people should keep the more detailed information on the stores, but it is a good idea for the account managers to also have access. At head office you need to know the people and how they interact. Their criteria for decisions can be very useful information. These change from time to time: it is not just a question of whether they make money out of the product, but depends on brand strength, media advertising and so on.

You need to know their systems and procedures. Have a list of the stores and their categories. Know how the planogram works and what it is for your section. Know what the rules of the chain are, and how you can break them, both at store level and at head office level. Try to find out what the chain's objectives are for your section. If there are any buzz words you find out about their thrust, build them into your own presentations.

182 Account profitability

Since there are so few chains that dominate your business, you should make an effort to measure your own profitability on these major accounts. There is a format you can use in Figure 18. This information is useful not only in seeing where you need to try harder with less profitable accounts, but also as a bargaining point with the trade. There have been some cases where the tabling of such information has caused the trade to back off, but there is also at least one case where the trade's view was that the supplier should keep on making a loss rather than change any other trading arrangements with that chain.

. . . .
Account SWOT

For any given chain you need to look at where you stand versus competitors, both direct product competition and other major players in your section or category. You should put together your own criteria for judging this. It might include terms, which is something you will have to try and estimate. You might look at the strength of your range, the brand strength of your product versus the competitors', and the amount of media advertising. If you find out the chain's criteria for decision-making include those in the SWOT for that account. In terms of opportunities, the gaps in their sales performance on a more detailed basis are those you identify and build into your presentations at head office. In the SWOT you should address any threats or opportunities on a macro level.

Name of account:

Account manager:	1995	1996	1997	1998
Invoiced sales				

Less rebates/allowances
   —volume
   —co-op
   —other				

= net sales revenue				

Less cost of goods
   —packaging
   —freight
   —credit				

= contribution				

Less sales costs
   —invoicing costs
   —sales support
   —media advertising				

= net contribution				
Less fixed cost allocation				
= net profit before tax				

Figure 18: Measuring account profitability

Notes
1 Where actuals are not available, allocations may be made.
2 Cost of goods should be based on standard costs.
3 Sales costs can be calculated as visits as a per cent of visits multiplied by total sales.
4 Fixed cost allocation should be provided by the accountant as a guide to how satisfactory the new contribution level is.
5 Make comparisons over time and between accounts.
6 Use information for planning as a profit diagnostic and in any negotiations.

. . . .
Opportunity growth search

This is a question of seeing if there are parts of the business of your products where the chain is missing out. You need to concentrate on how they can improve their results from trading. Look very specifically at volume sales, then margins or stock efficiencies. Be careful with margins,

183

because although you can point out that they are trading lower than others and can make the point that on brand loyalty there is no need to discount (if that is the situation), you must not suggest a price.

This part of the account management cycle is critical. You should be trying to see where the chain is missing out on sales by comparison with other states of the same chain, or this state but other chains, relative to your national figures on market share and volumes. They may miss out because they do not stock the product in all or any stores, because it is badly merchandised, in the wrong position, with too few facings and so on, or because of the wrong type of promotions. You need to recommend actions which will then form the basis of your presentation to the head offices.

You determine this by using the eyes and ears of your sales force, especially the in-store sales people who should be talking to the store managers and the category managers in store about what is happening. The most powerful tool is warehouse withdrawal data, coupled with other statistical information on the business.

184

. . . .

New products

There are more new products particularly shampoos, introduced in the grocery business than any other. The fact is that there are not too many really powerful new products which will increase the existing market. Too often the suppliers bring out line extensions (you have seen the basic product, then the apple-scented one, now look at the one which smells of mango or strawberry) which are simply variations on a basic theme. Most of these line extensions do not increase the market. Some people using the basic product will use the apple-scented one, and some of those may convert to the mango. You are just fragmenting customer purchases and nobody gains. The supermarket generally has very little to gain from it. There are rarely more overall sales, but there are more products to put up on shelf and more products to handle through the whole system, warehousing, stocking and administration.

The supplier probably does not gain. They also have higher stock and shorter runs in manufacturing and in packaging. There is money in developing the product and launching it and there is media advertising.

Because the trade has so little to gain from constant line extensions, they implemented a policy to try to discourage them. The deterrent policy was that the supplier pays new line fees to introduce a new product, ostensibly to cover the costs of putting new products on trade systems. Another policy is that you the supplier have a certain amount of space on shelf, and you are not getting any more. Assuming that you have the optimum number of facings already, if you want to put a new product on, you are going to have to take one of your other products off.

We might think that suppliers would see that line extensions which are not going to increase the market substantially are a bad investment from their point of view, and that they can sour relationships with the trade even further.

Suppliers would be better off to have a smaller number of new products, which are well researched and which are going to show some return for both them and the trade.

There are some areas of the business, for example health and beauty, where there is a perception that you have to keep bringing something new out, to keep up with changing movements in fashion and to keep the product in front of the consumer's eye. There is some truth in this, but the suppliers overdo it. Some old favourites always sell. 'Old Spice', for example, has been selling for nearly forty years and is still going strong.

This does not say that suppliers should not develop new products, but it does mean they should be far more selective. It is very hard for account managers to show head office another exciting line extension, the third in one year after some disappointing flops. It may be a very good product this time, but when the trade says what have you got for us today? and the account manager says 'A new product', the groan will be palpable. The more failures you have, the less your credibility for the next new product.

185

Using presenters

When you, the supplier, do bring out new products, tell the trade first of all what they are going to get out of it. Selling the product to the trade is not the same as selling to the consumer. The chain does not really care about the product—as long as consumers think it is all right and want to buy it, that is all the supermarket cares about. That needs to be established in the presentation, but it is secondary to what the trade wants to hear, which is what it is going to do for them.

If you develop new products that will increase the market and you can show that the trade is going to gain substantially, you will find that the new line fees get forgotten and room will be made on shelf. If you are trying to get more up on shelf, you would be better advised to make a few suggestions in the interests of the chain of what to take off the shelf. This does not have to be your product. There is nothing wrong with putting together a story which shows that there are some really poor performers on shelf in your category (maybe from a competitor or maybe even home brands), and showing a planogram which allows you to put in a new product and not lose any existing ones. You may offer to take off the poorest performing product of your own range, as well as some from other suppliers, to show willingness.

. . . .

The joint business plan

The joint business plan is the external document that you will use to get agreement at head office level to the basis on which you will do business for the next period. The supermarket business is well structured in this regard, and there are formalised planning cycles. You should look at the business on an annual basis with quarterly fine-tuning, very much like any distributive business. We will examine how such a plan/presentation might be constructed in the next chapter. The objective you have will be to reach certain target sales within a budget on spend, terms and co-op. The way you will do this is to get agreements on distribution, range through as many stores as you can, with the facings and position you want, promoting to an agreed sum, with your decision on which promotions and when.

There will be other things which you may want to achieve with the trade and these will be part of your own agenda, as described in the previous section in Part 2. It is recommended that you have a simple sheet similiar to Figure 16, which defines some actions that need to be taken with the chain or at store level. Many of those actions may be about relationships or about finding out information; there should be a sheet prepared for each chain on an annual basis and there may be a need to look at it on a quarterly basis, depending on how much of your own agenda you want to achieve.

186

. . . .

Implementing the plans

Most implementation of plans happens through ongoing contact between head office personnel and the account manager, but it is also important to ensure that what you, the account manager, are trying to achieve at head office is supported at store level. There are different approaches to this in-store job, which vary with what it is perceived you can achieve. For many of the chain stores the job has been reduced almost to a merchandising job, since the store manager is not empowered to make any decisions about the store which would affect the supplier's business. The sales representative finds it hard to change facings, position on shelf, range stocked and so on. Sometimes you might be able to persuade a store manager to change your end in a promotion for a better one, or put it up a day early and leave it up a day longer, but the days when sales representatives go into the chain stores and do a shelf relay have gone.

This reduces the job to checking the stock, making sure it is on shelf and monitoring stock outs, which has to be one of the most annoying problems encountered in selling through the chains. It is frightening how often they happen. Go and look on a Sunday afternoon or Monday morning and you will see for yourself.

Checking position and facings against what has been agreed is another task, and so is making sure that the conditions of promotions have been adhered to. The sales representative also has a role to play before the promotion in making sure that the store manager (or section/category manager) knows about it and has ordered the stock and made arrangements to get the promotion up.

It often happens that there is a job to do of putting the stock up, tidying it, and making sure any point of sales is clean and tidy and being used.

Some suppliers take the view that this role can be better handled by part-time merchandisers. Many such employees include women looking for a part-time job with flexible hours, students, and men and women who have taken early retirement.

Communication within the supplier becomes an important part of coordinating activities. For this reason there have been a couple of companies who decided to reorganise sales people from the traditional geographic area to having them organised round the chains, so one sales representative might call on only the Coles stores, and another only the Woolworths. This tends to mean that each sales representative has far more distance to travel and lowers their call efficiency. Generally this method of operation has not been deemed successful.

187

There is however, a trend in the sales force to organise account managers by customer, such that state account managers for (say) Woolworths report to the national account manager for Woolworths rather than a state sales manager. This aligns the supplier organisation more with the way the trade operates.

. . . .

Business review and development meetings

The review has long been entrenched in the way the chains do business. Every few months, there is a formal review where the supplier presents figures to the trade on what has happened in the prior period. These reviews used to be a bit like sales meetings—that is, very boring—mainly because they degenerate into going over a whole mass of sales results. There are often so many figures that the trade hardly gets a chance to work out what they mean. In fact some account managers have this as part of their strategy! But of course the trade does look at them in more detail afterwards. It is therefore much better for the supplier to keep control, and look at the figures, pick out the highlights, then decide what actions could be taken to address the anomalies from plan.

The review is the first part of a presentation in the sense that from this exercise come the strategies of what can be done to improve the results of both companies. It is where the opportunities are defined, and is the precursor to deciding the main plan for the next period. Traditionally many suppliers have sent the results to the trade first, so that they can look at them before the meeting and do not sit there shocked by the volume of figures. This certainly overcomes that problem, but it means that you lose control in presenting the information the way that you want to.

It is more effective to extract the main variances and the reasons as far as you can determine them. Put all the supporting data in an appendix so that the trade can go through them afterwards if they want to. But in presenting information, make it as easy to read and decipherable as you can. Organise it in sections, and examine product performance against plan and/or last year, versus national business and your overall shares, highlighting which areas are doing well and which are not. Then make some overall recommendations on what should be done. Even at this review stage your presentation is almost locked down. In fact, it is quite conceivable to have the two meetings in one. If you do have them separately, at least you will have agreed the ground rules at this first meeting, so that there will be few or no surprises when you do make your presentation and you will have presold it anyway.

188

The review is the opportunity for you to stress the successes in the retailing part of the business. You need to stress where your products have performed in making the trade money, volume and margin. You must keep focusing their attention on the money they make from selling your products, rather than the head office funds they want you to give them. This should be part of your aim in ongoing dialogue, but there is a real opportunity for you to stress the profit from trading, especially the gain over the previous period, when you have reviews.

. . . .

Non-chain supermarkets: the independents

Some 70 or 80 per cent of the supermarket business in each state is run by no more than two or three superchains, but there are also smaller chains and the independents. You may even decide once you have looked at the profitability on the business through the larger chains, that you will put a bit more effort into the others. If you are a manufacturer who sells OTC products through pharmacy only, you would be advised to hesitate before you embark into the grocery supermarkets as a method of getting more volume, because you will certainly find there will be far less contribution to profit on the same volume. You need to work out what extra volume you need through supermarkets to offset the drop in margin.

The independents have the advantage that you can work with the store on an individual basis, and that it does not cost you an arm and a leg to get things done. All the principles of merchandising we have discussed are valid for the independent stores.

This means that there is a real job to be done by the supplier sales force in these stores. It requires time, but the rewards can be significant. Many of these stores do not understand much about merchandising and will probably appreciate your attempts to help them sell more. If you can make a few suggestions which work, and they see an increase in sales, you will have gained their confidence to try a few more things out and to stock more of your products.

There are even local promotions you can do. Use the windows and point of sale material. A local store I know uses a blackboard. Some of the things they write are very amusing, or even a bit risqué, but people driving and walking along the street notice it and even look to see if there is anything new on the board. This has to pay off in terms of more store traffic and business. With independents, you can be a lot more creative.

At present the in-store selling job tends not to embrace some of these merchandising aspects, perhaps because sales representatives are so used to not being able to do anything other than police head office agreements at the chain store level and they fall into the rut of doing the same at the independents.

Make sure that your in-store sales representatives understand the merchandising issues of shelf management and store promotions, so that they can put together a financial argument to the store owner showing how they could gain in volume and contribution to profit by acting on the sales person's recommendation. There will be many store managers who do not understand concepts like ROII and shelf management, and these are the ones where you have the greatest opportunity. This approach may require some training of the sales representatives, and maybe a different attitude to their in store job, but it can be well worth it.

If, for example, your sales through independents are 8 per cent of your total sales, and in terms of contribution that 8 per cent represents 12 per cent of contribution to profit, and you are able to increase your sales through these stores by up to 50 per cent, your overall profit contribution increase will be 6 per cent. Making this sort of increase happen through the chains is much harder. It is therefore worth your having a look at this non-chain business, and considering putting much more sales effort into it.

For those of you who are interested in doing this, and who have not read Part 2, I recommend that you do so. It contains some ideas which I believe could be used in account management for independent supermarkets.

If you are a small supplier

Much of the background described in this chapter is well known to the account managers of the largest suppliers. They are used to the games, and play them well or badly depending on the company. However, the real losers are often the smaller companies, who have some good products to offer but do not have the resources to compete with the very large dollars some companies throw at the trade.

There is some merit in telling the trade that they should consider you as different. Most of the products produced by smaller suppliers are specialist products that tend to have higher margins for the trade. They tend to cater to niche shoppers, and are important because they attract people into the store because the people know they can get such products there. They are part of offering a full range and catering to special consumer segments.

The trade should see a role for such products and suppliers, and not demand the same high costs for those products to be given distribution. New line fees should be lowered or waived. Promotional activity should be looked at in a different light. There could be joint promotions of companion sales with other products from other suppliers which logically go together. There could be a 'gourmet gondola end' involving several suppliers of similar specialist products. The costs of shelf talkers and bins could be lowered. Some suppliers of smaller size and specialised products actually achieve this, and have a relatively smooth ride with the trade.

Another option is to use a brokerage firm. There are a few operating in the supermarket grocery business and in the hardware chain business. These companies do some of the packaging referred to above, and may represent a good alternative for the really small companies who have no experience in selling through chains.

. . . .

Summary

If it seems that much of account management in the supermarket chain area is about preparing for adversarial negotiation, that assumption is pretty much correct. The selling in of the deal to get the distribution you want, and the conditions on shelf and promotions which will help sell the product out, are settled during head office negotiations. This is why so much effort is expended on them. There is much less room to manoeuvre at store level, because the stores are all fully owned by the major chains who control them centrally and completely. In the non-supermarket area there is less rigidity in the rules, much less institutionalised negotiation, and far more room to do things at a local store level. This is true even for those groups which are fully owned chains.

The key issues are the presentation, and the negotiation.

So far we have discussed preparing for this event. The next chapter will look specifically at how these presentations should be structured and delivered.

10

Joint business proposals: the key to getting distribution

. . . .

Introduction

Following on from our arguments in the previous chapter, the key to getting sales through the supermarket chains is in negotiating arrangements at head office. This book is not about negotiating technique, although the subject comes up from time to time in the sense that account managing presupposes that the supplier ends up having a better quality of business, and that this is reflected in the sorts of agreements they negotiate with their customers. It is the return the supplier gets from the investment in creating the differentiation. In the case of the chains, if you can put together presentations which focus on how you contribute to the results of the trade through the products you sell and how you market them, this should take some pressure off the supplier to give money at the head office level.

There are several types of presentation which are made to head offices by account managers or sales managers. They could be on introductions of new lines, or they could be the sorts of things which govern the regular basis of doing business, such as terms or promotional program, or there are the reviews. New line introductions can happen at any time in the year, but it is recommended that you establish a pattern of the other meetings where you agree the elements of the business. You need to establish a schedule which meets the needs of the trade and your own needs, and for periods which make good business sense. The review should come first. Then the other elements are better handled all at one time, because it gives you greater room for flexibility in the negotiation. You are also handling more variables. For example, if you have made an agreement on trading terms, including a figure for ranging allowance, warehousing allowances, preferred supplier terms, a prompt payment discount, national terms or state terms and ullage, you do not want then to have to argue over a promotional program where there is little room to move. However, if the trade has new demands and the trading terms are not locked down, you have the option of turning some of the notional constants in this area back into variables. It is therefore suggested that after the review, you should present a plan for the whole business, including terms and promotions. This is really a joint business proposal, sometimes called a profit-improvement plan.

The joint business proposal is the same as the account plan—an external document which commits both sides to action. The only thing which is special or different is the dimensions of what is negotiated.

At the start of the last chapter I suggested that you list the concessions you currently make to the trade. Then list the things you would like back in return. You should get both of these lists out before you start preparing your presentation. You should resolve to try to get out of providing some of the items on the first list, but the most important list is the second one. It is here that you can start to build in some of the things which can help you regain some ground.

193

. . . .

Format of the presentation

There may be some rules about how presentations should be submitted, but you must ensure that these rules do not interfere with your presentation. Have the courage to put your presentations together your way, as long as they are coherent and persuasive.

The front page should have names and the logos of both trading partners and, like in the non-supermarket chain distributive businesses, have a desirable end result. Make the figures look as large as you can. Analyse them, use raw dollars if they look impressive, or use percentages if that seems to look bigger. The front page is designed to attract. The total package should look bigger than the previous year, it should include the money the trade will make from trading, and the money you are going to offer in terms and co-op. There is no doubt that whatever you offer the trade will want more, therefore you must offer in this presentation less than what you are prepared to, and must ask for more than you expect to get. You can always back down, and in reality you are going to be forced to give more than your first offer. It is therefore fundamental that this presentation is not your real position, but your 'aim high', from which you are going to negotiate.

The aim-high position needs to be credible, and you need to be able to sell it and support it. As you gradually retire from this position as the negotiation proceeds, by trading concessions, you need to make sure that it looks as if it hurts. This is the best way to leave the trade feeling satisfied.

Then there will be a sectional analysis of the business, by products or product groups. Try to group your products according to how the trade sees them, rather than how you organise or group them, if there is a difference.

For each product or group, you will look at the sorts of criteria which are normally included in the review. Show the performance through this chain, on a state or national basis. You should then analyse these results and draw some conclusions. An example of what this might look like is given in Figure 19. Use charts, and draw comparisons which help you justify the actions you are going to recommend. You should not put down things which are wrong or even misleading, but the art of presentation is to make what you are about to present look as attractive as possible, whether it is a meal, yourself on a Saturday night, or a commercial presentation to a supermarket category manager. The principles are very similar.

Use computer graphics. There are pie charts, bar charts and all sorts of other graphics available. All you need to do is put in the raw data and the computer will do the rest. If you are using graphs and charts, use a scale which makes the figures look good. That is, focus on any increases so that they are not just seen as a small movement on a large graph. Cut off the lower part of the graph and focus on the top part where the increases look far more dramatic.

The analysis should be clear. Have any supporting evidence in an appendix at the back. You need to keep the presentation itself as simple and as clean as possible. You will be very familiar with the information you are presenting, but your trading partner will not be. There is a limit to the amount of new information people can absorb, and this is even more true of figures. If I tell you a message you will probably understand the gist of it easily enough, but if I read to you a string of numbers, such as an overseas telephone number, you will not be able to remember much of it at all. This means that you need to express numerical data in a way which is easy to understand and assimilate. Expressing it visually is one of the best ways.

FRANWOLES–PRODUX FOODS

JOINT PROFIT IMPROVEMENT PLAN

ESTIMATED $143 000 EXTRA PROFIT

ON

19% TARGET INCREASE IN FRANWOLES SALES

VOLUME TO $3 000 000

1997 PERFORMANCE HIGHLIGHTS

- 5% growth in this market
- 3% growth in Franwoles sales
- Franwoles share of the market is 19% but their share of the total grocery market is 28%
- 1998 market is predicted to grow 5%

KEY ISSUES

Franwoles are missing out on sales and margins due to:

- not stocking the whole trange (neither 500 g High C, nor 100 g natural are stocked)
- facings of the High C product are not optimised
- selling a lower margin mix than other chains
- in store promotions were not as effective as anticipated

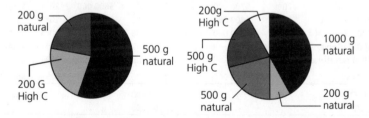

MIX IN FRANWOLES BUSINESS VERSUS THAT IN PRODUX FOODS BUSINESS

Figure 19: The joint profit improvement plan

RECOMMENDATIONS

1 Franwoles stock the 500 g High C and the 1000 g Natural in all Category A, B and C stores.

2 Higher margins (25% is the industry average) are available on these products relative to the rest of the range (20%).

3 All products to be company blocked in the Dried Goods Section on the second shelf, with facings as indicated in the attached planogram.

4 Promotion.

	1997	**1998**
CO-OP	$200 000	$220 000
DEAL	$ 80 000	$ 80 000

   a This will cover 4 one-week promotions of 500 g (both variants), with two promotions including the 1000 g Natural.
   b Produx recommends a price cut of up to 5% the week of the promotion and the week prior, to be funded out of the above figure by Produx, but any further cuts would be paid for by Franwoles.

5 National terms, warehouse allowances, state terms to remain at current levels. Settlement discount to be reduced from 1.5% for payment in 7 days to 1.2% reflecting the fall in interest rates.

FINANCIAL SUMMARY

PRODUCT	AVE INDUSTRY MARGINS	1997 PURCHASES	MARGIN	GP$	ESTIMATED 1998 PURCHASES	MARGIN	GP$
200 g Natural	20%	$700 000	20%	$175 000	$600 000	20%	$150 000
200 g High C	20%	$400 000	20%	$100 000	$320 000	20%	$80 000
500 g Natural	20%	$900 000	20%	$225 000	$720 000	20%	$180 000
500 g High C	25%	nil		nil	$300 000	25%	$100 000
1000 g Natural	25%	nil		nil	$400 000	25%	$133 000
TOTAL		$2 000 000	20%	$500 000	$2 340 000	21.5%	$643 000
CO-OP				$200 000			$220 000
DEAL				$80 000			$80 000

*CONSTANT DOLLARS
INCREASE IN YOUR PROFITABILITY $143 000
ON A SALES INCREASE OF 19% TO JUST UNDER $3 000 000

Making the recommendations

After the analysis, there should be a conclusion, followed by a recommended action. This may be, for example, that sales were lost because the products were promoted at the wrong time, or that the position on shelf had been changed and that caused a drop in sales. The recommendation you make follows straight after those two conclusions.

You might have determined that the promotions you did last period had a deep price cut, which worked better than a small one. You have to be careful, because you do not want to end up funding yourself deeper price cuts, so you might suggest that the trade participates in the cut, or that the extra cut be funded out of the agreed promotional funds rather than in addition (there are plenty of suppliers who manage to get case off funded out of the agreed promotional budget).

You gradually work through the business, looking at each area in detail and trying to get agreement in principle as you go along to the series of actions you recommend.

You need to have a page where you list all the conditions and terms which you want agreed, and which might emanate from your list of the things you would like in return. These are the general things about the way you do business, paying to agreed terms, compliance agreements, procedures, stocking and ordering, care of goods and point of sale, prior notice of intended changes, reasons for rejections, guaranteed tenure on shelf, and so on—whatever is an issue in your business where their actions could save you time and money, or allow you to make more money, or have more security in your business. Unless you ask for it formally, you will not get it.

. . . .

Their financial summary

You now come to the summary, the part the trade wanted to see all along, which is where you spell out the terms and the co-op. At the top of the page you should add up the expected volume sales and estimated contribution based on current margins, from all the products. It should be based on the estimates of sales if you both carry out the actions you suggest. This must show some increase, otherwise the trade will just want an increase in direct transfer of funds. It should be credible, and you may have to justify the figures through rational and well-reasoned argument. You may find that they accept what you say about each individual product or group, but that when you add it all together in the summary they will believe that the total is too optimistic.

Under this comes the part they really want to hear about, which is the offer on terms and promotional funds. If you have any new products as part of your presentation, include nothing for new line fees. Offer less than you are prepared to in co-op and terms. Try to reduce it from last year, but if there is a way of doing so make it look bigger. When you get to this point, they will say 'You have to be joking, this is not even as good as last year. You are going to have to do considerably better than that unless you want to lose distribution of most of your products.'

The presentation has started to move to negotiation.

. . . .

New line introductions

We have talked about the problems facing the trade with line extensions and new products which do not really grow the total market. Each supplier will nevertheless have new products which they want to introduce. These may not coincide with the ideal timing to include them in the joint business proposal. They will more often be a separate presentation and negotiation.

The first thing is to remind you, the supplier, that the trade only cares about the product insofar as it is likely to sell. What consumers get out of it exactly is of secondary importance. What really matters is whether consumers will buy it, rather than why they will buy it. Thus the marketing of new products to the trade is very different from marketing to the consuming public, and having a trade marketing department can be useful. The focus of these people is towards the trade, and it does not require split thinking between consumer and retailer.

With most product launches there are glossy brochures known as presenters, produced at great cost. These are usually put together by marketing. Unless you are careful, they will tend to have an overt consumer relationship focus, and will talk about the product as it might appeal to the consumer. This is quite the wrong approach. These presenters must concentrate first on what are the benefits to the trade.

A good example of this was the launch in the 1980s of a new hygiene paper product, New Generation Sorbent by Bowater Scott. The supplier had acquired the technology from North America to make an improved product. It was softer and stronger, and was a very good product technically and in terms of customer appeal. The original presenter, which was accompanied by a very professional and expensive video film, was organised badly. It started talking about this new technology, showing the plant in North America, and referring to the scientists and engineers who were travelling back and forth across the Pacific (who cares?). It talked about the processes which made the innovations possible, and described the results on the product performance. By this time most people in the trade would have been asleep.

Then suddenly, when no-one was listening any longer, it gave some amazing facts.

As a result of research in Australia and experience overseas, Bowater Scott were predicting, with evidence to back it, that:

- the new product would create 10 per cent market growth in the first year in its product category
- the product would take up 25 per cent of this expanded market in the same period
- the margins on this 25 per cent share of the market would be higher than on the current sales by a significant percentage
- stock turns would improve as a result of a different size case, and the fact that the colours would be packed separately so that individual regional preferences could be catered for.

Each one of these items was in itself a powerful reason why the trade should want to stock the product, and it was one of the best opportunities the trade had had all year to improve results. If only this total opportunity had been added together and presented as the desirable end result first, and then worked gradually backwards, the presentation would have been far more powerful. This would have been a good structure:

- $00000 opportunity to improve profit in one year—and more gains after that!
- The new product will:
  - grow the market 10 per cent; take a 25 per cent share of the total market
  - improve margins by x per cent
  - improve stock turns by xx
- Explain the product briefly
- Show the research and the evidence
  - Justify all the figures you have tabled
- Describe the media launch program
- More product details if there is interest in them
- Table the terms and conditions—the commercial part of the deal.

The trade might not have believed your opening statements, but they would have been interested enough to have listened to the rest of what you had to say.

In fact, the account managers tore the Bowater Scott presenters apart, and put them back in a different order. The story has a happy ending because it was a very good launch in the end, and the product performed well for all parties.

The point is that presenters should be constructed around how the trade benefits. Marketing people would do well to consult with the sales people to make sure that the presenters are going to be real tools in the selling process. It is the account manager who is going to have to use the presenter, and therefore he or she should have significant input into it.

Have your evidence ready

Just because you say the product will sell well and expand the market, the trade is not going to believe you. You have to back it up with reasons and evidence why your claim is true.

Test markets are the most powerful evidence, and local product testing and market research is the next best thing. When you talk about the experience in the USA or UK with the same product, you are skating on much thinner ice. At the state level, what happened in Geelong will not impress Queensland as well as Newcastle results will impress Sydney buyers.

200

Have a recommended shelf layout

As part of the presentation you need to recognise that the shelves are not infinite. You should have a desired position on shelf and know how many facings you want. If your product is to have space on shelf, then something else has to go. If you leave it to the trade to decide it is hardly going to advantage you. It is better to identify the poor performers in the category and propose reducing their facings or removing them altogether. Have a planogram with the rationale behind it. If the new product replaces one of your existing products, this makes it much easier to accommodate on shelf.

Decide how you want to promote it

Decide the best way to promote the product. Your preferred option will be for the promotion to be included as part of the agreed promotional activity, in other words to be funded out of the overall funds you have agreed for the period. You may also specifically not want any price cuts in the introductory phases. There may be a promotional pack designed to get people to try the new product. Try to avoid paying for promotions above what has been put in the program. If the worst comes to the worst and you get embroiled in arguing over new line fees, get those fees countered against extra-promotional activity.

An agreement to give the new product a reasonable time to prove itself is desirable. Specify the initial and ongoing buy quantities. Coordinate the introduction with media launch. Any product which is going to be advertised on TV will stand a better chance. Any new product which a competing chain has agreed to sell becomes a more desirable prospect for the other chains to sell too, but be careful how you play that card.

How strongly you are able to go in will depend on the extent to which this new product really is going to create extra profits for the trade. If you can demonstrate this, you will probably get the new product introduced on fair terms. If you cannot, expect that it is going to be a costly and not very satisfying result. This consideration should drive the product development strategy for marketing.

Costing out the negotiation

Whether you are making a joint business proposal or introducing a new product, you should always aim high in the initial presentation. This means that you will have an actual stance and an aim-high stance. Most experienced account managers will also be able to predict the sort of things their trading partners are likely to be trying to negotiate. In these negotiations very large amounts of money exchange hands, and it is a very good idea to monitor this cash movement.

You can calculate the expected profit to be made out of the deal if you get your aim high and if you get your actual result. You can calculate this by using a format into which you enter the aim-high stance and the actual stance figures, on a simple spreadsheet such as Lotus 1-2-3. You can then estimate what the trade is going to make out of the deal, and this will probably be part of your presentation. This will also change from your aim-high to your actual. It may be useful to cost the trade's aim-high and actual, as you assess them from experience.

The key issue is to focus the attention of the account manager on two points: looking at the deal from the point of view of the profitability to the chain, because that is how it is going to be sold; and looking at it as it relates to the profitability to the company. If the account manager keeps his or her mind on that throughout the negotiation, it will give them the fortitude to stick out for a better deal.

It is critical after the event to cost out what really happened. This means to calculate, based on the terms of the negotiated agreement, the financial impact on both parties and how that compares to the figures in the planned stances. You might even consider a walk-away bottom line, at which point the account manager withdraws from the negotiation with all offers made to date. The business may not be viable under the conditions that the account manager can procure it.

Formats you can use to cost out your plan and the actual result are given in Figures 20 and 21.

	BUYER'S POSITION	
	Based on seller's actual stance	Based on negotiated result
Estimated volume sales		
Estimated gross margin on sales		
Rebates/terms • head office • state • other		
Settlement discount		
Co-op		
Deal		
New line fees		
Total $		

$ summary based on estimated volume sales

Figure 20: Costing out results

The negotiation issue

Perhaps the key issue in all this is one we are not going to cover—the negotiation skills of the account manager. There are several models for negotiation, some better than others. Negotiation is a skill which improves with practice. The supplier must ensure that account managers have been given thorough formal training in negotiation and that they have plenty of opportunity to develop these skills through role plays. There are some negotiation workshops specific to the grocery industry and supermarket chains, which are far more applicable to the grocery business than the

SELLER'S POSITION

	Seller Aim High	Seller Actual Stance	Negotiated Result
Distribution			
Range			
Store categories			
Facings			
Deletions			
Positioning on shelf			
Blocking			
Volume purchases estimate $			
Financial summary			
National terms			
State terms			
Co-op			
Deal			
New line fees			
Settlement discount			
Other			
$ Impact on seller			

Figure 21: Costing your negotiated result

general ones where delegates might learn about negotiating on anything from tractors to houses.

It is important to make sure that you, the supplier, understand the difference between selling and negotiating when looking at training courses. There are some good sales courses which are geared to grocery, but they are directed towards in store selling. Negotiation is separate from selling. The selling must have happened at some point in the past before a negotiation takes place. No-one is going to negotiate over a product they have not decided to buy. Negotiation is the process of agreeing the terms and conditions under which two parties will do business. Account management prepares the ground for it, but unless your account managers are good negotiators, you will lose much of the advantage you will have worked so hard to secure.

PART 4

Selling to End Users

11

The account management cycle for end customers who use the product

. . . .

Introduction

The classic key account management approach was derived for customers who buy the product and service and then use it themselves, rather than selling it to the final consumer. This covers most industrial selling and quite a lot of selling of services, such as banking, printing, professional services, real estate, transport and some travel products.

The process differs from distribution businesses in that in this case the customer really does care how the product performs, and will compare product specifications and performance more than a customer in the distribution area, where they do not care about the product itself as long as people buy it.

This sort of selling includes ongoing consumable products such as plastics, packaging materials, chemicals, office consumables, manu-facturing intermediates, medical, institutional supplies and some services. It also includes one-off or project selling, including such areas as computer systems, equipment, construction and machinery. In all cases the steps are similar, and the account management model is the same.

This is where the concept of differentiation is fundamental, and where the focus must be deflected from price to value for money. The whole process of account management for these direct accounts must be geared to adding value to the package in some way, so that the pressure on price is reduced. On the one hand it allows far more creativity than in other ways of selling, but at the same time it requires hard work to deliver a differentiated package. The ROI of the whole operation must be looked at. You the supplier must be able to get more value returned to you through better negotiated agreements than it costs you to create the differentiation. It is bad business to invest money in differentiation which is not returned to you through the quality of the business you get. This has implications for the negotiating skills of the sales people, as well as their ability to sell a whole package rather than just product.

The account management cycle

The account management cycle for direct accounts very much follows the model described in chapter 3. Here are some comments which expands on the content of chapter 3, specifically with respect to direct accounts.

The marketing plans

In some of the industrial areas marketing plans are weakest, and the only thing the sales department can do is to push the marketing department until they get plans which are easy to interpret and useful. If you decide to hold a meeting to get key account management under way, invite the marketing people, because it will give them some insight into the problems the sales force faces in implementing programs with customers and gives them ideas on the sorts of plans they should be putting together to help sales create differentiation.

It often happens that the sales department holds up the account planning process because they have not received coherent marketing plans from the marketing department. In the long run, this lack of plans is a serious problem. However, it is not worth holding up account management because the marketing people have not got their act together. The account plans should be passed to marketing for their acceptance (in the same way that marketing plans should be passed to sales for acceptance before they become fact), and marketing will either need to accept any strategies used by sales in the plans or come up with some alternatives. Usually it is the former!

The more desirable way of operating is through a well-established marketing planning discipline, concentrating on how the company will achieve its goals, not just market definition.

The account profile

The account profile becomes very important, especially in industrial selling. This is because the larger organisations with which you, the supplier, deal can be very complex, and often make decisions in different ways. There will be individuals whose job it is to administer purchases, then there will be those who need to technically approve the product. The operations people, who actually use the product, may also have a say. In some cases a product may need to be 'specified' before you even get to make a commercial offer. In some selling, getting the specifications written so that they favour your own product can be a powerful way of selling. This happens when there are engineers, architects and developers involved in construction sites. Knowing all these people, how they operate and their role in the decision making process becomes very important.

It is also useful to know how they relate to each other, and who is likely to have the final say. As Australia develops its export market for manufactured products, there is a greater need for cooperation between supplier and purchaser to meet the needs of export markets. It then becomes important to talk with the customer's sales and marketing people.

An organisation chart is by far the most useful way of collecting information on the customer's organisation, because it allows you to express reporting and matrix relationships.

The account profile on direct accounts will include a section on how the product is used. This may mean a technical explanation, and may require detail of how your product specification and quality affects their productivity. You need to know how your products perform relative to others. This is not just a generic answer for all occasions; it may depend on the exact product the customer is making, and on their equipment and processes. There can often be opportunities for you to maximise their own productivity by either different operating conditions or by changing your product slightly to meet their processing needs.

The technical aspects of the account profile can be very detailed and complicated. In many cases it will require the input of technical people to get all the information. Partly because they understand it better, but also because you will often find that the customer's technical people tend to mistrust your sales people but will open up far more to your technical people.

One area often neglected is the market where the customer sells the final products, assuming that your product is used in a manufacturing process. You need to know what percentage of their total costs your product represents, and how critical it is to the overall product result. You need to understand who their customers and their competitors are. Do you supply their competitors too? Are there any useful alliances, whereby you can gain share through this particular customer's own share growth?

In a more strategic sense, there is the issue of corporate ownership, relationships and objectives. It can be important to see who is on whose board, and what kind of influence they might exert. This keeps changing, but you should try to keep abreast of the changes. The account management job is always complicated by the selling and buying of companies which has become a fact of life of Australian and international businesses. While you may not be able to influence or even predict who might buy and sell whom, you need to be aware of what is happening, and try to ally yourselves with the companies buying rather than the ones being sold. A fabulous way of growing your business with hardly any tears is when a customer of yours buys out a company which was buying from your competitor. The competitor usually does not even react, believing that there was nothing they could have done about it and that it was just your good luck that you won the business and they lost it. This is nothing like the way the competition is likely to react if one supplier wins the business from another, especially if it is perceived that it was done on price rather than service or other 'worthy' factors.

'Knowledge Equals Power' is right when it comes to knowing about your customers. It may take a long time to build up the sort of quality data bank you want, but at least the sooner you make a start the sooner you will reach your goal.

The account SWOT

The criteria used in distributive businesses for choosing suppliers are well understood and mainly easy to predict. They should revolve around ROII per shelf space, and a few long term strategic considerations. They might even extend to generosity in rebates, promotional funds and terms. In these businesses most elements can be quantified.

But in direct accounts the situation is not always quite as clear. You need to really find out how your customer decides, recognising that the customer will always tell you that price is the key issue. You need to understand how important to them are items such as:
• specification of product
• quality and consistency of quality
• delivery
• packaging
• technical back-up
• trouble shooting capability
• Australian component
• availability.

It can be useful to try to rate these items, and although it will never be an accurate assessment it might point to the issues where you are best advised to concentrate your efforts, simply because they are the most important issues for the customer.

It is most important that the issues from this SWOT analysis are brought forward into the plan for action.

Value-added search

In distributive businesses the opportunity is fairly straightforward. You, the supplier, are looking for where you could sell more product into the marketplace and therefore increase volumes for both yourself and the customer.

In direct selling the identification of ways of adding value is the key to differentiation. You can try to bring your capabilities to bear on any area where the customer could be making or saving money. Traditionally this has been achieved through product differentiation and, to the extent that your company can still develop differentiated products, it is the best differentiation you can find because it takes a long time for competitors to catch up. Price differentiation can be matched easily. This is why some of the most successful companies are pouring money into product development. The problem is that development costs are so high and there are now so many players in the business, that there is less product differentiation. This is exacerbated by the fact that many products are coming out of patent.

211

The facts of life are that companies are having to find non-product ways of differentiating themselves. This means looking at all the aspects of supply, which have an effect on customer costs, and even looking outside the normal areas of supply to see where our total abilities as a company can meet any customer needs. There is no reason why these cannot in principle be divorced from the product they buy from us. It is a question of looking at our ability to contribute to their bottom line in whatever way possible.

How well you, the supplier, can come up with ways of adding value depends on a couple of things, one of which is how well you know the customer. The better you know the customer, their people, how they operate and the results they get, the easier it is to find ways of helping them do better. The value-added search exercise is much harder for customers you do not know well. The first time you do the exercise, you may just end up saying that there are so many areas of the customer's operation which you do not understand that you need to build the account profile first. That is fine, as long as you then do it. The account management system is a long-term commitment: it is not all going to happen in the first six months.

The other issue is how flexible your organisation is and the extent to which resources from anywhere in the company might be available to support work at customers. There is a danger in overcommitting resources in a total account management program, and this must not be allowed to happen. The person who controls the resources must always be asked before a commitment is made to include them in a plan.

A real commitment to key account management implies a readiness of the whole organisation to accept that they may be called upon to assist the sales effort.

At the end of the process of working through a value-added search, you should be able to identify some key items with which you choose to work.

> Key items will be the ones which best meet these criteria:
> * consistent with your own marketing plans
> * consistent with the customer's objectives and priorities
> * availability of resources within your organisation
> * the ROI you will get—the recognition of added value relative to the cost to you of providing the differentiation.

Pick a few issues which you know you can handle well. These few points should form the backbone of the account plan, which is the next step.

Key account plans

These plans are internal plans written by the account manager and used to manage the business on a daily basis. They represent the synthesis of all of the previous steps. You need to decide over what period the plan should be written. This can be quite flexible, since it is an internal document, so that you can have plans for a shorter period when the account is active, and a longer period when there is not as much activity. You should also spread the plans so that not all of them have to be written at the same time, and not all the BRADs, at the end of the planning period, need to be conducted at the same time.

The main decision, however, which needs to be made, is whether to use a full format such as that in Figure 9, or a reduced format. For large accounts or ones where there is a lot of activity the full one should be used. Since the plan reflects the collecting of information and ideas from a number of sources, it is important to start the process by doing exactly that—collecting your ideas from all sources. If this is not done there is always the risk that there are important issues which are forgotten. The headings to be addressed include:
* any areas of the account profile where there are gaps you need to fill
* any relationships which need to be expanded or built up

- the key opportunities from the value-added search
- any actions which need to be taken as a result of the SWOT analysis
- any other issues in the business which need to be taken into account.

Objectives and strategies

At this point you have everything ready to go, but before you start transferring items from the first page to the plan itself, it is a good idea to set your objectives independently from the work you have done so far. The reason for this is that sometimes what appears to be a good idea can get carried into a plan, when in fact the idea may not have really been consistent with the objectives at that account. In other words, we tend to plan to do things because we can or think it would be nice or good fun, and sometimes lose sight of what we want to achieve at that account. The discipline of setting objectives involves standing back from the previous work and asking yourself what you want to achieve at this account. You may ask the question over a short term, such as the currency of the plan, or you might look at much longer-term objectives.

There will of course be quantitative objectives, generally about sales results. They could include something on your share of the customer's business. But there might also be other quantifiable objectives. These could include:

- delivery performance
- share
- penetration
- cost of transport
- margins on certain products
- growth.

Some of these items might derive from a profitability analysis, and others may be from the SWOT analysis. There will also be some qualitative, or nonnumerical objectives. These should still be measurable and desirable end results. Examples might well include:

- gaining certain business
- becoming the accepted partner in the customer's export business
- changing the basis on which you do business (removing clauses from contracts)
- becoming the favoured supplier
- initially gaining a supply position on a minor product in order to establish your ability as a supplier.

The strategies are the ploys you will use to achieve these objectives, and these should depend on, or at least be consistent with, the items from the first page, especially the selected items from the value-added search. It is debated sometimes whether something is a strategy or an objective. This matter was covered in the first part of the book: the key issue is that objectives are the results you want. If the overall achievement, for example, a target sales result, is very dependent on a certain issue, although that issue may be more of a strategy but is described as an objective in the plan, because of its importance, it really does not matter. What is important is that the way the plan is written forces you, the writer, to think through what you are doing with the account, so that the activities support what you want from the account.

It is worth giving more thought to what the objectives and strategies are, as they set the direction of the whole plan, and just putting in the sales budget figure is not going to do justice to the art of account management.

If there are longer-term objectives beyond the currency of the plan, they may be included to provide context for the objectives of the current plan. If you have a more formalised planning discipline, it can be useful to number the objectives and the strategies. An objective might be numbered 1. The strategies to support that objective might be 1.1, and 1.2. The activities reflecting that strategy become 1.1.1, 1.1.2, 1.1.3 and then 1.2.1, 1.2.2 and so on.

214

This is fine in principle and it is a disciplined way of making sure that activities do flow directly from objectives. The problem is that some strategies may serve more than one objective, and some activities may support more than one strategy. It is always better to list the activities in chronological order, and if you do that the flow of the numbering system is lost to a certain extent. If you use a computer you can do it both ways.

Strategies, since they are ploys, tend to be less easy to measure than objectives and activities. There is a danger therefore that if you take the activities from the strategies, you may end up with some rather 'woolly' plans.

· · · · · · · · · · · · · · · · · · ·

Activities

The activities are the most important part of the whole plan.

Activities must be:
• detailed
• complete
• capable of being determined
• timed
• indicate who is responsible.

All the items on the front page including issues to be addressed from the account profile, account SWOT, value-added search and relationship-building actions must all be brought forward so that they appear in the activities. You should check that this is so, unless at the point where you considered the objectives you decided to delete some items from that first page. This might happen, for example, to an item selected from the value-added search, which on further thought and analysis did not fit with the objectives at that account.

Remember that these plans should be made accountable documents, and should be signed off by the account manager and his/her supervisor, both when the plan is accepted as valid, and at the end of the period when the plan should have been completed.

. . . .

BRAD meetings

Reviews are an integral part of the way that the supermarket chains conduct business with their suppliers, but have traditionally not been so much a part of life for those selling to direct accounts. Reviewing business regularly becomes very important, because it allows a reassessment of the total business relationship and ensures that both sides are getting the best out of the business relationship. Even when there is project selling, such as in the construction business, there should be a BRAD at the end of the project. The occasions when one sale is made to an organisation and never repeated are very rare. Wherever there are key accounts, the business tends to be ongoing.

In direct selling there is less rigidity in the sorts of agenda which may be appropriate, and they will depend very much on the mutual issues in the business. This makes it much more important for the supplier to add agenda items from the customer to their own.

The feeling of the meeting must be one of mutuality, openness, constructive discussion and trust. Where the supplier has been doing a reasonably good job, this will happen without much effort, but where it has not, the chairperson of the meeting (normally the account manager) might need some very good skills in running meetings (see *The Effective Sales Manager*, Chapter 14). There is an element of soft sell in these meetings, where you, the supplier, are seeking to establish with the customer that you have indeed added value to the package. There is likely to be some degree of 'manipulation' in that you may want to force the purchasing people to recognise a technical advantage you have created with their technical people, or perhaps in the service area. Opening up communication requires different skills from the normal one-on-one selling. Such issues must really be hidden agendas in that you do not want the customer to transparently see that you are in any way being manipulative, yet at the same time you must be. The art of subtlety is critical.

It also means that getting the right people and the right mix of people to these meetings is very important. The better the reputation of your BRAD meetings within the customer organisation, the better the chances are that you will get the people you want. It means that the first meetings you hold are very important. If you mess those up you will find it hard to get people to the next ones. This makes life difficult because the first meetings are not likely to be as good as later ones. The implication is that when you first start holding these meetings you need to 'cut your teeth' on some easy ones, usually with customers where you both have good relationships with a wide range of people within both organisations and where you have performed well, particularly where there has been differentiation created and where you can show that you have added value to the package.

This will give the account manager some experience in organising and running these meetings before they have to conduct one at a more difficult account. The principles of BRADs for direct accounts follow those expressed in Chapter 3.

The challenge in the longer term is to keep up the interest. As long as you have some reasonable account plans you should be able to run some good BRADs with most customers until there seems to be not much new to say. This may be the time to reduce the frequency with which you hold BRADs. There will always be ongoing things which will need to be covered, but unless you are careful, they can become mundane. Changing the venue can help, and combining them with a plant visit is a good idea. You may look for other people within your organisation to make a presentation, as long as it is on a subject where the customer derives some benefit. You could even consider doing some joint workshop work with a professional external facilitator, or getting an independent person to address the group on a subject of mutual interest.

Like any relationship, it needs a bit of spice from time to time to keep it healthy.

Businesses where there are specifiers

There are some businesses, especially anything to do with the construction industry, where there are several people, such as architects, contractors, specifiers, owners, civil engineers and so on, who could be involved in a buying decision. This complicates the normal selling process.

There is a need to have contact with the major players in each of these areas to establish the right relationships, promote your company and products and services in general, and to lobby for specifications to be written round your offerings. This is an ongoing work in preparation for when or if a project might be born which involves them. It is what I call 'tilling the soil'—preparing the ground for the day a seed drops.

This is an account management job, and it should be done for the key players in any of the areas where there are influencers in your business. However, in any year there may be more or less projects which happen and which involve that particular party.

When a project does happen, there needs to be a coordination of what the company does at whoever the organisations involved in the project turn out to be. This would be a cross between an account plan and a project plan. If one mentally substitutes the word 'project' for account, and then operates the account management system as normal, including actions and steps in the cycle involving possible several influencers, it will work well. Often there needs to be a team handling such projects. The leader could be considered as the project account manager.

217

. . . .

Negotiation

It is inevitable that the subject of negotiation should arise. In direct selling the plans are internal, unlike distributive businesses where the plans are the presentation from which agreement will be negotiated with the trading partner. In direct selling the negotiation might take place at any time, either as decreed by the end of a contractual arrangement, or because a need has arisen. The negotiation is important because it is through the result of the negotiation that you find whether you have managed to achieve one of the objectives of account management, that of less focus on price.

There are many approaches to negotiation and quite a few miss what I believe to be an essential point—the question of when you handle a commercial objection.

In selling, when you are trying to persuade what must be assumed an initially reluctant person to change their mind, there is a different process at work. The objections are generally real or perceived problems with the whole concept of the purchase. There is no harm therefore in dealing with these as they arise and getting them out of the way. There may be another objection, but the resolution of that next one will normally not be affected by the resolution of the first one. It is just a question of removing the barriers to the concept of buying one by one.

The 'commercial objection' is different, in that it might affect the exchange of money or concessions. It is not when the customer seeks further clarification or asks a general question.

> Commercial objections are:
> - we would need to have longer payment terms than that
> - the price would need to be lower
> - we could never commit to that sort of period
> - you would need to provide a longer warranty service
> - we want more free service calls than you propose
> - we could not place single orders that large.

If you handle each commercial objection as it occurs you will start to exchange concessions, or even give concessions away for nothing, without knowing what other things the customer is likely to bring up. This means that there is a very real danger of trading all the concessions you had intended when the customer hits you with one you had not expected, and you end up having to give away more than you wanted to or ought to have given.

The way round this is to avoid haggling over any single issue until you know all the issues that the customer wants to argue over. Once you know what the negotiating arena is going to be, you can start handling each item against the background of the other items. Any approach to negotiation which does not make this specific point must be treated with suspicion.

When you make your presentations you should include a list of concessions you want from the customer. If you do not specify items which might help you, even if it is only forecasts or to stop deducting items off their invoices without specifying them, or returning pallets, it will be much harder to get them included later.

Be very careful about introducing clauses which could disadvantage you if things change, especially when long term contracts are involved. Anything which ignores the fact that the world is a capricious place is dangerous. Fixed prices, assumptions about interest rates or exchange rates can lead you into an unprofitable deal from one which appeared very good when it was agreed. Even price escalation clauses linked to CPI can be wrong because CPI is not a fundamental measure and is affected by non-business cost factors. Do not assume that the future will be like the past or you can get caught out.

Negotiation is the one area of the relationship between supplier and customer which is mostly combative. In the major areas of negotiation a concession by one party leads to benefit of the other, and vice versa. Inevitably this leads to tension and problems in the relationship. However, the overall relationship built up through account management should be such that both parties will recognise the advantages of coming to agreement. There should be more mutual ground in relationships, and this needs to be worked upon.

If the account management process is working, there will be more of a desire for give and take in the negotiation in order to not jeopardise an arrangement which serves both parties well. For this reason it is better to negotiate at a point at the end of any given cycle, after the cycle has been completed and the BRAD held.

Creative differentiation strategies

. . . .

Introduction

It would be wonderful to provide readers with an exhaustive list or menu of creative differentiation from which they could pick, according to their company situation. Unfortunately life is not that easy. To do that would in any case produce an incomplete list, and it would deflect thought into existing channels rather than force the reader to think about individual accounts.

The process of determining the opportunities to add value and to differentiate yourself from other suppliers must be a combination of the opportunities at that particular account and the capabilities of your own company. It is a process of thought and enquiry which should be original for each account. There may be certain avenues of differentiation which you as a company in a total sense are intending to create and which would be part of the marketing strategy. This might include the intent to provide a certain level of technical back-up, or application technology, or packaging or delivery method. But the search for differentiation is best when it goes beyond these ploys, it incorporates them then builds on them and individualises them to the situation.

A list to choose from is therefore not going to be provided. However, some ideas are given which might spark more concrete thoughts in the reader.

. . . .

Product differentiation

As was said before, if you can develop products so that you can stay in front on the basis of product differentiation, that is the best differentiation you can create. With technically based products that is quite difficult to achieve, and very costly. The fact is that the amount of product differentiation is decreasing, in a world dominated by ever more complex technology, which means that there has been enormous waste with several companies spending money on developing the same products. Internationalisation of business and takeovers have to a certain extent attenuated the process.

It is a bit easier to develop product differentiation in the service industries. To do this effectively marketing people need to find out what services customers expect, especially any items which are not currently being provided. Market research plays the major role in such enquiry. Surveys on services are part of life in many service organisations, but even then it is questionable whether surveys are the best way to find out what the customer wants and is not getting. The reason for this is that those who fill out the surveys are not encouraged to think laterally about what they would like, but rather to respond simplistically to the services currently being provided.

A better way may be a group discussion, if you can get the right people, meaning those who use the services regularly, who are good conceptual thinkers and communicators, and are mature and even creative. During the group discussion a professional facilitator can direct discussion along new paths, with those present feeding ideas off each other, leading to the identification of some good workable ideas.

This process works well for the service industries, but can be considered also for manufacturing industries. This requires much greater care, in the same way that caution was recommended in chapter 3 in involving customers in a value-added search exercise. Even so, as long as you make it quite clear that your company is looking for ideas, not making any premature commitments to action, there can be some value in getting a few individuals together from a small number of customers. This should not be restricted to product development, but should include things like packaging, delivery methods and so on.

If you work for a company which has good product differentiation, good luck to you. If not, you are going to need to look for non-product ideas and, for heavily product-oriented companies, this is quite a challenge.

Building on technical advantage

There are two ways where the technical ability of a company can be capitalised on. One is in the ability to trouble-shoot, that is, when problems arise, to go and solve them effectively. This is something like insurance. If a customer buys a technically complex product and there is a chance it could go wrong, unless the customer can fix it themselves, the speed with which the problem can be fixed is an important consideration. In some businesses this is such an issue that service contracts are more lucrative than selling the original equipment. This has certainly been true of products as different as computers, medical equipment and elevators, for example.

The other technical issue is in terms of application technology. If you, the supplier, are able to develop an expertise in how to use the products you sell, such that you can outperform your own customers and do so better than your competitors, you have some valuable differentiation. The question becomes how to make it a sustainable advantage and capitalise on that expertise.

This may not be a good strategy for all businesses. It works well when the efficiency in using the product substantially affects the results obtained, and where the savings to the customer are therefore substantial. Then it is worth investing money in keeping on top of the application technology.

Reflecting technical advantage in price

The trick is to get such an advantage reflected in price, rather than letting it become a service which is provided free of charge. If the process used by the customer in using your product is discrete from other processes, one idea is for you to set yourselves up to perform the whole operation. As long as you are confident that you can consistently get better results than the customers, you can offer to take over that operation and provide a service incorporating your product and the application technology, and charge accordingly. This may have considerable advantages for the customer, who can cut down on fixed costs. The advantage to you the supplier is, especially if there are not other competitors who can provide this forward integrated service as well as you can, that it takes the price of the product out of the equation altogether and defies easy comparison with other suppliers. It also means that the customer is tied much more closely to you the supplier. This may be seen initially by the customer as a barrier, as they would be putting themselves at your mercy. On the other hand, if there is a mature relationship, both parties need to recognise that if one can perform a service more cost-effectively than the other, it makes sense to find a way of using the ability of the more competent party. This has been used in the mining industry, and it has worked well.

The main message about technical service is that it costs a lot of money, and it should be directed to where the most differentiation can be created and where the best trade off for the service can be won. Generally that tends to be in application rather than in trouble-shooting. People are more likely to buy something giving them an advantage every day, rather than buy insurance.

The other way, which is good when the process using your product is part of a more complex operation involving other products and equipment, is for some kind of service fee or contract which is built into supply. This is almost like running your own consultancy business alongside the product business. You can make a modest charge for this, on the basis that people value less the things they get for nothing, or you can set an overtly higher price for the package but include a defined level of consultancy service.

The technical people must see themselves very much as part of the sales and marketing arm, and ideally should report through marketing rather than through research and development or a separate technical manager. There needs to be careful coordination between what the technical people do and the requirements of account management. If you are using technical muscle as part of the differentiation strategy it makes sense to have the technical people involved in the process of writing and implementing the plans.

The role of technical people in the traditionally technically based multinationals needs to be reviewed. Unless they are making a real contribution to creating differentiation, it should be considered whether they should continue to be there. This does not mean that I am advocating getting rid of technical people, but many of them should be redirected into different operations with a different focus.

The commercialisation of technical people should be a priority. Too many technical people feel divorced from the business of making money. They may not even understand how their own endeavours fit into their company profit, and even less the financial impact they can have on the customer. Technical people need to understand basic business operation and be able to recommend actions to customers on the basis of sound business common sense. They should be able to talk to customers about the financial impact of the work they do and the recommendations they make.

. . . .

Materials management

As companies have been forced to look at every aspect of their operations in order to see where they can save money and prevent losses, one of their priorities has been inventory and transport of goods. The first thing companies have tried to do is conserve their working capital by holding exactly the right level of inventory. Thus we have seen JIT systems appear. In many cases of course the initiative for these improvements has come from the customer not the supplier. The supplier plays a role in the degree to which they can help the customer make programs like JIT work.

This depends not only on the operational abilities of the supplier to plan to have goods at the right place at the right time, but also on the communication systems both parties set up to handle any changes from the expected norm, because that is where the system usually falters. Often when the customer carries the minimum stock and expects immediate delivery to keep at that level, the costs saved by the customer are more than offset by the extra costs incurred by the supplier. This is not good business for either in the long run. It is much better to find a way of cutting costs by making the materials handling issue more efficient for both sides, and share the savings. This requires discussion, tabling of how materials are handled by both sides currently, and working together to find the efficiencies.

Usually there are plenty of opportunities for savings. Transport in a country like Australia is expensive. The question of where stock points should be located, whether decentralising stock requires greater stock to supply the market, and methods of delivery are all key issues which need the consideration of experts.

There have been various attempts by suppliers to offer customers something other than price. One of them has been consignment stock. The problem with consignment stock is that while it does make life easier for the customer, it also encourages lazy stock control practices. This adds to the costs of the supplier, considerably reduces stock availability for other customers and means that more stock is required to support the business. Once it has been introduced it is also quite difficult to take away. Unless you have a customer in Dry Salt Creek, 500 km out of Longreach or Tennant Creek, where you are better advised to put in consignment stock, don't touch it. It costs an arm and a leg in wasted inventory and is a pain to administer. It often leads to arguments about the condition of the stock, the age of the stock, and the insurance cover. Inevitably the supplier is the one who usually bears the losses. Instead ask the customer what he or she thinks consignment stock would achieve, and then look for another way to achieve it.

Payment terms

Another area to be wary of is extended terms. Many companies have tried to gain advantage, while others had to equal the offer by extending terms. In the plastics industry in the late 1970s and the early 1980s there were customers paying on 120 days from end of month invoice (effectively getting up to 150 days free credit), rather than the usual 30 days. This created some terrifying exposure problems and there were many nervous finance directors. The sales people refused to see this as a problem, until there were a few nasty bankruptcies which cost some multinationals (who should have known better) sums of money they could ill afford to lose.

Once you create the cash flow for the customer to do other things (the customer will tell you to expand the business for both of you), it is very hard for the customer to rein in the payment terms again. They need to create cash flow to do so from other sources. The worst scenario is when the business turns down and when the interest rates rise, which is what happened at the end of the last decade. As a result suppliers have learned the dangers of extended credit, although we wonder whether the same mistakes will be repeated. More fashionable lately has been paying a rebate for early settlement. If the customer pays within seven days there is a 1–2 per cent discount. Even when corporate overdraft rates were at 18 per cent per annum, or 1.5 per cent per month, a rebate of over 1.2 per cent for payment three weeks earlier was not attractive to the supplier. Now that corporate overdraft rates are far less, even 1 per cent is costing you the supplier money. It is just another way of throwing money at your customer, although there may be times when some financial assistance could be a good idea. If you can get a licence as a moneylender (some companies have one), you can provide bills so that the customer pays the interest, but you carry the risk. This helps the customer over points where the cash is tight, but does not become an ongoing arrangement.

225

Delivery and packaging

How you deliver can also be an issue, including the size of the orders, the way product is stacked, how much damage occurs in transit, type of pallets, return of pallets, ease of stacking and unstacking, and transport around the customer's plant. The chances are that any improvements which can be made here will reduce costs for both sides, and thus is well worth investigating.

Packaging becomes another issue, especially when there are export markets being developed by Australian manufacturers. All these areas are best looked at by pooling the ideas and experiences of the supplier and the customers. It is true that in the area of packaging, changes generally need to be made globally rather than on an account-by-account basis. You might even argue that this is a marketing issue rather than an account management one, but the two disciplines need to be brought together in any case.

Do not be afraid to invest money in looking at what is happening overseas. We as a nation have been good about travelling to see what the rest of the world is doing, but we need to adapt and adopt more ideas.

There have been many innovations in delivery and packaging, such as bulk, minibulk and so on for fluids. The ownership of silos and bulk facilities and questions of contamination arise, but generally the supplier who has facilities on the customer's premises tends to have an advantage. It can be quite a good investment to take the initiative to place them there.

. . . .

Sales and marketing

One area of customers' business where we tend to be weak is in the knowledge of their sales and marketing and in knowing their sales and marketing people, and what their priorities are. There are real opportunities which can arise from a closer relationship between the sales and marketing staff of suppliers and customers.

Sometimes the supplier may have experience or ideas and expertise where the customer does not. It may require diplomatic handling, but there have been cases where the customer has been ready to accept some help from the supplier in areas where they see themselves as being weak.

This can particularly occur where the supplier has already established an export business, and the customer has not but wishes to. There can even be contacts for possible representation in the overseas markets which the supplier can pass on. Export is a very different business, and however many seminars people attend there is nothing like being able to talk to someone who has practical experience, and who can tell you the pitfalls to watch out for.

I have seen a customer ask the assistance of a supplier in putting together their presentation for a large contract. They recognised that they did not have the expertise themselves.

When your marketing people travel overseas to see what new things are around, they should also have a brief to look at the markets for the products which are made using your products. On their return they should be expected to talk to some of the major customers about the opportunities they have discovered.

There may be opportunities to invest in activities which will create business for both parties. This was the original concept of cooperative advertising which was discussed in earlier chapters, but that became part of the rebate system. This needs to be kept in mind, but there are more opportunities for joint investment in projects to sell more product for both supplier and customer. This may be for some initial price break (but make sure that this is not invested in price in the marketplace, as it could prejudice profitability of the whole business). It is far better to invest in promotional activity of some sort. Again, this is an area where you may have expertise, and where the customer does not. The advantage of getting involved with new projects like this is that you are perceived by the customer to have some moral ownership over the business, which is a very useful thing to have. Maybe it even needs to be written into the contract somehow, as long as you do not break the law (on restrictive trade practices).

227

Management and administration

This is the area where unless you really manage to create the right working relationship between supplier and customer, it is hard to capitalise on joint strengths. But if you can, there are some very interesting opportunities for creating differentiation. They cover virtually any aspect of the operation of a company, and there is plenty of opportunity to be creative.

Some of the areas where I know suppliers have worked with customers to share expertise and add value to their relationship and the total package are in:
- communications systems
- information processing systems
- management systems
- industrial relations issues
- safety
- environmental control
- laboratory design and testing procedures
- legal advice
- economic assumptions and market assumptions for planning purposes.

There are as many possibilities as there are activities which a company undertakes. If you as a supplier know your customer so well that you know exactly how they operate and where their cost centres are across the whole range of operations of the company, and where they could do better, you have one side of the equation right in finding opportunities.

The second side of the equation is to know what you as a company do well. This can be forced on you by unforeseen circumstances. When I was working as National Sales Manager at Union Carbide Australia, we had the longest lock-in in Australian industrial history, basically over the issue of the thirty-five hour week. There were many customers who were facing exactly the same challenges in their business. The Managing Director of Union Carbide Australia at the time was an American, Vern Larson. He made a point of giving upper management of our major customers his analysis of what had happened, with some tips in hindsight on what worked and what did not in the negotiation process, and the resolution of the strike. This I believe was of invaluable help to many of the major customers, and they were very appreciative of the offer made by him. It also enabled some very useful relationships to be forged at the highest levels, and some in principle commitments were made about the way the companies were to work together.

It is the account manager who must know the customer and know the capabilities of his or her own company so well, that he or she can match them to the benefit of both. Many large organisations are placed at a disadvantage to smaller ones producing or selling essentially the same product, because of a larger and more expensive overhead structure (although many of these have been reduced dramatically over the last few years). At the same time, these larger companies have general expertise in areas where the smaller ones do not. An example is the experience ICI Australia had with communication systems. They had studied them all in some detail and were in a good position to tell people what they had found out. If you are a large company with a large overhead and with some good sound management and administration expertise, make it work for you by sharing this with your customers. The lower-overhead competitors will not generally be able to do it. It becomes a way of getting a better return on the money you have invested in corporate overheads.

. . . .

When products move to commodities

There are many areas where there is less and less product differentiation. Many of the products which were specialised products ten years ago, have become commodities. Patents expire, the customers become more technically competent, and there is a tendency to feel that the only place for the discussion with a customer to go is price. This is where consideration of an account management approach becomes even more important. It may be easier to operate account management when there is real opportunity for product or technical differentiation, but in some ways it becomes even more important where there is a real need to find some other way of differentiating, and these elements are absent. In other words, when the products turn into commodities. It is very important for a company to recognise when this is happening, preferably before it does! That way they can reposition themselves on their own terms. The marketing people will need to change their strategy, and you the company may even be better advised to bring in new people who have more expertise in the marketing of commodities. For multinationals, in particular, who have had the prestige, the products and the technology, there has been a tendency for them not to market or to sell. The sales people have been order takers and consultants. But once the differentiation of product and technology has disappeared, it leaves an enormous gap. The sales people tend not to be very street wise, or even service or customer oriented. There are still a few multinationals who have a reputation of being dictatorial, inflexible bureaucracies.

This means that a change in culture is needed. Some organisations are not able to adjust to this change, but unless they do their long-term prospects are dim. We have all seen that although a company has been large and dominant in an industry, this is no guarantee of survival.

When you find yourself selling what have become commodities, you need to change. You may need to reassess the role of technical resource, you may need to change your marketing strategy, and you certainly will need to find some other ways of differentiating yourself in the market. That is most likely to be in the areas already covered in this chapter.

You can try to cut overhead or offer a commodity service with a commodity product at a commodity price, but unless you are able to be the lowest cost producer in the market, do not attempt to sell on price. If you are not the lowest-cost producer and you cannot create any differentiation which the customer will value, such that they are prepared to pay some kind of a premium, unless the business is returning you a comfortable ROI you can only get out of the business as soon as possible.

Usually there are options to create differentiation, and maybe only when the drastic option just stated seems to be real will companies look seriously at account management.

PART 5

Making Key Account Management Work

13

Interpersonal relationships and account management

. . . .
Introduction

Most of this book is about the basic subjects of gathering information, thinking through the business, and planning activities with major accounts, implementing them and then reviewing them. This is a necessary part of the success of doing business with customers, but it is not sufficient. There is one very important area which we should discuss—the fact that all the account management program is implemented through people dealing with other people. Account management is closely intertwined with establishing and maintaining the right interpersonal relationships.

. . . .
Establishing relationships with the right people

Apart from the question of interpersonal skills, the first issue is identifying the people within both the supplier and the customer organisations who should have some kind of relationship.

The rule of thumb must be that you the supplier should establish a relationship with all those people within the customer's organisation who do or could influence the purchasing decision, or are involved in making it. It is also dangerous for the supplier to leave all those relationships in the hands of one account manager who could leave or move to another position, and thus create a void. The supplier should ensure that there are relationships with several people within the supplier organisation. This is not easy. The candidates to be involved, such as sales managers, product managers and marketing people are also busy with their own direct tasks. It means that the contacts will be less frequent than with the account manager, but they should be planned as part of the account plan visit schedule.

Ideal opportunities for such contact is in BRAD meetings, where relationships can be established involving several people at the same time. Industry meetings or even social events can be useful. Entertaining clients in the evening is a good way of doing it, because the individuals are more relaxed and do not feel that the meeting is detracting from their work in the day.

234

Generally there will be a need to match levels within companies. There are very few suppliers who have managed to build up the status of their account managers to the point where on their own they can get the CEO of a customer out to dinner. It happens occasionally in the USA, but very rarely here. If you the supplier want to get to know the CEO of your customer, the chances are that you will need to field your own CEO to manage it.

The starting point in deciding who you need to know is the account profile, in particular, the organisational chart. Identify the influencers and the decision makers, and anyone you believe who could be a target for an approach by your competitors. Then decide how, when and with whom the relationships should be built, and then include those as part of the account plan. You will also find that there will be people in the customer organisation you need to know in order to find out where there are opportunities for you to grow their business. For example, one of the areas where few suppliers know the personnel of their customers is the sales and marketing area, yet there can be some very useful relationships established there. The supplier gets a better idea of what the customer's needs are in his or her own market, which in turn may influence the supplier's product. Furthermore, when marketing people get together there are sometimes some opportunities for synergy.

The customer's sales and marketing people may not influence the purchasing decision directly, but they are certainly important people to know if you want to find value-added opportunities.

Rational versus emotional decisions

This book has been very much focused on the rational value for money business decisions we expect our customers to make. But do they always make rational business decisions? Some psychologists believe they often do not; that especially when it comes to some large decisions, there is a rational thought process which the decision maker undertakes, but at the last minute they make an emotional decision then rationalise it. It is certainly true that there are usually advantages and disadvantages with all of the options when making any major decision, which lead to Festinger's cognitive dissonance. Because there are negatives attached to the chosen option, the individual still feels some internal conflict. The way they try to overcome that is to minimise them in their own mind, and build up the positive aspects of the option chosen. That is why there are some very entrenched opinions either in favour of Ford and against Holden, or the other way around, when in fact the offers of the two companies are very similar.

What certainly is true is that people like doing business with the people they like. There is more business lost through poor relationships or service than are lost through poor quality. I don't have statistics to prove it, but I would bet that poor relationships have lost more business than high prices.

Do as you would be done by

If you think through your own personal experience of buying or using a service, the chances are that when you have changed supplier it has often been because you thought they had not treated you right, or that you felt you had been taken for granted, or even abused. During the pilots' strike, prior to which I had been an Ansett customer, there were several annoying things Ansett had done to me, but one night one of their supervisors in reservations made what I considered to be a totally offensive remark. I have never flown with them since, and am now Gold Frequent Flyer status with Qantas, and very satisfied overall. One remark by one person lost them an account which is worth tens of thousands of dollars a year. What is even worse for Ansett is that even though they had the chance to come and talk about it with me, and indeed said they would, they never did. I feel no hesitation in telling as many people about that experience as I can. The point is that it can take years to build the right relationships, but they can be destroyed in a second.

The most sound common sense in relationships is to 'do as you would be done by'. If you are about to treat a customer in a way you would not like to be treated, or you are about to say something which would offend you, or use a tone of voice you would object to if someone adopted it with you, then stop and do not do it.

General rules

Everyone is different, and these differences are what makes up personality. But there are far more similarities in terms of people's expectations in how they are to be treated than there are differences. It is therefore possible to set some overall good rules for dealing with people. Note, however, that these rules are culturally based: in other countries and in other cultures these need to be revised and maybe reinterpreted. If you take a word like 'respect', it may mean different behaviour in different places. One of the keys to exporting, especially to countries with a very different culture from our own, is to ensure that you get to know the culture and modify your behaviour accordingly. The most important thing to learn is patience.

236

Some elements of behaviour you should adopt, at least in Australia:
- show respect
- address people in the way they want to be addressed
- focus your conversation on them not on you
- listen carefully to what they say
- listen carefully to what they do not say, and you might have expected them to say
- do not interrupt when they are talking
- wear appropriate dress for the situation
- be on time and keep to other deadlines
- watch your body language
- don't tell the customer about your problems
- put things from their point of view
- choose your words carefully
- show a genuine interest in them and their business
- show you remember, and keep notes to remind you if it helps
- keep confidences
- information on current topics is fine, but do not gossip
- do not patronise
- provide information in a humble way
- watch your own ego
- know the 'no-no's' to avoid
- if in any doubt, do not say it
- think before you speak
- always let the other person save face.

Individual differences

It is the differences between our personalities which make us individuals, and to be completely successful in interpersonal relationships we need to address these differences and respond accordingly. This does not mean that the account manager should change personality depending on the person with whom they are dealing. You must always be yourself; you should never try to change your basic personality. What you need to modify is your behaviour. This means that you need to be sensitive to the personality of the person you are dealing with, and modify your approach through the right choice of words and the way you go about things, so that you are most likely to get on well with that person and avoid annoying them. The best sales people tend to do this naturally, and women tend to be better at it than men. But anyone can develop skills in this area, especially if they stop and think about it first. The key is to recognise some of the different personalities and then modify your approach to fit in with them.

Understanding personalities: trait theory

Much psychology is based on theories of personality. Out of these theories come approaches to motivation, therapy and so on. Most of the psychological testing which was so popular in the 1970s, and is now coming back into fashion is based on trait theories, which say that a person can be described by the extent to which they exhibit certain elements or traits. The normal way you find this out is to get the individual to answer a battery of questions, then analyse the answers to understand their profile. Some of these tests have been well tested and normed and some have not. There are extroversion—introversion models, there is needs for power, achievement and affiliation, and so on. One of the best tests from my own experience is the Humm-Wadsworth test, which is operated in Australia by Chandler and Macleod. This sees the personality as a mix of seven different elements or traits.

Christopher Golis has simplified the Humm-Wadsworth model into an approach to address the subject we are discussing. He has called it 'empathy selling'. It gives some hints on how you recognise the major personality types and combinations (most people will have two or sometimes three major traits, there are few pure stereotypes), then gives some tips on how to handle them.

The strength of this approach is not perhaps so much in the ability to recognise specific personality types, which in fact is quite a difficult task. It is more in the fact that it highlights to account managers the need to think about the people they are dealing with, and how to get the best out of that relationship. This book does not purport to be a book on personality theory. In fact many of the models I find too full of jargon. I prefer to use my own list which most people can identify with, because the words come out of everyday usage.

Some classic personality types and characteristics are shown in the boxes.

Status seeker:
- wants social and business recognition
- likes to be seen to be in control
- deals only with the boss
- is dismissive of minions
- looks at your background and social standing
- tends to ask where you live
- mixes with the right people and talks about them all the time
- has monogrammed clothes and personalised number plates
- needs to keep up appearances
- cares what other people think.

Security minded:
- does not like risk
- prefers not to make decisions
- lives in the comfort zone
- is conservative
- resists change
- follows rather than leads
- saves money rather than invests it
- buys heaps of insurance
- finds reasons why not
- is often a hypochondriac.

Withdrawn personality:
- is shy
- is hard to get a response from
- listens but does not give much feedback
- does not easily reveal what they are thinking
- seems a bit vulnerable
- has still waters—often running deep
- thinks far more than they say.

Likes to be liked:
- needs recognition
- tries to please everyone
- fears giving offence and losing friendship
- tends to go overboard in servicing but does not get anything in return
- avoids confrontation
- lacks assertiveness
- promises everything to everyone.

Social personality:
- is always ready for lunch
- talks a lot
- is very friendly
- is good fun to be with
- is genuinely pleased to see you
- is hard to get down to business with
- never seems to get things completed
- is easy to get on with.

Entrepreneur:
- has a knack for making money
- sees opportunities clearly
- is a hard negotiator
- is loyal mainly to themselves
- is a person of action
- is not good at managing others
- likes to leave the details to others
- has an autocratic style
- is out to win.

Dots every 'I':
- gets bogged down in detail
- often cannot see the woods for the trees
- takes a long time to do things but—completes them perfectly
- is more involved in the task than with people
- is methodical and logical
- values facts and truth above anything else
- is idealistic
- often carries lots of pens in their shirt pocket.

> **Butterfly mind:**
> - has poor concentration
> - tolerates lots of interruptions
> - has an untidy desk
> - is easily distracted
> - is not consistent.

In each of these cases you would think through what you are trying to achieve with a customer, then you would look at how this person's personality might cause them to react. What are the things which could be problems? How will you try to appeal to this person? What are the pitfalls you should avoid? How should you put your case? What arguments or statements will work best?

As an exercise you might want to decide what things you would need to modify in your approach to meet the needs of these classic stereotypes. Remember that most people are not a pure type, but a combination.

240

. . . .

Summary

Good relationships can enhance your business, and poor relationships can ruin it. The account manager, or anyone involved in any relationship with a customer, needs to think about the person they are dealing with, and modify the approach. Not only will that ensure you establish and maintain good interpersonal relationships, but it eases the path to business success.

14

Implementing account management

. . . .

Introduction

It is good to read a book on account management or even run a workshop with your people, but the step between that and getting an account management program up and running seems to be a very large one. There are a number of reasons for this.

Firstly, sales people are primarily people of action. They like to be out and about with the customers, doing what their main job is supposed to be, getting orders. Their personality type is such that they are less likely to enjoy the rigid discipline of a rigorous planning system. They may see the benefit in account management, but they will not enjoy doing it.

They may not even see the advantages of account management. Managers tend to overestimate the ease with which sales people will understand what account management is all about. It seems that managers tend to operate at more of a conceptual level, but that sales people are far more action oriented. Even after a two-day workshop, with considerable time spent on discussion and gaining agreement to the approach, there will be many people who have still not understood the concept of account management.

There is a danger that sales people will see account management as just a form-filling exercise to keep the boss happy. They secretly hope that, in common with many of the things management tries to introduce, they will be flavour of the month for a short time and then with a bit of luck everyone will forget about it.

Account management must be seen as a process, not a series of forms

It is essential that sales people see account management as a process and as a way of managing their business. There are forms to be filled out, but those are there only to provoke thought about the business and to collect information on the account and bring ideas together. The central part of the whole plan will always be the activities sheet. That is what commits the company to action, and what will produce the results once the actions are complete. All the other steps in the process support the activity sheet. It helps enormously in getting the sales people to give it a go, if they see the tangible output of the process as a series of actions rather than a completed form.

Generally, once a company has managed to get the account management program running, and the cycle has revolved a few times, the sales people start to see the benefits and therefore are more likely to be committed to it. The difficulty is the initial stages where, unless management is careful, the impetus will be lost, creating a major barrier to introducing the subject again. The first steps in getting an account management program implemented are therefore extremely important. Here are some hints about avoiding some of the pitfalls.

Show you take it seriously

You will need to get the team together either formally using a consultant or informally by running a session yourself to introduce the subject and explain what is involved. At that meeting you should try to get the most senior people in the company to make some introductory comments and to provide a summary. These comments should be most supportive of the program, and you would probably be wise to write them yourself.

Make this meeting a bit special. Hold it off site in a location which is pleasant, avoids interruptions, and allows discussion in the evening. It is best if it is residential.

The managers should talk about account management as often as possible, at sales meetings, conferences, in memos and at every oppor-tunity. It needs to become integrated into the company jargon as a buzz word. Ensure that the senior managers keep talking about it too.

Include it in the job descriptions

Unless the words and the steps in the process are integrated into the management system, no-one will take it seriously. Unless the job descriptions of the sales people have a section on account management as near to the top of the list of accountabilities as possible, the chances are that sales people will not see it as being important.

Since account plans should be written for the top accounts which might be expected to produce 70 or 80 per cent of the results you want, and the plans define both the results and the activities most likely to achieve those results, the account plans become a good basis on which to appraise sales people, particularly because the plans are devised by the sales people themselves and managed by them, so that they control the whole process with guidance from the manager.

The plans are accountable documents. They should be prepared by the account manager and signed off by the account manager's immediate supervisor, normally the sales manager. The sales manager should then discuss with the account manager on a monthly basis the progress made towards the implementation of the plan.

At the end of the period covered by the plan, the sales manager will review the total plan and sign it off, ready for the plan for the next period to be accepted. It is not just the account plan which needs to be managed, but also the ancillary activities such as account profiles, account SWOTs, value-added search, and the BRAD meetings.

If the account management process is integrated into job descriptions, ongoing management and reviews and appraisals, it becomes accepted as part of daily life. Unless there is a management system in operation with a dedication to sound sales management practices, the chances of account management being properly implemented reduces. If you doubt whether you have got effective sales management systems operating, you should read *The Effective Sales Manager*.

. . . .

The initial meeting

We have talked about the advisability of having a separate off-site meeting to introduce the concept of account management. This is in essence a training event. Training is about knowledge, skills and attitudes. In this case your aim is to impart the knowledge of what account management is and how it works, and you will try to give the attendees some opportunity to gain skills in some of the steps. Unless you address the attitudes issue first, however, they may never listen to the rest of what you have to say.

The important point is that you must demonstrate clearly that there is a need for account management, even before you talk about what it is.

A good way of approaching the subject is to talk about how your own company makes money, introduce the concept of ROI, and look at the sales force's impact on the various elements of contribution and ROI. It is then useful to talk about price, and gain agreement that the company needs a different strategy than having to lower prices to meet the competition. This inevitably leads into a discussion on differentiation and added value.

If you then look at the fact that the resources of the sales department are limited, you can lead into the need to set priorities in customer categorisation, and how important it is that you focus efforts on those activities which are really going to make a difference to your sales results. This includes the concept of key account management. You are not going to implement the account management program for all accounts, only the main ones.

If you can reach agreement on all these steps, it is usually only a short step to the next point, that of explaining account management and how it fits in with what was discussed at the start. Many of the points you would want to bring out would be the sorts of things which are covered in the introductory chapter of this book.

Once the overall concept of the cycle has been explained, you should go through each of the steps of account management, talking about what is involved. Allow plenty of discussion and encourage questions. Through the discussion you will get the concepts across, and it will allow the leader of the meeting to asses the extent to which people have understood the concept.

At the end of the meeting you need to ask for commitments from the sales team. You will usually get this, purely on the basis that the team will have correctly assessed that is what management wants. They are not likely therefore to refuse commitment. But by listening carefully to the words and watching the body language the leader should be able to assess whether the commitment is a real enthusiasm for the idea. Usually it is somewhat tentative at this stage because the attendees are not quite sure how much time it is going to take and whether this means an extra workload.

. . . .

'We won't have time'

One of the greatest concerns sales people have about account management is that it implies more work and will actually reduce their productivity. Sales people say they agree on the importance of sales planning, but very few of them actually believe it deep down inside. Part of the introduction of account management will be selling planning as a discipline. This is hard in cases where the sales department has not been subject to a planning discipline before. You may just have to use your charm to persuade them to give it a go.

The amount of time required to produce plans for an account, including SWOTs and value-added searches should be estimated as accurately as possible. It really depends on how much information there is to analyse, and how good the support systems are. Generally, the first time a plan is written for a large account, it will take up to a full day. But once people have got used to the process it will be faster, and you should calculate on less than half a day per plan.

In a distribution business, these plans need to be written once a year with quarterly fine-tuning, and for direct accounts you will probably need to write them twice a year. I estimate that for an account manager with a normal load of key accounts, the time invested in operating the account management system—that is, keeping the account profiles up to date, doing the account SWOT and the value-added search or opportunity growth search, writing the plans and preparing for the BRADs—should take five to seven per cent of an account manager's time. (I do not count visiting customers, because sales people should do that anyway.) This figure is the time investment in operating the process.

Looked at that way, it is reasonable to invest up to seven per cent of your time in planning the business at major accounts. In fact, there should be a net time saving at the end of the year, in that the account management process should help avoid problems, so that there ought to be less time spent solving customer problems. The main productivity gain is in indentifying and carrying out the actions which will deliver results.

A reasonable load is generally about eight to twelve accounts, depending on how many are A or B accounts. Most account managers will have some of each, so the abridged format will be used for the simpler accounts or the smaller ones (these two things tend to go together). My experience is that most account managers end up having seven or eight accounts for which they use the full account plan format. If they have more than ten the chances are that either they are using the full format for some accounts where they should be using the abridged one, or they have more work than they can easily handle.

In the initial stages of writing plans, there will be a greater workload because there will be some deficiencies in the account profiles. As we discussed in the section on account profiles, it is better to take the process of getting the profiles into shape step by step. Write down for two or three accounts a month what you know. This whole process may take four or even six months. Then start to systematically find out the information to fill the gaps in your knowledge. This way you can build up the profiles without it seeming an enormous task, without distracting the sales people from their normal jobs, and without creating a demoralising barrier to account management.

Agreeing formats

One of the things which impedes progress is the lack of agreed formats for the various steps. The format you choose will depend on the business you are in and the capabilities of your data base. There are formats to be agreed for:
- the account profile
- account SWOT analysis
- value-added search
- the account plan or joint business plan.

With respect to the account profile, the format should be such that the space available for information is flexible, but that the information is always collected in the same way under the same headings and in the same order. That way it is much easier for everyone to find their way around the profiles, and everyone is keeping the same sort of information.

The account SWOT format really needs decisions only on what the criteria of the customer are likely to be in deciding on supply, or any areas of possible differentiation. This will vary from business to business, and you need to make up your own lists.

The value-added search for direct accounts will most usefully follow the format in the book, where there are a number of prompts which revolve around most company cost and profit centres, and will require amendment.

The distribution model focuses on identifying opportunities for both the supplier and the dealer/outlet/retailer to make more money through more market share, market growth affecting volumes and retail margins. You the supplier need to segment your business so that you can look at each segment on its merits, in-so-far as there is a different market, maybe different customers with different product groups. How you segment will depend on your own business, but as far as possible use a segmentation which makes sense to your customer. In other words try and split up the business into the same segments as they split their business.

This format then leads on, in the case of distribution businesses, to the joint business plan, since this analysis forms the basis of where the opportunities are, with a view to agreeing what needs to be done to make them reality.

The joint business plan format will therefore to a large extent evolve from the format you use for defining the opportunities. You will have to decide the depth of analysis to which you want to go, remembering to put as much as you can in an appendix. For smaller accounts you will have a somewhat shorter format.

The situation is similar for the direct accounts. The large ones will require a full format along the lines of the ones in this book, which you amend to meet your needs. For smaller accounts you need to agree on a one-page format similar to the one in the book. Unless you agree all these formats before you start to implement the program you will find yourself in trouble. All sorts of formats will be used, many of them inappropriate. Then there is always the excuse for not getting down to the task, that the formats have not been agreed so that they cannot make a start.

The right organisation for key account management

There are several ways you can apportion responsibilities in a sales group. You can do it geographically into territories, by industry, by product or by type of account. For sales representatives there is a lot of sense in a geographical arrangement, since it helps minimise travel time.

You could give everyone in the sales team a spread of A, B and C accounts as well as prospecting work. But there is good reason to consider making some people responsible for key accounts, As and Bs, and others for non-key accounts. The reason is that the key account managers, as we have already discussed, need to be freed from sorting out the background noise of these smaller accounts if they are going to devote the right amount of time in developing business with the key accounts. Furthermore, the qualities required for a key account manager are different from those required for a more straightforward sales job. Good account managers are even harder to find than good sales people. And if you make a clear distinction in role, job title, and job description, you can also differentiate in remuneration.

Remuneration for key account managers

It is true that a remuneration system which relies on at least part of the package in commission is counterproductive to account management. This is because commission works best in shorter term selling, and where the results come from individual effort. Account management is all about a long term development of the account, team approach, more project style selling.

So if you do not provide commission to key account managers, how can you provide an incentive? The best way of doing this is to provide some bonus scheme. In this way you can actually reward teams. To avoid the problem of the individual either not cooperating with the team, or else coasting and letting the team work for the overall result, a good idea is to have a two-level bonus. If, for example, the individual achieves their goal there is a 2 per cent bonus, and if the team gets their goals the team members get 2 per cent, there could be a further 2 per cent bonus to the individual if both the individual and the team reach their goals. There is therefore a 4 per cent penalty if either the individual or the team fails.

Another advantage of a bonus scheme is that you can be very flexible in the sorts of results you set as goals. Financial results can be part of it, but you can also include activities. These could be virtually any measurable activity which relates to the achievement of results at the key accounts handled by that particular account manager. One of my clients, who generally pays an annual 10 per cent bonus, made half of that bonus contingent on the account managers getting their account plans written according to the agreed schedule.

What makes a good key account manager?

Only a quarter to a half of sales forces I come into contact with are capable of becoming really good key account managers. The job of an account manager is different from a representative, and the skills and knowledge required are different. Good key account managers have more knowledge about how businesses work, have a better grasp of finance and are more capable of putting together good financial arguments in favour of their propositions. They are mature people who are able to conduct themselves at any level within the customer organisation up to CEO level. They generally have highly developed interpersonal skills, and have a high verbal intelligence. They must be good at problem solving, and are analytical in their approach. In their organisational capacities they must pay sufficient attention to detail to make sure nothing falls through the cracks, yet at the same time they need to be able to stand back and look at the total picture.

A good account manager has to be able to make sound commercial presentations, negotiate, sell new ideas and propositions. They have to be at least as good at listening as they are at talking. They need to know the market, their own products, the competition, and their own company and its capabilities. They do not necessarily have to be experts technically, although this depends a little on the type of business. An account manager can often resource specialist knowledge from within the company, if required. But above all, the key account manager needs to know the customer inside out.

Yes, of course it is a big ask. But on the other hand these people are handling the business from which around 80 per cent of the company's results are going to come.

Setting a schedule

It is critical to set dates and to manage them. Have a schedule for getting one or two per person completed, perhaps giving them a month. Once those have been completed, set a schedule for the remainder, perhaps one or two a month. If possible have a rolling schedule so that not all plans become due at the same time. This eases the load for writing them and spreads the BRADs at the end of the cycle.

Once you have set the deadlines, stick to them. Make them part of the objectives you agree with the sales people, assuming that you operate some sort of management by objectives system.

Writing the first plans

The first plans are the hardest to write because people have little experience. The next ones are easier and faster. It can help in writing the first ones if you do it in a group. Have a one day workshop, if you like, where the sales manager acts as a facilitator. Perhaps the single most important thing you can do to facilitate the whole process is to have a plan for an account everyone knows prepared which shows what you want.

This comes back to the point that account management operates at a conceptual level, and most sales people tend more to be people of action. You can bridge this gap by showing sales people what a good completed plan should look like. Take either a very typical customer, or one which they all would know, and go through the various steps in the account management cycle. That is, you need to complete the account profile, a SWOT, an opportunity or value-added search first, then write the plan. Either the sales manager should do this for an account, maybe working with one of the sales people, or a senior person in the team should do it under the guidance of the sales manager.

Until the sales people have got used to the system you may find that your pro forma plan is 'copied' by the sales team for their own customers. This does not really matter for the first few. As they become more familiar with the process, they should start being more creative and deriving strategies which are specific to their own accounts.

Do not expect perfection first time. As long as the first plans make some contribution to moving the business in the direction you want, it is better to let people start using them, see some advantage in them, and aim for a higher standard the next time plans are written. If you spend too much time getting the perfect plans written first time, you will find that the sales people get disheartened and lose interest. And while people are perfecting the plans, there are no activities with the customer, and that after all is the reason for writing the plans in the first place.

Checklist for implementation of key account management system
- Marketing plans
  - segmentation and priorities
  - levers in the business
  - 4 Ps
- The right organisation to support key account management
- Job descriptions
- Appraisals and a management system
- A remuneration system which is not complicated by key account management
- The agreement and support of upper management to the concept and the program
- Support and management by first-line supervisors
- The right culture, where cooperation is encouraged across functional boundaries, and there is a company-wide dedication to customer services issues
- Clearly defined communication channels and areas of authority and accountability
- Establishment of a formal internal review mechanism
- The hardware and software necessary to operate the system
- Having the right information available in a format which is easy to understand and to use
- Measurement of current sales productivity, setting of targets for sales productivity
- Freeing up of account managers from non-sales-productive tasks which detract from their productivity
- Allocation of people and financial resources to operate key account management
- Nomination of a key account champion to coordinate the implementation process
- Definition of which are the key accounts (distributors, end users or influencers)
- Agreement on the formats for the account management steps.

Some of these items need to be worked on before any formal commitment to the program. Others, like the formats, will only become obvious when preparation of the program is under way. But ideally all of these items need to be thought about and acted on before training sales people.

. . . .

Common errors in plans

Starting with the account profile, it is usually found that there are some major deficiencies in your knowledge. This is particularly true of direct accounts, where you the supplier often do not know enough about how your product is used, and particularly where the final products are sold. This is because your own sales people tend to have most contact with purchasing, and sometimes operations, but rarely with the customer's sales and marketing people. This is fine as long as you recognise it and plan to do something about it. The problem is that sales people forget to carry forward into the plan itself the need to find out more information. This runs the risk that the next time a plan is written you find the same gaps in your knowledge.

Not enough account profiles have a customer organisation chart. These are important, because it helps you see who reports to whom and gives you some clues in finding your way around their organisation.

The main problem area with the account SWOT tends to be the lack of objectivity. You often do not have direct feedback from customers on how they see you versus other suppliers. The sorts of comments they make in a negotiation cannot be taken too seriously, as they are putting pressure on you, and will always seek to give you the impression you are not good enough, in the hope that you will lower the price to them to compensate! You will get far more accurate feedback once you have the account management cycle operating and get some good BRAD meetings completed. These meetings have no negotiation and they are far more relaxed, and you are much more likely to get some good information on how customers see you, especially if you give them the opportunity to comment.

In the distribution businesses, when it comes to the opportunity search expressed in the final summary at the end of the plan you will present to the customer, you are talking about their opportunities, which are of course opportunities for you to increase your volume too. The key thing is that the joint business plan for these customers is also the plan which you are going to present as the basis for agreement on how you will do business. It must be written as an external plan.

With all plans, the strategies developed for business at that account must be sound. I have seen plans where the strategies seem to revolve around dropping price to gain share. Generally it does not work. By all means promote more or sell more; that is harder to beat and is just as effective even short term. Dropping price invites an easy response from competitors, and ruins the profit for everyone.

Another issue is the 'fairyland' syndrome. There is no point in hoping for a wonderful new product if it has not yet been developed by your company. You must work with the products you have. Certainly generate ideas for new products, but remember that the trend is towards less not more product differentiation. If you can create it, it is the best strategy (look at Honda), but the fact is that very few companies are able to support their business very often with product innovations. You certainly can't rely on it in writing plans.

I often see plans which have got some good material in the value-added search, and some points to be addressed from the SWOTs, but when you come to the activities there is almost nothing there. The activities page is the most important. Without some good solid activities nothing is going to happen. It is critical that this page expresses everything which needs to be done at the account, otherwise it just will not get done. You must take each of the prior points and carry them forward so that there is an activity to make it happen.

Do not forget the relationship issues. You need to plan on expanding relationships across more people. There may be people within your customer's organisation whom you need to know and currently do not. This has to be planned for.

Day-to-day management

Things operate best when they are integrated into the way people do things. The worst thing that can happen is that the plans are written, then put in a drawer and forgotten. It is most important that the sales people use these plans to plan their time and to run the business at key accounts. This means that the sales people should be encouraged to plan their time using them, and that they be used in preparing for visits. The sales manager can assist by making a review of the plans part of the regular monthly reviews held with the sales people.

. . . .

Summary

This book has discussed a systematic way of managing the major accounts which provide most of the sales results for the company. It is logical, it is well tried, it works, but it requires some dedication and discipline to get the system working. The best testimony I can think of to finish with, is from one of my clients, who weathered the recession in the early 1990s well. They said that key account management was the most important factor in their being able to actually improve their share position in the marketplace, and only slightly drop margins, in what was the worst recession in Australia since the 1930s.

As we move into a period of growth again, it is perhaps even more important that the principles of account management be respected. As we put direction and substance in managing these major accounts, the growth we create should be more sustainable and relationships between supplier and customer develop, so that when the next slump comes we will be in the best possible position to weather the storm.

It all leads to better profitability for both supplier and customer.

Index

locators in **bold** indicate figures

account management
   activities 17, 70, 214–15, 252
   classification 13–14
   commitment of 19–20
   company relationships and 10–12,
      44, 110, 115–16, 136, 137, 215–16,
      222–9, 233–4
   cycle 31–84, **34**, 79–81, 116–25,
      208–15
   direct **33**
   discipline of 17–18
   distribution **34**
   efficiency 85–7
   formats 246
   implementing 241–53
   internal review 79–80
   interpersonal relationships and 10,
      44–5, 87–8, 152, 233–40
   meeting, initial 243–4
   multisites and multi-SBU contracts
      81–4
   and negotiation 80–1, 217–19
   objectives 69, 193–4, 213–14
   and organisations 247
   philosophy of 3–7, 125
   productivity and 71
   profiles 37–45, **39–43**, 117, 182,
      209–10
   profitability 182
   schedule 249
   setting direction for 23–4
   strategies 69–70, 193–4, 213–14
   SWOT 182–3, 210–11
   through distribution 112–16
   see also distribution; information,
      account manager; outlets; plans,
      account management;
      supermarkets
account manager
   defined 248
   efficiency 85–6
   information 88–91
   qualities 248
   remuneration 247–8
   training role of 136–7
advertising, media 148
agenda, your own 142–4
agents and distributors 106–7

balanced corporate scorecard 29
business
   direction, flow of **28**
   needs 10
   plan 125–35, **127–33**, **135**, 186
   specifiers 216–17
business review and development
   meetings (BRAD) 49, 74–9, 144–5,
   187–8, 215–16

category management 169–70
commodities 228–9
computers 86, 92–4, 120, 166–7, 194